INFORMATION AND COMMUNICATION TECHONOLOGIES FOR DEVELOPMENT IN AFRICA

Volume 3

Networking Institutions of Learning – SchoolNet

Edited by
Tina James

International Development Research Centre
Ottawa • Dakar • Cairo • Montevideo • Nairobi • New Delhi • Singapore

Council for the Development of Social Science Research in Africa

© International Development Research Centre 2004

Jointly published by the International Development Research Centre (IDRC)
PO Box 8500, Ottawa, ON, Canada K1G 3H9
http://www.idrc.ca

and the Council for the Development of Social Science Research in Africa
(CODESRIA)
PO Box 3304, Dakar, Senegal
http://www.codesria.org
ISBN 2-86978-117-2

National Library of Canada cataloguing in publication data
Main entry under title:
Information and communication technologies for development in Africa.
Volume 3: Networking Institutions of Learning – SchoolNet

Co-published by CODESRIA.
ISBN 1-55250-008-X

1. Information technology – Africa.
2. Communication in community development – Africa.
3. Community development – Africa.
4. Computer-assisted instruction – Africa.
I. James, Tina
II. International Development Research Centre (Canada)
III. Codesria.

HC805.I55I53 2004   338.9'26'096   C2004-980230-5

Contents

Chapter 1

Contextualising Education in Africa: The Role of ICTs

Shakifa Isaacs, Irene Broekman and Thomas Mogale

Chapter 2

Introduction to the Evaluation Study

Shakifa Isaacs, Irene Broekman and Thomas Mogale

Chapter 3
Emerging Pictures – Lessons Learnt and Recommendations
Tina James

Chapter 4
Starting National Schoolnets
Malusi Cele and Shafika Isaacs

Chapter 5
Internet para as Escolas in Mozambique
Ephraim Siluma, Daniel Browde and Nicky Roberts

Chapter 6
Youth Cyber Clubs in Senegal
Ramata Molo Aw Thioune and El Hadj Habib Camara

Chapter 7
SchoolNet South Africa
Edward Holcroft

Chapter 8
Schoolnet Uganda: Curriculumnet
Anne Ruhweza Katahoire, Grace Baguma and Florence Etta

Figures

Tables

Acronyms and abbreviations

AISI	African Information Society Initiative
Acacia	IDRC Initiative for Communities and Information Society in sub-Saharan Africa
AISI	African Information Society Initiative
BRVM	*Bourse régionale des valeurs mobilières* / West African Stock Exchange (Abidjan)
CAD	Canadian dollar
CAERENAD	*Centre d'Application, d'Études et de Resources en Apprentissage à Distance* (Senegal)
CD	compact disc
CEM	*Collège d'Enseignement Moyen* (Senegal)
CETDE	Centre for Educational Technology and Distance Education (South Africa)
CIUEM	*Centro de Informatica*, Eduardo Mondlane University
DDSP	District Development Support Programme (South Africa)
DFID	Department for International Development
ECSN	Eastern Cape Schools Network
EIG	Economic Interest Group (Senegal)
ELSA	Evaluation and Learning System for Acacia
EMDP	Education Management Development Programme (South Africa)
ENS	*Ecole Normale Supérieure de Dakar* (Senegal)
FCA	African franc / franc CFA (Senegal)
FET	Further Education and Training
FLE	Family Life and Education (Senegal)
gbps	gigabytes per second
GDP	gross domestic product
GEEP	*Groupe pour l'Etude et l'Enseignement de la Population* / Group for Population Studies and Education (Senegal)

GEPE	*Gabinete Técnico de Gestão de Projectos Educacionais* Mozambique)
GET	General Education and Training
GNP	gross national product
GSN	Gauteng Schools Network
HIPC	high interest paying country
HIV/AIDS	human immunodeficiency virus / acquired immune deficiency syndrome
I*EARN	International Education and Resource Network
ICT	Information and Communications Technology
ICEIDA	Icelandic International Development Assistance Agency
IDRC	International Development Research Centre (Canada)
IICD	International Institute for Communications and Development
IIP	Intergovernmental Informatics Programme (UNESCO)
ISAS	Institute of Southern African Studies (Lesotho)
ISDN	integrated services digital network
ISP	Internet service provider
ISPA	Internet Service Providers Association
LAN	local area network
MEN	Ministry of National Education (Senegal)
NCDC	National Curriculum Development Centre (Uganda)
NGO	non-governmental organisation
NSN	National Schools Network (South Africa)
OBE	outcomes-based education
OECD	Organisation for Economic Cooperation and Development
PC	personal computer
PDEF	*Programme décennal pour l'éducation et la formation /* "Quality Education for All" programme (Senegal)
PDIS	*Programme de développement intégré de la santé /* Extended Health Development Programme (Senegal)
PLE	Primary Leaving Examination (Uganda)
POP	point of presence
PRC	Provincial Resource Centre (Angola)
PTA	Parent-Teacher Association
ROSA	Regional Office for Southern Africa
SABC	South African Broadcasting Corporation
SACOL	South African College for Open Learning

SAIDE	South African Institute for Distance Education
SAITIS	South African IT Industry Strategy Project
SAP	Structural Adjustment Programme (World Bank)
SIDA	Swedish International Development Cooperation Agency
SNP	SchoolNet Project
SNSA	SchoolNet South Africa
SPRU	Science Policy Research (Sussex)
STDs	sexually transmitted diseases
STSI	School-to-School Initiative (Uganda)
TBLISS	Technical-based Learning in School Science (Uganda)
TDM	*Telecomunicações de Moçambique*
TELI	Technology Enhanced Learning Initiative (South Africa)
TURP	Trade Union Research Project (South Africa)
UCAD	Université Cheikh Anta Diop de Dakar (Senegal)
UK	United Kingdom
UN	United Nations
UNDP	United Nations Development Programme
UNEB	Uganda National Examinations Board
UNESCO	United Nations Educational, Scientific and Cultural Organisation
UNFPA	United Nations Population Fund
UPE	Universal Primary Education (Uganda)
USA	United States of America
UVA	*Université Virtuelle Africaine* (Senegal)
VAT	value-added tax
VSAT	Very Small Aperture Terminal
WCED	Western Cape Educational Department
WCSN	Western Cape Schools Network (South Africa)
WorLD	World Links for Development (World Bank)
ZAR	South African rand

Foreword

The story of schoolnets in Africa is a fascinating tale of a pioneering attempt to apply new information and communication technologies (ICTs) to resource-poor environments as a means to enhancing education and development, and bridging the much-vaunted "digital divide". This process unfolded amidst immense skepticism among development practitioners about prioritizing ICTs particularly in poverty-stricken Africa. The African schoolnet story is a short tale of this experience, rich with lessons of successes and failures, of difficulties and triumphs, of many frustrations but also of incredible hope.

Yet, too little of this tale is written. And even less is written in a way that involves the actors in the storytelling and involves local researchers in investigating the story. This study marks the beginning of writing the African schoolnet story, written and researched by Africans. And by initiating the telling of the tale, by involving a number of schoolnet stakeholders in a protracted yet systematized process of learning, the IDRC's Acacia Program has made a path-breaking contribution, not only by producing a highly accessible and readable product but more importantly, by beginning the process of developing a learning system amongst various actors in the growing African schoolnet movement.

Schoolnets are essentially national organizations that promote learning and teaching through the use of ICTs. The idea emerged in Canada and Europe where the first schoolnet formations were set up in the 1980s and early 1990s. At the heart of the schoolnet process lies a revolutionary transformation in the way learning and teaching happens. Since the early 1990s, the schoolnet initiative took root in Africa and mushroomed across the continent. It is a movement that began as nodes of community access to ICTs, often initiated and catalysed by organizations like the IDRC's Acacia Program and the World Bank's WorLD Links for Development Program. Today, many have moved beyond points of community ICT access and represent tiny beginnings in educational transformation at school level. Unlike their Northern counterparts however, the typical national schoolnet in Africa is a small-scale, donor-supported pilot initiative that is grassroots-focused and led by local champions who have found and developed local African solutions, thereby "Africanising" the schoolnet concept. The evolution and eventual formal establishment of SchoolNet Africa over the past three years, as an independent organization to promote and support the growth of national schoolnet organizations in Africa, is testimony to the growth of an Africanised schoolnet movement, a process also supported and promoted initially by the IDRC. Throughout this evolution, more and more research questions have emerged, highlighting the need not only for ongoing learning but for continuously diffusing the learning among practitioners and policymakers to inform daily practice.

Whilst much of our successes imbue us all with hope, we cannot gloss over the very real, often formidable challenges that most schoolnets are still facing today – challenges which are sometimes not very different from the typical donor-supported development project in Africa. Some of these challenges include:

- Integrating ICTs in the very life of the school, as an essential part of an educational solution and not just as a technology-centred project;
- Creating awareness amongst policymakers and convincing them about the usefulness of investing in education through ICTs;
- Developing beyond donor-dependency and creating integrated national programs that are affordable and sustainable in the face *inter alia* of education budgetary cuts, the HIV Aids pandemic and short term donor support; and of course
- Monitoring whether ICT-interventions in schools really add educational value to learners, teachers and school management, etc.

These are all questions that remain uppermost in the minds of schoolnet practitioners, for which we have more questions than answers, at a time when many schoolnets are also struggling to survive and are seriously grappling with ways to become sustainable. Evidently, a massive intervention remains a necessity if we are to stem the tide of the education crisis and make a major difference to the lives of Africa's youth through the schoolnet initiative. Here research and learning, whilst not enough on its own, will always play a very important role. Continuously defining the right research questions, conducting the research process in a way that encourages stakeholder participation and ownership of the research and disseminating the learning from the research experience but above all, acting on the lessons that have been learned through the research process remain central to our future success as a schoolnet movement.

This study marks the beginning of such a process. The network of schoolnet practitioners across Africa, their international partners and the unfolding commitment by the New Partnership for African Development to support tele-education in schools, have much to gain from this study.

Shafika Isaacs
Executive Director
SchoolNet Africa

Preface

Every year donors donate books, pens and paper to African schools, which never seem to get enough of them. Every year innumerable teachers from developed countries come to Africa to make up for the shortfall in qualified teachers. Every year millions of school children in Africa graduate without the appropriate tools needed to make it in this world.

In the 1990s, with the advent of the Internet, digital pioneers envisioned a school, delivering quality education, where there would be no need for books, paper, pens...maybe even no need for teachers. Could this be the solution for Africa's educational problems? And if so, how do we go about it?

With these questions in mind, IDRC's Acacia program set out, in 1997, to facilitate research in this area by supporting schoolnetworking projects in each of the four Acacia focus countries (Senegal, South Africa, Mozambique and Uganda). These "action-research" projects focused on connectivity in schools, due to the severe access problems. An evaluation framework was also set-up to learn as much as possible from the experiences.

This evaluative study on school networking in Africa is the fruit of five years of experimenting and research with schoolnet projects in Africa. It may not be the definitive answer to the question of whether school networking is the solution to Africa's educational woes, but it certainly goes a long way to explaining the benefits and pitfalls of setting up connected African schools.

Donors, development practitioners, policy-makers and even school-workers would be loath not to assimilate the lessons that emerge from this study. It is a key to understanding what environment must prevail for a school networking project to be successful. It is also very useful for Acacia, as it highlights the key issues that still need to be better understood and thus sets our future research agenda in this area.

Quality education, as well as access to it, are essential conditions for Africa's development. Hopefully this study will bring us one step closer to understanding how we meet those conditions.

Thank you to all involved.

Laurent Elder
Acacia Program
International Development Research Centre

Acknowledgements

A research project of this magnitude depends on immeasurable contributions from a wide range of people for its success. I would like to acknowledge the many people who made this compilation possible.

This book does not reflect the individual contributions that made it possible as clearly as it should, as the nature of the research requires they be integrated as a coherent document. Nevertheless, each effort was crucial to the final composition, and is therefore worthy of acknowledgement.

Authors and researchers who worked on the country case studies:

Ramata Molo Aw Thioune (Senegal)
Irene Broekman (South Africa)
Daniel Browde (South Africa)
Grace Baguma (Uganda)
Neil Butcher (South Africa)
Malusi Cele (South Africa)
Michael Cross (Mozambique)
Hadj El Habib (Senegal)
Florence Etta (Uganda)
Edward Holcroft (South Africa)
Shafika Isaacs (South Africa)
Anne Ruhweza Katehoire (Uganda)
Ephraim Siluma (Mozambique)
Thomas Mogale (South Africa)
Nicky Roberts (South Africa)
Terry Smutylo (Canada)

Editors
Irene Broekman
Florence Etta
Tina James
Nicky Roberts

We are also indebted to those who shared ideas and insights through workshops, interviews and email and fax correspondence, especially the staff and steering committee members of the SchoolNet projects in all of the nine African countries. The comprehensive nature and scope of this report is due to their efforts.

Special acknowledgement is due to the following:

- South African Institute for Distance Education (SAIDE) for providing an invaluable information base, extensive expertise and support for this study.
- World Links for Development (WorLD) Programme for its participation in the research workshops for this study, and especially for its support and collaboration in conducting the case study on SchoolNet Uganda.

Finally, on behalf of IDRC Acacia, I wish to thank Linah Hlatshwayo and Muriel Reneke at IDRC for handling administrative matters relevant to this project.

Shafika Isaacs
Project Team Leader

Executive Summary

Introduction

The International Development Research Centre's (IDRC) Acacia program has, since its inception in 1997, invested considerably in promoting the establishment of school networking projects in a number of African countries. Schools are institutions where members of different communities converge – learners, educators, school managers, parents of learners, unemployed youth, women and other community residents. It therefore made sense for schools to serve as a base for community access to Information and Communication Technologies (ICTs).

The introduction of computers and the Internet, when first introduced in 1997, was a new phenomenon to African communities. For this reason, an institutional mechanism had to be established to promote the application of ICTs in schools and to test the efficacy of ICTs in enhancing school education. This was the rationale for setting up SchoolNet projects as new entities and to test various models in differing contexts in Africa.

SchoolNet projects were established on the premise of three assumptions:

- ICTs based in schools will enhance access to information and facilitate communication in school-based communities as well as various communities based in the residential areas surrounding the schools;
- ICTs in schools will enhance access to education to those who have been deprived of education in the past; and

- ICTs can contribute to new pedagogical methodologies thereby enhancing learning and teaching particularly in the context of the education crisis in Africa.

The projects under evaluation

During its first three-year phase, Acacia promoted the start-up of SchoolNet projects in nine countries in sub-Saharan Africa: Angola, Lesotho, Mozambique, Namibia, Senegal, South Africa, Zambia, Zimbabwe and Uganda. The size, scope and activities of these projects differ significantly from one another, and are at varying phases of development. The projects were evaluated using a combination of in-depth interviews (face-to-face and telephonic), e-mail surveys, site visits and photo-documentation, and a review of project documentation.

Angola

The school-networking project was based at the Catholic University of Angola in Luanda. The start-up activity entailed connecting three schools in Luanda to the Internet and training teachers at these schools in basic ICT skills. The start-up process did not involve setting up SchoolNet Angola as an institution, nor did it support the employment of full-time personnel to run the institution.

Lesotho

The Lesotho project, was set up to provide connectivity to a Centre for Rural Business and Community Development in Liphering, providing ICT access to ten schools and four tertiary institutions in the area. The project also trained teachers, rural development workers, students and trainers.

Mozambique

Acacia supported the establishment of a project in ten schools, in partnership with the Centre for Informatics based at the University Eduardo Mondlane (CIUEM) in Maputo. Teacher training and technical support were included.

Namibia

Acacia supported the development of a business and strategic plan to set up SchoolNet Namibia as a formal institution. SchoolNet Namibia was set up in partnership with a range of education, private sector and government institutions.

Senegal

Acacia supported the Youth Cyber Clubs project, which involved the establishment of 12 cyber youth clubs as part of a national network of youth clubs in schools. The project is an experiment in secondary schools that allows for continuous dialogue and increased public awareness on adolescent issues, using ICTs, in Senegalese schools.

South Africa

SchoolNet South Africa (SNSA) was established as a non-governmental organization, housed in the IDRC offices in Johannesburg. SNSA's original start-up objective was to provide one to three computers to 48 schools and hold eight educator-training workshops, although this was far surpassed.

Uganda

Acacia collaborated with WorLD in their start-up of SchoolNet Uganda. The partnership took the form of regular communication between Acacia and SchoolNet Uganda, which laid the basis for the establishment of CurriculumNet, a project geared towards developing local education content on the Internet. CurriculumNet commenced in December 2000 with support from Acacia.

Zambia

Acacia supported a project that provided the basis for the establishment of a national SchoolNet structure by targeting 14 provincial teacher resource centres situated in each of the nine provinces in Zambia. These centres were already equipped with computers, telephone lines and electricity.

Zimbabwe

Acacia supported the development of a WorLD SchoolNet project, SchoolNet Zimbabwe, by providing financial support for a national workshop on ICT in basic education, the training of trainers and of schools involved in the networking program, and the development of provincial business plans.

There are therefore cases where Acacia actively promoted and supported the development of an institution called a SchoolNet, while in others it supported start-up activities under the aegis of existing institutions. In the case of both SchoolNet Zimbabwe and SchoolNet Uganda, WorLD played an instrumental role in setting up these institutions, whereas Acacia supported two start-up activities in Zimbabwe.

Lessons Learnt

Lesson #1: Small is beautiful, large is necessary

All the SchoolNet projects in this study were conceptualised and implemented as pilot initiatives, in some cases very small-scale pilot initiatives. The experience with most pilot initiatives is that they rarely progress beyond the pilot phase. What works well at the micro level can be disastrous at the macro level, because it may require levels of complexity that a large system is unable to accommodate sustainably.

More often than not, models of successful ICT use at the micro level are evolved by dedicated, highly proficient individuals, and depend on these people's personal traits and commitment for ongoing success. Such models do not translate easily or at all to the macro-systemic level and attempts to escalate such models of operation to the systemic level may have a seriously destabilising effect on a large system.

Lesson #2: Pushing the concept of ICTs or 'ICTs in education?'

SchoolNet projects have developed a stronger technological than an educational approach, with their activities mainly focused on installing and making accessible the technologies, and less on using them for educational purposes. This has been a necessary first step for SchoolNets given the problems associated with gaining access to ICTs in the first place. However, the reason for setting up SchoolNets is to demonstrate the beneficial effects of ICTs on education and it therefore becomes imperative to initiate content-based projects.

Ways need to be sought to integrate ICTs effectively into the curriculum. This requires close partnering with departments of education because of the implications for teacher-based and school-based curriculum development models. Since the integration of ICTs into educational systems is still largely uncharted territory in Africa, it becomes clear that more research is needed on how such integration can be managed.

Lesson #3: The realities of contexts need to shape the project

Contextual factors such as infrastructure, shortage of ICT skills, geographic location, and lack of culture of use of technologies affect a project, as do the working conditions of employees. Projects should start by doing an infrastructure and ICT skills audit at the national level. If ICT skills are concentrated in one province or city, then the project should be initiated where there are available skills and resources, or where these are likely to be developed relatively quickly. This will reduce the initial risk of failure and allow the initial project implementation to be undertaken in a less risky environment, thus increasing the likelihood of achieving successful implementation. Access to electricity and telephone lines should determine the selection of schools in a SchoolNet project.

Lesson #4: Simple and clear project objectives are important

Key objectives must be clear. Where a project is being implemented on a long-term basis, clear phases of implementation with clear objectives for each phase are needed. Timeframes and measurable deliverables for the completion of project phases must be made clear to all stakeholders. Accountability for deliverables should also be clearly articulated so that there is no confusion as to who will be held responsible for completing tasks and activities. This will make the ongoing monitoring and evaluation of a project easier and ensure that project deliverables have been met, that problems are picked up in time, and that the project is implemented effectively and efficiently. Regular meetings and updates are necessary to keep stakeholders informed of progress on the project.

Lesson #5: Dedicated ICT champions – Blessing or curse?

The most successful SchoolNets appear to be the ones that have dedicated champions. A champion considered a good leader for a school networking initiative should provide visionary leadership, and possess good communication and project management skills. Champions should also have excellent lobbying and negotiating skills, and strong networks in both the public and private sector. Generally champions are characterised by high levels of enthusiasm.

Dedicated champions should not be equated with full-time paid staff. In some cases, the role of a champion can be fulfilled on a part-time / volunteer basis, by a person who is driven by the vision and future potential of the project. This person may be a key stakeholder in government or a community member, and may not even be the project manager, although having the latter fulfill the 'champion' role does appear to bring many advantages to a SchoolNet project.

There is the danger however of developing a dependency on one or a few individuals. This poses problems for sustainability as projects easily collapse when those individuals move away from the project.

Lesson #6: Volunteerism may put your project at risk

In countries where incomes are very low, and where there is no culture of volunteerism, it is difficult to sustain the necessary momentum with volunteers only. In most cases, volunteers appear to expect some payment for their services and are unlikely to stay with a project if this is not forthcoming. Volunteer staff (usually teachers) also present difficulties when their regular workloads become too heavy to cope with the additional demands of teaching and supporting ICTs at the school level. This is particularly noticeable in cases where schools relied on volunteer teachers for technical support.

Lesson #7: Train and sustain scarce management resources

Project management and implementation skills are scarce in Africa, and even more so in rural areas. This also extends to weak capacity in the private sector, where both ICT skills and entrepreneurial capital are much more limited than in other parts of the world. This makes it significantly more difficult to generate innovative local solutions to educational problems, and also raises the cost of attempting to maintain technology-dependent projects.

Lesson #8: Create flexible management structures

For a successful start-up phase, there needs to be a very flexible management structure, a structure that allows exploration of different ideas and is very responsive to an environment that requires quick decision making. Because of its inflexible bureaucratic nature, the public sector may therefore not be the optimal structure to run a SchoolNet project, particularly during the start-up phase.

Lesson #9: Incubate within an existing organization but retain independence

Incubation in existing institutions (whether universities, Ministries of Education or the private sector) has been the appropriate starting point for most SchoolNets. It serves to consolidate partnerships with established education institutions, encourages outreach within universities and from a SchoolNet development perspective, promotes an awareness of the potential that ICTs hold for the promotion of education.

Another essential ingredient for success is the establishment of the SchoolNet initiative as an independent organisational entity. Not only does this reinforce ownership and control by the SchoolNet governing structures and staff, it also widens the scope for decision-making and determining SchoolNet activities and partnerships. While establishing an independent organization is essential, this has to be coupled with the development of the network through partnerships with government ministries, the private sector and civil society structures.

Lesson #10: Understand the implications of donor support on financial sustainability

At the design stage it is important to factor in the possibilities for moving beyond the pilot phase and develop a framework for sustainability at inception. Partnerships with a number of stakeholders have proven to be an important criterion for success. They can assume different forms, in terms of both financial support and in-kind contributions. While most SchoolNets will essentially remain non-profit entities, organizing the project on sound business principles has become critical for longevity and sustainability. This involves generating products and services with potential revenue streams and developing aggressive marketing strategies. Sustainability models will also have to factor in the development of public private partnerships where the private sector can be shown the positive effects of partnering with SchoolNets.

Lesson #11: Broaden available connectivity options

The main issue that affects the use of ICTs by various communities was, and continues to be, connectivity and its availability and affordability. The problems of using dialup connections were highlighted but even schools currently using wireless connections complained about the low bandwidth. SchoolNets need to explore in detail the various technical options available and affordable to schools so that they can make informed choices in relation to connectivity.

Lesson # 12: New computers versus refurbished computers?

Second-hand computers are useful for demonstration purposes and the teaching of keyboard skills, but mechanisms need to be in place to test the computers before they are despatched to schools, and for refurbishment and upgrade facilities to be readily available. Refurbished computers are not always cost effective due to high support costs and shorter life spans. Most of the technical breakdowns and connectivity problems were blamed on the fact that old, slow computers were used. This was exacerbated by the fact that users were frequently new to computer technology.

In view of the technical problems experienced with using old computers, the lesson is that faster and newer computers are needed to access the Internet and download materials; this would also assist in ensuring that telephone bills are not too high for users. In countries where technical support is likely to be scarce in rural areas, a strategy of using refurbished computers is unlikely to work unless a concomitant strategy is put in place to develop local technical support skills.

Lesson #13: Improving access

The use of schools as an access point for ICTs has been very successful. Different models of access can be applied:

- Access only by users from the school concerned, where the range of usage varies between only the principal who uses the one computer available to the school, to learners, educators and principals using computers in a computer lab at a school;

- Access by users from both the existing school and the surrounding community; and
- Access through a school that acts as a hub site for servicing surrounding schools and the community.

Lesson #14: Develop technical troubleshooting skills

The development of local capacity in technical skills, a team of troubleshooters, people capable of upgrading and refurbishing computers, and setting up help-desks, are particularly necessary. Mechanisms for improving technical support, particularly in remote areas, need to be addressed during teacher training, if only to deal with basic troubleshooting skills. More emphasis should be placed on technical training for teachers and learners so that they can undertake their own local first-line technical support. Furthermore, mechanisms are required to provide teachers with continuous ICT support e.g. through help-desks.

Lesson #15 Longer courses and ongoing training for teachers

Training should not be a once-off intervention, but has to be continuous and followed up, with an emphasis on longer training courses. Different levels of training should be considered for teachers at varying levels of competencies.

Lesson #16: Local content development needs to build on a strong technology base

Much of the content now available through the Internet was developed elsewhere and is not always relevant to the local situation in African countries. Of all the components of SchoolNet activity, the development of education content online or through the use of ICTs was extremely limited, or was marginalized completely, even though these activities were part of the original SchoolNet design. There is therefore a need to revisit the need for local African content development.

Lesson #17: Different approaches to policy for ICTs in education

ICTs do not yet constitute a significant policy or financial priority. There are several competing priorities – budgetary constraints, administrative and management challenges, teacher supply, impact of HIV/AIDS on education, and so on – all of which vie for the attention of local policy makers. ICT-related education policy still needs to establish itself within this set of priorities.

Close working relationships with policy-making entities are important for SchoolNets. The close involvement of policy-makers in implementation processes has proved to be the single most enabling factor in policy development around the use of ICTs in education. Policies addressing ICTs in Education could take the form of:

- Broad policies on the use of technologies in education, and strategies – at national and provincial levels – to promote the specific use of ICTs in education emerges from this broad policy framework;
- Specific ICT in education policies, where the policy focus is specifically on the use of ICTs in education; and
- Specific policies on schools and ICT infrastructure and how schools should be equipped with the appropriate technology.

Conclusion

In conclusion, the outcomes of the evaluation of the Acacia-supported SchoolNets reveal that the projects have ranged from being limited in their achievements to those that can be regarded as very successful. Connectivity is still one of the biggest stumbling blocks and will continue to be so until stronger emphasis is placed on universal service in underserved areas. The integration of ICTs into school curricula requires stronger emphasis in future phases, particularly as more students and educators are exposed to the technology and start demanding school-based content material that is more relevant to the local context. Finally, the need to address sustainability, financial and human resources remains an area of concern, which can only be addressed by applying stronger business principles, and by emphasising capacity building for improved project management.

Chapter 1

Contextualising Education in Africa: The Role of ICTs

Shakifa Isaacs, Irene Broekman and Thomas Mogale

Africa and the Information Age

Dizzying changes in the scope and reach of information infrastructures were the hallmark of the 1990s and have continued until present. Information technology and networking use have reached both developed and many developing economies, albeit to varying degrees and levels of intensity. The ubiquity of these changes has manifested itself through the extraordinary expansion of the Internet and the World Wide Web, as well as the rapid deployment of wireless networks, giving rise to the term 'networking revolution'. Developed societies have taken advantage of these changes with astonishing rapidity, gaining broad access to modern digital networks and significant economic and social spin-offs for their communications and business sectors. These countries have made inroads toward e-commerce opportunities, while their counterparts in developing countries have yet to achieve satisfactory levels of connectivity. The proliferation of e-business has heralded the so-called 'new information economy', with further positive ripple effects for information-intensive industries.

There is little doubt that sub-Saharan Africa's underserved populations are missing out on the boons of information and communication technology (ICT). As a region lagging behind in adoption, use and innovation in the ICT sectors, its populations are missing out on a better education, well-paying

ICT jobs, investment possibilities and opportunities to use information technology to facilitate the delivery of basic services, such as health and education.

The long-term effects of ICTs and of domestic and international digital divides remain considerably unclear. Yet, ICT yields have increased income and cultural and political advantage to those who can apply it to their benefit. The networking revolution has unrivalled potential to open up new digital opportunities for developing countries, particularly in the area of education. The potential benefits from advances in ICTs could mean an acceleration of economic and social development and greater inclusion of isolated – particularly rural - populations into the mainstream of society and economic activity.

By bringing ICTs into the education environment, there may be opportunities for undertaking broader education initiatives that will bring youth into the information era. The evolution of school networking initiatives in more than 23 African countries should be seen against this background; thus it is crucial to embrace and appreciate tis potential for reducing the digital divide.

Status of education in African schools

School enrolments

While in many African countries formal education remains the largest sector and consumer of public revenues, educational participation in sub-Saharan Africa is only now approaching this level of significance. Between 1960 and 1990, the total number of persons enrolled at the three main education levels (primary, secondary and tertiary) in Africa rose on average 5 per cent (UNDP 1992).

Figure 1.1 illustrates the educational situation in terms of enrolment ratios at primary and secondary levels in the sample countries included in this publication. There have been remarkable escalations in enrolments at both the primary and secondary levels. However, the dropout rate of children from primary to secondary school is a major cause for concern. While significant improvements in educational provision at primary and secondary levels are evident, a large section of African youth is still excluded from education and will concomitantly be deprived of opportunities to benefit from the new economy.

Figure 1.1: School enrolment for selected countries,
1980 and 1994–97 as a % of total schoolgoing-age children

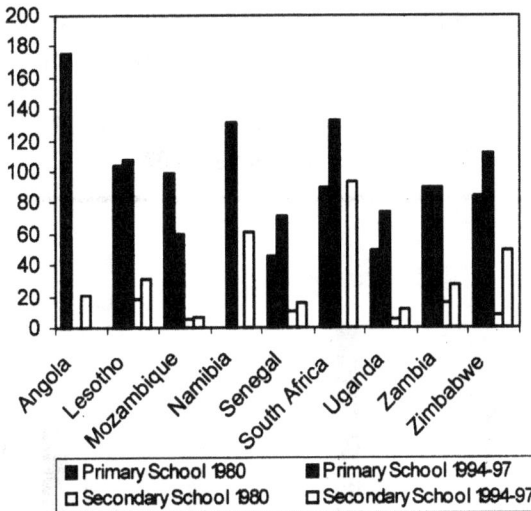

Source: World Bank (2000)

Public educational expenditure

Following years of serious economic and political instability, African countries have only recently begun to show the macroeconomic stability needed
for educational financing. Finally, African population growth rates are consistently growing at a faster rate than economic growth. For instance, between 1988 and 2000, the average per capita economic growth rate in many
of the sub-Saharan African countries was -0.1 per cent, as opposed to the
average annual population growth rate of about 2.7 per cent since 1990
(Ibid.). Against this backdrop, one would have expected increases in revenue allocations for education to keep pace with population growth. This
has not materialised, instead, spending has only been sufficient to maintain
current enrolment figures.

Figure 1.2 shows that, with the exception of Lesotho, Namibia and South
Africa, most of the selected countries have maintained relatively low revenue
expenditures on education as a percentage of gross national product (GNP).
By comparison, education spending per capita in industrialised countries is

roughly 20 times that of Africa, and almost twice as high in Asia (UNICEF). This is hardly surprising, given that many African countries have just emerged from periods of civil war, thus sufficient revenues have not yet been generated to establish education as a major priority. Many of these countries also carry heavy debt burdens that have to be serviced – they are classified in the current language of development as high interest paying countries (HIPCs)

Figure 1.2: Education expenditure as % of GNP, 1980 and 1985 versus 1990–97

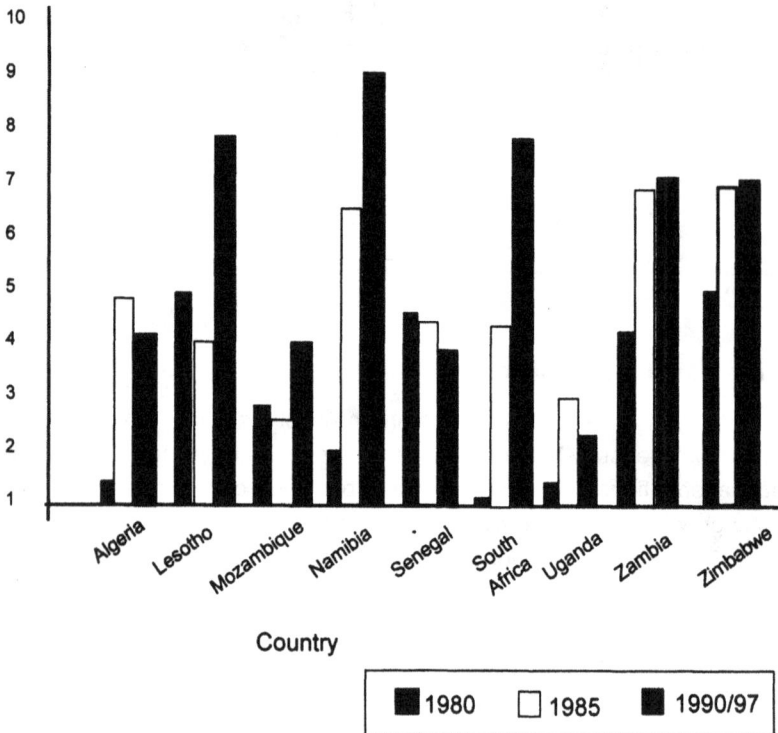

Source: African Development Bank.

Illiteracy

Figure 1.3 highlights the problem of adult illiteracy levels in the region. A notable feature in this figure is the high adult illiteracy level in Senegal relative to other countries.

Figure 1.3: Adult illiteracy rates, 1995 as a % of age 15 and over unable to read and write

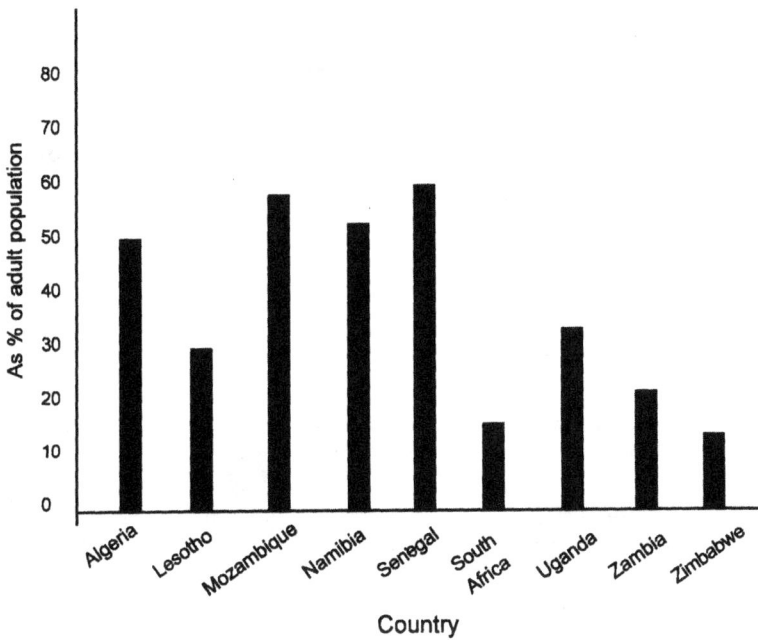

Source: African Development Bank.

Connectivity

By its very nature the ICT phenomenon is relatively new and extremely time sensitive. Available data, which are generally not as recent or as detailed as needed for many African countries, suggest that the majority of poor countries in sub-Saharan Africa are lagging behind in the information revolution.

Not surprisingly, the quest for connectivity has been problematic and will require fundamental shifts in the regulatory environment, as well as renewed attention to public-private partnerships and social services. For example, developed countries have 80 per cent of the world's Internet users, while the total international bandwidth for all of Africa is less than that of the city of São Paulo, Brazil (UNHD 2001).

Table 1.1: Number of Internet users, 1999 and 2002 (NUA)

Region	Number of Users (millions)	
	1999	Feb. 2002
Africa	3.11	4.15
Asia/Pacific	104.88	157.49
Europe	113.14	171.35
Middle East	2.40	4.65
Canada & USA	167.12	181.23
Latin America	16.45	25.33
World Total	**407.10**	**544.20**

All 54 African countries now have an Internet presence (Jensen 2002). Few countries from the region are, however, able to keep pace with the developed countries along a number of dimensions, which include:

Telephony

In 1998 there were 146 telephones per 1,000 people in the world, but only three per 1,000 in countries such as Uganda (World Bank 1998). More recently, there has been a rapid growth on the African continent in mobile telephony, which has far surpassed the number of landlines in countries where it is available (Table 1.2).

Computers

In 1998 for the world, there were 70.6 personal computers (PCs) per 1,000 people, with 311.2 per 1,000 in developed countries, compared with 7.5 per 10 000 in sub-Saharan Africa.

Bandwidth and speed

The amount of bandwidth a country has tells how much information can quickly travel from one country to another. By late 2000, the bulk of Internet connectivity linked the United States (USA) with Europe (56 gigabytes per second) and, to a lesser extent, the USA with the Asia-Pacific region (18gbps). Africa had extremely little bandwidth reaching Europe (0.2 gbps) and the USA (0.5 gbps). The latest figures indicate that the total international incoming Internet bandwidth is now well over 1 gbps, while outgoing traffic is estimated at about 800 megabytes per second (Jensen 2002).

Table 1.2 Estimated number of mobile phone users
in selected African countries, 1998–2001 (NUA)

Region	Number of Users		
	Dec. 1998	Dec. 2000	Nov. 2001
Mozambique	–	–	101 ,000
South Africa	2,552,900	7,060,000	9,400,000
Uganda	–	–	280 ,000
Zimbabwe	–	175 ,000	330, 000
Africa Total			**23,000,000**

Africa, with its 739 million people, has only 14 million phone lines, a figure lower than that of Manhattan or Tokyo. Some 80 per cent of these lines are found in only six countries. The *United Nations Human Development Report* (UNHD 2000) indicates that industrialised countries with only 15 per cent of the world's population are home to 88 per cent of all Internet users. The geographical distribution of Internet hosts further illustrates the wide differences in connectivity between industrialised and developing countries.

Table 1.3: Telephone, mobile and Internet penetration in recent years, 1997–99

	1997	1998	1999
Telephone Mainlines per 1,000 persons			
Asia-Pacific	52	60	71
Eastern Europe	197	212	227
Latin America & Caribbean	109	121	139
Middle East & North Africa	90	99	109
Sub-Saharan Africa	30	33	35
Excluding South Africa	6.7	7.3	8
OECD Countries	541	551	561
Mobile Phones per 1,000 persons			
Asia-Pacific	12	20	31
Eastern Europe	13	27	45
Latin America & Caribbean	25	41	66
Middle East & North Africa	20	28	40
Sub-Saharan Africa	10	15	19
Excluding South Africa	0.7	1.6	3
OECD Countries	195	268	332
Internet Hosts per 1,000 persons			
Asia-Pacific	0.6	1.0	1.1
Eastern Europe	0.9	1.4	2.4
Latin America & Caribbean	0.5	1.0	1.5
Middle East & North Africa	0.6	1.1	2.1
Sub-Saharan Africa	0.7	0.8	0.9
Excluding South Africa	0.013	0.036	0.041
OECD Countries	34.3	49.6	64.1

Source: World Bank (2000)

In 1999, there were only one million Internet subscribers on the entire African continent, compared with 15 million in the United Kingdom (UK). The average country of the Organisation for Economic Cooperation and Development (OECD) has roughly 40 times the per capita number of computers of a sub-Saharan African country (South Africa excluded), 110 times as many mobile phones, and 1 600 times as many Internet hosts.

The differences are less marked with respect to the forms of technology that have been around longer – particularly television sets – but are still noticeable.

To summarise, the available information suggests there is a digital divide between Africa and the developed world. At the same time, however, there has been significant growth in ICTs. This creates opportunities for addressing some of the major educational problems the continent faces. The establishment of school networking projects in Africa is therefore an opportunity to bring youth into the global information society.

The role of school networking projects in Africa

The development and deployment of ICTs in education are perceived as important priorities for a nation. Howell and Lundall (2000) state that:

> ... the literature strongly indicates that the effective use of ICTs in a country impacts strongly on the competitiveness of that economy within the global marketplace as well as the ability of the governments to deliver on their social goals.

While the causality expressed in this claim is contestable, the strong positive correlation between economic development and use of ICTs could invite such a perception. Many countries thus cite the use of ICTs as a strategy for economic development, seeing an investment in ICTs as an investment in the future. Believing these developments are, 'Exposing today's kids to new ways of thinking to be able to compete tomorrow in a global environment,' (IDRC 2000) they express this view. ICTs then become part of the vision for both globalisation and the development of communities, with the promise of a medium that is not bound by time and space. Meanwhile, time and space remain barriers to the development of ICTs in education in Africa. What is not questioned is that ICTs have become a means for communication, between people and of information, and that these means promise to be cost effective.

> [T]he growing use of databases and information warehouses, together with the explosion in the use of e-mail to facilitate quick, low-cost communication, are two relatively simple applications that can prove very cost effective (James 2001).

SchoolNet projects – What they aim to achieve

The aims of SchoolNet interventions vary enormously across projects and regions. For some the aim is to increase exposure to and awareness of computers through leisure or social use, for example in the Sayi Centre in Benin. Others require tangible changes to content and curriculum. Most aim explicitly for the improvement of communication and access to information through connectivity. Broader goals include global and local awareness, such as Partners for Internet in Africa, and SchoolNet Zambia (IDRC 2000). The development of local content is a goal expressed by several projects. The Information Policy Handbook (James 2001) regards the design and development of course materials as prerequisites. Though costly, these can be updated frequently and delivered rapidly, besides reducing paper costs. The development of local content is also posited for political, social and pedagogical reasons. It has been considered in relation to capacity, and whether or not the development of content is seen as part of the process of capacity building rather than purely as a product. Beyond new knowledge, capacity includes development in the use of ICTs as well as critical thinking skills through both developing and critiquing local and international content:

> [T]he impact of ICTs on learning is connected to the extent to which learners become critical evaluators of information to solve problems and develop new insights and understanding (Howell and Lundall 2000: 34).

Applications of ICTs in African schools range from offering optional courses in computer studies to plans to introduce ICT as a compulsory, non-promotional subject for all learners from Grades 1–12, as is the case in Namibia. Some interventions work with specific student projects – examples include the 'Laws of Life' project of the Partners for Internet in Education in Ghana, and SchoolNet Namibia's Insect@thon project on the digital classification of indigenous insects. Others include the broader community. SchoolNet Nigeria, for instance, has a problem-based learning approach that is community based and includes formal links with the United Methodist Church.

Yet others work towards national education goals for the development of the curriculum to include computer education, for example, the application of ICTs in schools and rural training centres in Lesotho (IDRC 2000).

Goals can be specific and measurable (e.g. the acquisition of funding), or they can be more general and intuitive, such as the goal of sensitising policy makers to the importance of ICTs in education. Some cite maintenance of the technology as a goal. Yet others make explicit the importance of incentive reward mechanisms for ensuring sustainability.

Some goals are research based, such as that of SchoolNet Uganda whose stated intention is to undertake a needs assessment for integrated ICT curricula and to establish the status of and requirements for connectivity in schools in different geographical locations. Others include researching the role and value of ICTs in enhancing the quality of teaching and learning. Many projects explicitly stress the importance of sharing information.

Goals thus vary from working with learners, to providing the community with information resources. Some of the specified objectives are quite vague. For instance, the University of Lesotho's school networking project aims to create an enabling environment for the innovative development of information technology in rural communities (IDRC 2000:8). Some are very ambitious. In Morocco for example, the vision for school networking is to enable young people to undertake projects designed to make a meaningful contribution to the health and welfare of the planet and its people (IDRC 2000:9). SchoolNet Nigeria's aims include leadership development, character strengthening and capacity building toward political empowerment, economic development and social revitalisation (IDRC 2000:11).

Policies for SchoolNet projects

Most policy work on ICTs in education in Africa has been funded by donor agencies rather than national governments. Countries have various approaches to policy, ranging from having no policy, such as in Angola and Malawi, to having broad policies, in the case of Mozambique and Namibia (James 2001). In some countries, education policies are established within technology policies, or educational policies are aligned to general policies, such as with the Computer Education Trust in Swaziland. Where national visions exist, computer networking tends to align with the policies (IDRC

2000:14). Where these are being developed, one finds indications of attempts to influence such policy development, for example SchoolNet SA.

Policy formation in a context of social justice would need to take account of the diverse and competing needs of the countries concerned. Importantly, without policies:

> ... that promote economic growth, the historically under-resourced public educational sector is unlikely to receive sufficient investment to allow it to adequately deploy ICTs effectively. Simultaneously, the relatively small populations and the sheer geographical challenge of reaching people require sharing of resources in order to build economies of scale (James 2001).

In Mozambique, operating from a low skills base, policy is ambitious, with the planning of incentives to develop learning and teaching using ICTs, and the provision of computers in schools. However, it remains to be seen how such plans will be implemented in relation to other pressing educational needs, such as the need for classrooms and basic classroom furniture and resources (Joint Technical Mission 2000).

According to the *Information Policy Handbook*,

> The policy positions ... when contrasted with the realities of implementation, highlight the enormous challenges (and high risk of failure) presented by education in developing countries. The low institutional, human resource and infrastructure base raises barriers to entry because ICT policies focusing on education are forced to engage with all of these related gaps and weaknesses, massively increasing the scale of the challenge. Simultaneously, this significantly increases the cost of possible policy interventions (James 2001:103)

For parts of Africa, "ICTs are not yet a high policy or financial priority" (James 2001:98). and "ICT-related education policy still needs to establish itself within this set of priorities" (Ibid.:98).

The development or redress perspective is an overall concern for many developing countries. If teaching online requires ongoing teacher development and learner support, it is unlikely in the short term that goals of mass education will be addressed through ICTs.

> Several of the broad challenges facing education systems are magnified by a low skills base, significant resource constraints, and a range of non-educational social problems that make the creation and sustenance of any stable social system harder (James 2001:92).

Reach of African SchoolNet projects

Some projects target the least privileged, like the 21st Century Kids Club project in Egypt, while others invest where the infrastructure is more reliable. Project activity is more common in secondary schools than in primary schools. In Lesotho for example, one of 1,250 primary schools and 15 of 204 secondary schools were computer active in 1999 (IDRC 2000:7).

These projects range in scope. Some aim to reach all schools in the country, while others focus on smaller pilot studies or projects. In Côte d'Ivoire, for example, two pilot schools assessed whether or not they could manage educational costs, whereas a pilot study in Egypt involved 150 schools and was followed with plans to cover all schools and develop content for all school grades (IDRC 2000:3). SchoolNet Namibia plans to have all schools connected by 2004, while SchoolNet Zambia plans to connect schools that already have computers. In Botswana and Swaziland, the policy is for all senior secondary teachers to acquire basic computer literacy and for schools to have enough computers to permit all students to develop computer skills.

Emerging models

Project activities within countries are contingent upon the perceived needs and resources available. The range of approaches that respond to context can be seen in the different paths taken toward ICT development. For example in Egypt, the 21st Century Kids Clubs aim to meet their educational goals through clubs, and the Sayi Centre in Benin through cyber centres (Ibid.:3). Telecentres were seen by some projects in Lesotho and South Africa as a way to influence education in schools and, at the same time, to provide access for the broader community (Ibid.:8,13,24).

Different partners have been solicited. The Youth Cyber Clubs project in Senegal has worked with partner schools in Canada, while SchoolNet Zimbabwe opened centres to the commercial sector during non-school hours. In some projects, innovative plans are being tested, for example a 'cyber bus' that provides mobile access and raises awareness of the possibilities of using ICTs in South Africa and Zimbabwe.

Emerging data will inform the future development of these initiatives. Tentative indications are that while telecentres may provide exposure to ICTs and raise awareness about how they can be used, ongoing use of telecentres is limited because of the difficulties in getting to them. Also, because of the number of schools linked to a centre, these may have limited impact on the schools. Despite some negative findings, some projects intend to capitalise on centres already established (e.g. SchoolNet Namibia) to improve their facilities and maximise their use. The context is dynamic, and clear indications of best practice are still to emerge, which may in any event be context specific.

The role of champions

Initiatives vary from being government led, such as in Gambia, Ghana and Senegal (Ibid.:5–12), to champion or donor led. The identification of champions or dedicated personnel, such as computer teachers, is cited as important for project success (Howell and Lundall 2000:6). For SchoolNet Namibia, the identification of champions is stated as an explicit goal: to 'highlight' and "encourage the critical role of ICT champions and mechanisms to ensure sustainability" (IDRC 2000:11). Where champions exist, it appears that schools can overcome barriers caused by inadequate resources, but that successors need to be developed to sustain the work. Where parents and governing bodies of schools become more involved in the management of schools, imperatives for ICTs in education become stronger (James 2001).

Donor support

Prominent protagonists are the World Bank's World Links for Development (WorLD), the International Development Research Centre (IDRC), the International Education and Resource Network (I*EARN) and the Department for International Development (DFID), Schools Online, and the Swedish International Development Cooperation Agency (SIDA). Shifting to the goals of donors rather than projects per se, these goals are often broad and ambitious. For example, the aims of WorLD are the provision of Internet access, training, leveraging partnerships, advocacy for educational rates in telecommunications, and evaluation. Areas of particular interest for WorLD are collaboration, cultural awareness, knowledge management and improved teaching (WorLD 2000:2). Its aims include a concern with distance learning, cultural sensitivity, economic and social development and teacher training to integrate ICTs in the classrooms.

Donor organisations support the interventions either independently or collaboratively. For some, collaboration and complementarity are seen as ideal. However, collaboration can lead to difficulties if the basic conditions

14

for participation are not established, and especially if these are dependent on infrastructural conditions and human resource capacity that have inadequately been taken into account. Partnerships are generally seen in a positive light. South Africa's SchoolNet SA is a partnership with four national government departments, the private sector and informal school networking, non-governmental organisations (NGOs) and donor communities. Some companies invest where their direct interests may be positively influenced – as with British Aerospace – (IDRC 2000:5–12), while others require an intersection of the needs and their interests. For some, the focus is one specific event, such as the International Schools Cyberfare sponsored by Cisco Systems.

Donors have undertaken much work. WorLD for example, aimed to connect at least 1,200 schools in 40 developing countries by 2000, and has projects in progress in several African countries. However, projects built on money from funding sources have uncertain futures. Unless sustainability is developed as part of the project and ownership of the project is in the hands of the recipients, the impact is likely to be limited (James 2001).

Challenges facing ICTs in Africa

The principal factors that prevent schools from using computers as tools for teaching and learning are insufficient funds, insufficient numbers of computers, lack of computer literate teachers, lack of teacher competence in integrating computers into different learning areas, and the absence of properly developed curricula for teaching computer skills (Howell and Lundall 2000). This section discusses areas that school-networking projects should address and provides examples of how countries in Africa are coping with the challenges facing them.

Availability of infrastructure

Infrastructure for online learning is crucial. Many African countries have a very low base from which to implement ICT interventions in education. It is estimated that less than 1 per cent of people in Africa use or have access to the Internet (African Development Forum 1999, as quoted in Howell and Lundall 2000:48). The figure of 139 students per computer is given for WorLD participants (WorLD 2000:6). Listed in order of rank, aspects that inhibit schools from acquiring computers are an absence of electricity, lack of funding, insufficient building space, lack of available and trained staff, and poor security. In Malawi, where most technology infrastructure is government controlled, very low levels of infrastructure for and use of ICTs are found and many government departments have themselves not yet acquired computers. In sub-Saharan Africa, the low teledensity and high costs of installing and maintaining lines are major barriers. Wireless technology is seen as a possibility for rural schools (e.g. in Lesotho). Some countries have implemented pilot projects for wireless technology in rural areas, for example SchoolNet Uganda.

Computer access and use

The development of computer use in Africa is very uneven. In some countries like South Africa, some sectors of schooling are using computers in education to an extent on par with the developed world, while others are only beginning to explore the possibilities of introducing school networking, for example SchoolNet Malawi. A few are in the start-up phase and most of the developments have been established since 1997.

Time spent on computers in SchoolNet activities in Africa is generally limited and is related to the type of access and use. Students doing computer studies will spend more time working with the technology than other students. While teachers and students in schools that have computers learn basic computer skills such as word processing, the integration of computers across learning areas happens in only a minority of schools. Pedagogical use is more common in the areas of mathematics, science and technology than in the humanities, especially since some funding is targeted at these areas, as with Microsoft in South Africa (IDRC 2000:26).

Budgeting for ICTs

Schools do not budget adequately for maintaining the use of computers, and instead dedicate their computer budgets, where these exist, to the purchase of computers and software. In schools: 'the costs of installation, maintenance and expansion remain hidden unlike in the commercial sector where the capital costs of a PC represent only one fifth of the yearly cost of running that PC' (Lynch 1999, as quoted in Howell and Lundall 2000:47).

Costs include teacher training, and additional advisory and technical staff as support, both in the technological and pedagogical fields. The Internet for Schools Project in Mozambique, for instance, has both technical and pedagogical coordinators. In addition, hardware, software, telecommunications, infrastructure such as phone lines, and content development have to be budgeted for. Fewer than 5 per cent of South African schools with computers budget for teacher training in the use of ICTs (James 2001). Initial expenditure has to be considered along with the recurrent costs in order to sustain the use of ICTs in education, in particular the investment in the human capability (Ibid.:46).

Budgets tend to derive from fees, fundraising and donations, although in some countries such as Nigeria, government funding is provided. Evidence of the cost effectiveness of spending on ICTs rather than, say, libraries has not yet been established (Ibid.:47).

Training in ICT skills

The lack of infrastructure may be compensated for by the commitment of the teachers. In some countries projects focus on training for the implementation and sustainability of ICT-based interventions in education. Some see preservice training as essential, such as the revised national policy on education in Botswana and the aims of SchoolNet Namibia (IDRC 2000:2), while others consider in-service training the appropriate response. Some hope that "cascade" models will work, like in the Ministry of Education in Gambia (Ibid.: 5). Some claim that it has already done so, as in the case of Ghana (Ibid.: 6). Others still rely on volunteers, both young and old, to sustain the intervention. Such is the case with the I*EARN Project in Côte d'Ivoire (Ibid.:4) and SchoolNet Namibia (Acacia Workshop 2001).

Training goals vary but most are based on training schedules using workshops to cover the various skills. In general, training is seen more in terms of time spent on training than in terms of outcomes such as proficiency in the skills, comfort with the technology or experience in integrating use of the Internet into curricula (Telkom).Training generally includes basic computer literacy, exposure to the basics of email, search engines, website design and the integration of technology in the classroom, in a concentrated period with groups at various levels of competence. Training may take place over a single intervention of a few days or weeks, like the Telkom 1000 Schools Internet Project in South Africa, and WorLD, I*EARN and Global

SchoolNet training in Ghana. Many teachers are new to computers and the training for this group has been ambitious.

Diverse approaches are evident in the literature. And teachers have not been the only focus for training iniatives: SchoolNet Uganda has called for the training of trainers and SchoolNet Zambia trains selected learners.

The provision of support for teachers and the development of networks form part of teachers' training. These networks offer coordination and support functions for educators and are cited as one of the factors enabling a school to overcome barriers created by inadequate resources (Howell and Lundall 2000:6). In some countries that have established associations, such as Ghana's Partners for Internet in Education, the aim is to bring together schools, companies, organisations and individuals interested in promoting and using the Internet in learning and teaching, within and across countries, which can serve to promote online learning.

The pedagogical value of ICTs

Although computers have been used in some schools in Africa for up to a decade, for example for "drill and practice" exercises in conventional curricula, the infusion of computers into all subject areas, integrated into classroom practice in a way that transforms pedagogy, is relatively new. Shifts in pedagogy include a move to problem-based or investigative learning, which not only requires learners to assume increasing responsibility for the learning process but also requires teachers to surrender the type of control over the learning process they exercise in conventional pedagogy. Learning becomes more open ended, with the teacher's role changing to one of "facilitator" rather than "provider". The assumption is that work becomes more collaborative and learners become more engaged in the learning process, seeking out new knowledge and skills motivated by need. Learning is assumed to last longer and be more "meaningful" than in more conventional models of learning as acquisition. Students with online access can manage information and communicate their ideas effectively (Sherry 1998). Learning becomes participation and acquisition in a more interactive context.

Calls for ICTs to be integrated into the curriculum have been made globally. Both developed and developing countries, such as Ireland, the USA and Canada, as well as some of the countries studied in this evaluation, are drawing up and effecting new ICT policies that make novel demands on teaching and learning. Policies for curriculum development using ICTs in some African countries are still visionary rather than material (e.g. Botswana, Egypt and South Africa).

Changing teaching and learning practices

Many ICT interventions have ambitiously stated that integration of ICTs across the curriculum is one of their major goals (e.g. the Telkom 1000 Schools Internet Project in South Africa), but the literature indicates that the widespread realisation of this goal is unlikely in the short term. Drawing on emerging data from existing interventions, reasons given for anticipated difficulties include Africa's more recent and far more limited exposure to ICTs, the lack of appropriate infrastructure such as telephony and electricity, the lack of human resource capability, and generally underserved populations. Further, a common belief is that time is needed to develop familiarity with computers and their possibilities before computer technology will restructure classroom activities. Sherry (1998:113–145) draws on Hall's (1987, as quoted in Howell and Lundall 2000:6) model of stages of concern in change. Each stage is characterised by specific questions, concerns or anxieties about the innovation and changes to practice.

Stages of development cited are those of general familiarity with the technology, with a focus on the technology itself, to a stage where the person can begin to use the technology for certain tasks, for example, writing reports or keeping records. The final stages are the competent pedagogical use of the technology, which significantly alters practices in problem solving and the critical evaluation of information found online. Although contested, some claim the longer the school has had computers, the more likely it is to be integrating them effectively into the curriculum (Howell and Lundall 2000:6). Sherry (1998) claims that the learning process in technologies for teachers who are being trained in a "train the trainer" approach are learning from peers; experimenting and adopting; co-learning and co-exploring with their students; and reflecting - rejecting or confirming the uses while becoming the next cohort of peer trainers. Shared vision is central to the model. However, strong voices for "back to basics" or the massification of traditional approaches may scupper attempts at integration, especially if dissension festers among those who can strongly influence the success of the projects.

The integration of ICTs in curricula and teacher training and confidence are integrally related. Factors that accompany the successful implementation of ICTs in schools are both networks of connectivity and ongoing teacher training, together with the uses of computers in administration and management (Howell and Lundall 2000:2). The more confident the teachers, the more integrated and innovative uses are made of ICTs. It is claimed that teachers who have attained a high sense of self-efficacy and comfort level with telecommunications are usually those who have adopted them in the classroom (Sherry 1998).

The concept of situated cognition is useful to draw on here. In "communities of practice" newcomers to the practice become legitimate peripheral participants, gradually moving to full participation over time and with more responsible participation in the practices (Lave 1991). This has implications for both teachers and learners who are new to ICTs. Two levels of community exist: the surrounding social community in which the learner participates, as well as the virtual community on the Internet. The development of ICTs in education becomes part of a learning process for teachers, learning new roles in relation both to the technology and pedagogy, and to the value they can add within developing contexts.

Using a notion of learning as participation in a community of practice makes interventions difficult to assess. Indicators, observations and perceptions can be compared if baseline studies are available, but many changes cannot be causally attributed to the intervention, nor are they likely to be seen in the short term. WorLD has benchmarks that it uses, relative to context. These pertain to measures for implementation and impact. The former include teacher training support (received and given), access, time, nature and purpose of ICT use, student-centred pedagogy, cognitively complex learning activities, collaboration (within schools and across countries), and gender participation. WorLD evaluation studies look at student technology skills and attitudes, communication and information reasoning skills, cultural awareness, attitudes to school, impact on young women, teachers' technological and pedagogical skills and attitudes, and perceptions of the potential employability of students. Sometimes, however, the effects of an educational intervention are intangible, though subjectively present.

ICTs have clearly made new demands on an already stretched sector while simultaneously offering opportunities in support of current difficulties.

The enthusiasm for ICTs may well ultimately be the catalyst for transforming dominant education practices (James 2001: 29).

Meeting the needs of diverse stakeholders

Many different interest groups are involved in online learning. These include learners and their teachers, their organisations and communities, governments, as well as the development and private sectors. All have stakes in the successful development of online learning. However, different voices about the importance of online learning are present. The optimistic voice cites the radical possibilities provided by online learning for the development of critical thinking and problem solving. The "inevitabilists" (Howell and Lundall 2000:6,24) see ICTs as part of life and believe that learners need to be equipped to deal with them, or at least not be totally disorientated by them. Pessimism is voiced about the possibilities of already underserved educational sectors in developing countries being able to invest in ICTs where other needs are more pressing.

Research and evaluation

More research is needed to evaluate the influence of online learning. Some claim insufficient evidence to attribute positive benefits to computers, while others state that if the right questions are asked, the value of ICTs in learning is certainly positive (Lundall 2000:41). Literature suggests that the more systemic the changes, the more effective ICTs will be in education (Ibid.: 42). This systemic approach includes uses of ICTs in administration and management, and in broader management of the education system. Data can be more easily collected from schools, for instance, and educators can have an easier access route to government departments where two-way communication is possible. A more holistic approach requires that schools be receptive and open to the changes ICTs may make, and to the ongoing evaluation of these changes for the schools' purposes. There is evidence from countries such as Botswana, Namibia and South Africa that investments in ICTs in some countries are now becoming sufficiently significant for systemic impact (Ibid.: 36; James 2001: 27).

This brief literature review would be incomplete without some reference to the process of evaluation itself. Evaluation research is seen as critical to understanding and directing the process of integrating ICTs in education, in this case in African SchoolNets and school networking projects. Many of the funded ICT interventions include an evaluative component such as this book provides. Evaluation is not only dynamic in that it takes account of research and development in a developing context, but the technology and approaches to evaluation change too. Evaluation processes themselves become more holistic, moving away from studies that provide reasonably certain but limited data, to a broader, richer view. Taking a view of a curriculum that includes participation in a community of practice involves looking at aspects of ICTs in education that consider developments in technology, changes in learning and teaching practice, individual and organisational learning and so on. This is not an easy task. Studies may need to become longitudinal, which will require funders to invest in longer-term initiatives, so that influences, or hypothesised influences, of the technologies may be investigated over time. Shorter studies include perceptions of participants and research the lived experiences of stakeholders in the interventions. For example, the WorLD study in Mozambique showed that WorLD had a positive impact on Mozambique teachers, with 78 per cent claiming satisfaction with the programme and 82 per cent claiming more professional satisfaction (see also SAIDE 2000a).

Sherry (1998) speaks of a structural model for ICT interventions that comprises the following components:

- Technological – access, cost, type and age of computers and hardware, physical aspects of the school network, reliability and interface;
- Individual – user characteristics and perceptions, such as motivation, need for control, attitudes, anxiety, prior experience and skill level;
- Organisational – complex needs of the educational institution, district, community and the broader community; and
- Teaching and learning factors – instructional goals, pedagogical strategies and espoused learning theories.

This is an expanded version of previous adoption models where technological barriers, user characteristics and organisational issues were studied in relation to the success of ICT innovations. This promises to be an interesting aspect of research for later evaluation studies, and teaching and learning questions could be a possible point of intervention.

Conclusion

Time and research may foreground new perspectives. One line of thinking is that Africa cannot afford to exclude itself from globalisation and global connectedness and has to "get on board" with ICTs, while others express the concern that connectivity and technology compete with more pressing priorities. Exclusion is a concern not only nationally, but also internationally. As urban centres are "better places" for digital technologies than rural areas, fears are expressed that urban-rural digital divides may intensify. With exclusion goes fears of increased antagonisms between rich and poor, young and old, urban and rural and boys and girls, across and within nations. All these tensions threaten the potential success of school networking initiatives and pose the biggest challenge for practitioners and decision makers. It is against this background, with its particular challenges and constraints, that the IDRC's evaluation of selected school networking has to be considered.

Chapter 2

Introduction to
the Evaluation Study

Shakifa Isaacs, Irene Broekman and Thomas Mogale

The IDRC's Acacia programme has, since its inception in 1997, invested considerably in promoting the establishment of SchoolNet projects in a number of African countries. Because schools are institutions where different communities converge – learners, parents, educators, school managers, unemployed youth, women and other community residents – it made sense for schools to serve as a base for community access to ICTs.

At the time, the introduction of ICTs, particularly computers and the Internet, was a new phenomenon in African communities. For this reason, an institutional mechanism had to be established to promote the ICTs in schools and to test their usefulness in enhancing school education. This was the rationale for setting up SchoolNet projects in Africa as Acacia sought to test models in differing contexts. During its first three-year phase, Acacia promoted the start-up of SchoolNet projects in nine countries in Africa: Angola, Lesotho, Mozambique, Namibia, Senegal, South Africa, Zambia, Zimbabwe and Uganda. Acacia further promoted partnerships with regional SchoolNet initiatives, such as the WorLD programme, and specifically worked with WorLD in Mozambique, South Africa, Uganda and Zimbabwe. Acacia also promoted collaboration between national school networking projects through pan-African regional workshops, which laid the basis for the promotion of SchoolNet Africa as a flagship regional initiative. By July 2000, total investment in school networking by Acacia approximated CAD 2.3 million.

The decision to evaluate the IDRC's school networking experience in Africa thus far is timely, particularly in view of its considerable investment and learning in the education arena, and the growing number of global initiatives for bridging the digital divide that have identified education as a priority area.

The IDRC-supported SchoolNet projects were established on the premise of three assumptions:

- ICTs based in schools will enhance access to information and facilitate communication in school-based communities as well as various communities based in the residential areas surrounding the schools;
- ICTs in schools will enhance access to education to those previously denied opportunities; and
- ICTs can contribute to new pedagogical methodologies, thereby enhancing learning and teaching, particularly in the context of the education crisis in Africa.

Objectives and scope of the evaluation study

This study specifically evaluated the school networking projects, otherwise known as SchoolNets, to which Acacia provided support in varying degrees during the period 1997 to 2000. This signals the end of the first phase of Acacia's support for various school networking projects. The projects included in the evaluation were selected from the following countries: Angola, Lesotho, Mozambique, Namibia, Senegal, South Africa, Uganda, Zambia and Zimbabwe.

The basic unit of analysis for the study was the specific SchoolNet project, with particular reference to the component supported by Acacia. Its main areas of investigation were the nature of the inputs, activities, outputs, effects and lessons of these SchoolNets. Given the recent nature of these SchoolNet developments, it remains too soon to conduct a comprehensive assessment of the impact on learning and teaching. Such a study may well be carried out at a later stage.

General objectives

The general objectives of this study were to:
- Document school networking projects supported by the IDRC in Africa between January 1997 and July 2000;

- Inform subsequent phases of evaluation on school networking;
- Inform the IDRC's future programming in ICT application in education;
- Inform subsequent evaluation processes and projects;
- Take the first step in the establishment of a repository of information regarding school networking experiences in Africa that can be shared with a broad range of interest groups and stakeholders; and
- Inform potential pan-African research studies related to the social dimension of ICT application in Africa.

Specific objectives

The specific objectives of this study include an attempt at investigating various start-up models for school networking in an African context, and to building upon the experiences of mature SchoolNets, with respect to the following:

- Establishing computer access and connectivity to the Internet;
- Developing the capability of educators to utilise ICTs to enhance learning and teaching;
- Developing local education content; and
- Determining the extent to which national policy on the use of ICTs in education has been developed either under the influence of the SchoolNet or whether it has influenced the development of a SchoolNet.

Conceptual background

There are varying models of school networking at different stages of development (Isaacs and Sibthorpe 2000). The suggested evolutionary stages are premised largely on functional criteria rather than time-based criteria or on the number of schools connected. The time horizon for reaching different stages differs with different SchoolNets. The stages in the life of a typical SchoolNet project are depicted in Figure 2.1, with an indication of the status of the nine projects evaluated here.

Figure 2.1: Stages of school networking

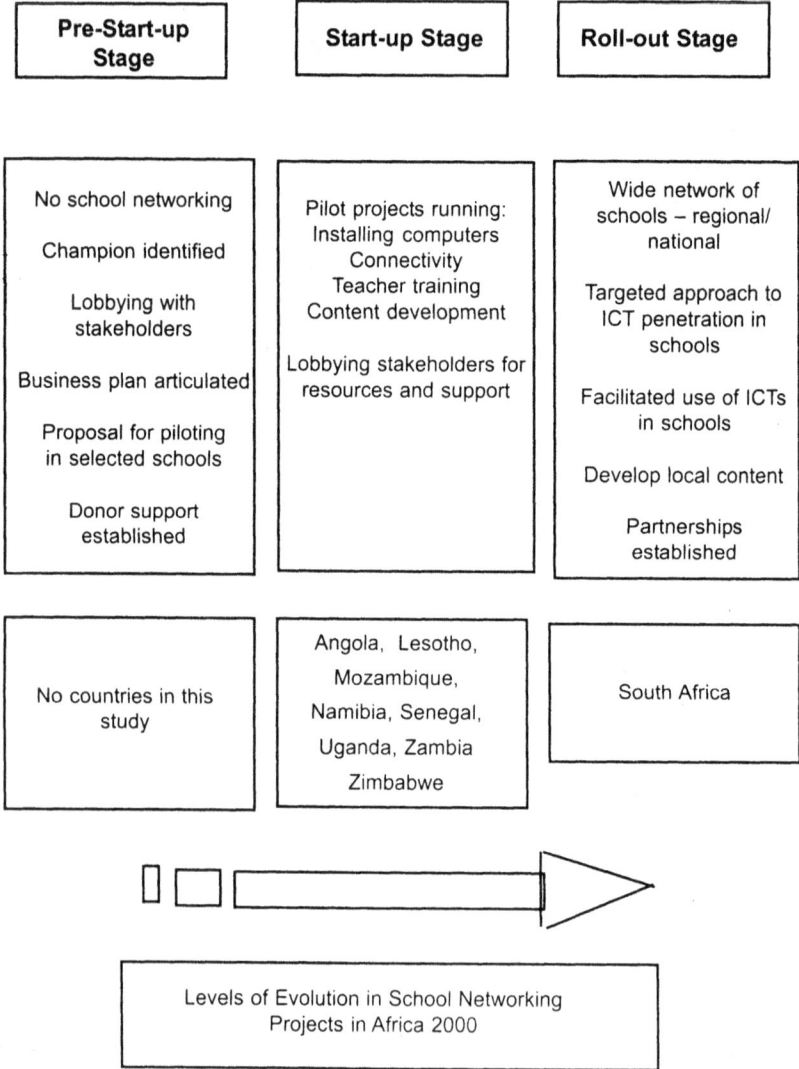

Pre-Start-up Stage	Start-up Stage	Roll-out Stage
No school networking Champion identified Lobbying with stakeholders Business plan articulated Proposal for piloting in selected schools Donor support established	Pilot projects running: Installing computers Connectivity Teacher training Content development Lobbying stakeholders for resources and support	Wide network of schools – regional/ national Targeted approach to ICT penetration in schools Facilitated use of ICTs in schools Develop local content Partnerships established
No countries in this study	Angola, Lesotho, Mozambique, Namibia, Senegal, Uganda, Zambia Zimbabwe	South Africa

Levels of Evolution in School Networking
Projects in Africa 2000

Pre-start-up stage

The pre-start-up stage is typically characterised by activities involved in setting up a structured school networking initiative, from conceptualisation of the project to its formal constitution as a school networking organisation. The pre-start-up stage bears the following characteristics:

1) A formally constituted school networking project does not exist in the country;
2) Champions to initiate school networking have been identified or have articulated interest in setting up a school networking structure;
3) Interest has been expressed and lobbied by various groups and potential partners;
4) A framework or business plan has been devised to establish a school networking project;
5) A proposal to pilot a school networking activity usually involving a few schools has been developed; and
6) Donor support has been expressed or provided to assist the pre-start-up stage.

Thus the pre-start-up stage characterises all activities that lead towards the formal constitution of a SchoolNet. The period of time for the pre-start-up phase varies from country to country, but on average appears to take between one to three years.

Start-up stage

The start-up stage commences once a SchoolNet has been formally constituted. Usually donor support has been provided to initiate the start-up stage. The SchoolNet is typically engaged in the following activities:

1) Piloting individual projects such as teacher training and installing computers in schools;
2) Piloting Internet connectivity with a few schools;
3) Developing content; and
4) Lobbying various stakeholders for resources and financial support.

Roll-out stage

The roll-out stage is characterised by a well-established SchoolNet that has:

1) Facilitated connectivity at a number of schools on a national scale, and has reached a critical mass in defining its core competency as a SchoolNet organisation;
2) Developed a targeted approach towards achieving higher levels of ICT penetration in schools in that country;
3) Developed a systematic approach towards facilitating teacher capability to use ICTs effectively in education;
4) Encouraged the development of local education content at a national level; and
5) Promoted well-developed partnerships with key school networking stakeholders.

Key concepts

It is important to provide conceptual clarity of the terminology that has been used in SchoolNet projects. This evaluation makes a distinction between school networking and SchoolNet projects. In addition, it explores four themes related to school networking activity – connectivity, teacher training, content and policy. Definitions for the various concepts explored in this book are provided below.

Information and Communication Technologies

ICTs broadly refer to:

> ... all forms of technology used to create, store, process and use information in its various forms (data, voice, image, multi-media presentations and other forms including those not yet conceived) and which enable, facilitate and support communication. More specifically, ICTs refer to the convergence of micro-electronics, computers and telecommunications which make it possible for data, including text, video and video signals, to be transmitted anywhere in the world where digital signals can be received. They include networks such as fixed, wireless and satellite telecommunications, broadcasting networks and applications such as the Internet, database management systems and multi-media tools (Howell and Lundall 2000).

While ICTs clearly encompass a wide range of technologies, for the purposes of this study ICTs refer specifically to the use of computers, email and the Internet, as these are the technologies that are used predominantly to promote school networking in the Acacia-supported SchoolNet projects.

Connectivity

This refers to the technologies that specifically allow computers and other electronic devices to communicate with each other. Telecommunications technologies, computers and Internet protocols power this type of networking, particularly the use of email and the Internet. These technologies facilitate communication between various school communities and provide the means to access information.

School networking

School networking is defined as the process that involves the installation, application and use of ICTs to enhance education in schools through the development of communication networks between learners, educators, school managers and administrators at local, national, regional and international levels. Usually the school networking process is implemented by a number of implementing agencies, of which a SchoolNet project may be one.

The "network" assumes both technical and social dimensions:

- The *technical dimension* involves the development of network technologies installed in schools that will enable school communities to have access to education information and to communicate effectively; and
- The *social dimension* of school networking involves the development of communication networks at school, local, national, regional and international levels between and among learners, educators, school managers, administrators, and ministries of education. Communication networks are also developed between these and other stakeholders such as NGOs. ICTs enhance the development and effectiveness of these communication networks, which can assume a variety of modalities.

SchoolNets

A SchoolNet project or SchoolNet typically refers to an institution or organisation that facilitates school networking activities. In the context of this evaluation, a SchoolNet typically assumes one or more of the following characteristics:

Organisational structure

- A school networking organisation is established, which facilitates school networking in a specific country;
- A few schools in the country are associated with the SchoolNet in different ways, hence forming a network of schools;
- The schools associated with the SchoolNet project have at least one computer in each school, which is used for educational purposes;
- At least one computer per school is connected to the Internet; and
- The SchoolNet project establishes partnerships with a number of stakeholders, including government, the private sector and civil society organisations.

Services

The SchoolNet facilitates the following activities:

- Sourcing of computers to be installed in schools;
- Installation of computers in schools and connecting the computers to email and the Internet;
- Provision of technical solutions and support to schools;
- Provision of teacher training in using computers to improve teaching and learning; and
- Development of educational content on the Internet.

The typical SchoolNet is also involved, to varying degrees, with policy development addressing the integration of ICTs into school education.

Access

Access refers to the ways and means in which individuals, communities and/or institutions are exposed to ICTs. It takes into consideration such elements as affordability, availability of the technologies, geographical locations of access points, and the times at which the technologies are available.

Teacher training

Teacher training refers specifically to the development of ICT skills among teachers through the efforts of the SchoolNet projects. Teacher training includes training in basic computer skills, otherwise referred to as computer literacy. It also includes methodologies for showing teachers how to use ICTs to enhance teaching. Teacher training models in a SchoolNet context typically assume the following features:

- A donor agency or private company provides funding to the SchoolNet to support a teacher training project;
- The SchoolNet project hires a service provider or experienced individuals to produce a teacher training manual or CD-ROM to provide training for teachers;
- The SchoolNet project develops criteria for selecting teachers and schools to attend the training;
- The training takes the form of a one-off introduction to ICTs, usually over a period of one to two days; and
- The donor agency works with the SchoolNet project on evaluating the teacher training project.

Content development

Content development refers to the development of a curriculum on an ICT platform. This could take the form of the production of curriculum content on compact disc (CD), as well as the development of curriculum content for interactive use by learners and educators on the Internet. In the context of this study, the following features typify education content development in a SchoolNet project:

- A donor agency, the public sector or a private company provides funding to the SchoolNet to support a pilot project on the development of local education content on the Internet for use by educators and learners;

- The SchoolNet project selects areas and schools where teachers and learners will be involved in the project;
- The SchoolNet project hires a service provider to work alongside the learners and educators in developing local content; and
- The SchoolNet project and its service provider evaluate how local content is utilised among learners and educators.

Policy

Policy refers to the role played by SchoolNet projects in the development of policy or by influencing national ICT policy processes in general. More specifically, it applies to educational policy that accommodates the application of ICTs in education.

Evaluation approach and methodology

This evaluation study was conducted within the framework laid down by the Acacia Evaluation and Learning System (ELSA). ELSA makes a distinction between ongoing performance monitoring, which tracks whether actual performance and results are on target, and more discrete evaluations, discontinuous data collections or analytical studies, which assess issues such as effectiveness, sustainability and the impact of programmes. ELSA is based on the premise that a series of feedback mechanisms are in place between the various stakeholders so that they will receive timely information to support management, investment or other decisions (Whyte 2000).

In the case of school networking projects up to July 2000, the projects were evaluated retrospectively. These summative evaluations are intended to serve as baseline data for continuous, formative evaluation in subsequent phases of Acacia's school networking projects (July 2000 onwards), should these projects continue.

Figure 2.2 illustrates the process that was followed in each of the SchoolNet projects under evaluation. What it illustrates is the level of interaction between the in-country evaluation teams and others involved in the evaluation process.

Figure 2.2: Process followed for the evaluation of Acacia-supported SchoolNet projects in Africa

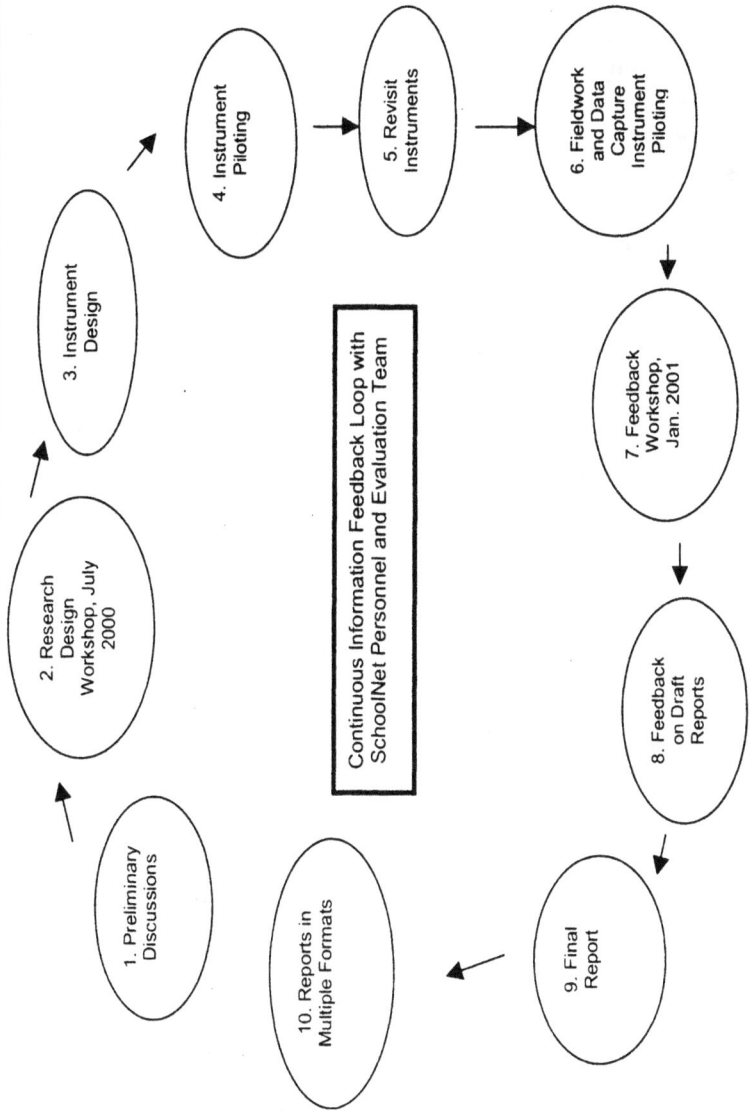

1. Preliminary Discussions

2. Research Design Workshop, July 2000

3. Instrument Design

4. Instrument Piloting

5. Revisit Instruments

6. Fieldwork and Data Capture Instrument Piloting

7. Feedback Workshop, Jan. 2001

8. Feedback on Draft Reports

9. Final Report

10. Reports in Multiple Formats

Continuous Information Feedback Loop with SchoolNet Personnel and Evaluation Team

Following preliminary discussions, a research design workshop was held in July 2000. This was attended by SchoolNet project managers from Mozambique, South Africa and Zambia, and representatives from the IDRC's Acacia programme. The workshop agreed on the focus on starting up SchoolNet projects in Africa, and on conducting in-depth studies of the SchoolNet projects in the four Acacia national strategy countries – Mozambique, Senegal, South Africa and Uganda.

Existing documentation was reviewed and research instruments were designed and piloted. Appendix 1 includes an example of an evaluation framework developed for the SchoolNet South Africa case study, and which formed the basis for the development of the research instruments.

With subsequent refinement of the instruments, fieldwork was undertaken, which entailed site visits, questionnaires and interviews. A feedback workshop was held in January 2001 with the evaluation team researchers. Representatives from the school networking agencies in each of the nine pan-African research study countries were present to comment on the research that had been undertaken in their specific contexts. A final research report was compiled with the intention of producing it in multiple formats (books, website and CD-ROM versions).

Overview of the evaluated SchoolNet projects

Table 2.1 outlines each of the nine SchoolNet projects investigated in this evaluation study. Acacia supported all of them to a greater or lesser degree. The size, scope and activities of these projects differ significantly from one another, and are at varying phases of development.

Angola

The school networking project was undertaken in partnership with the Catholic University of Angola based in the capital city Luanda, Ebonet – the local Internet service provider, and the Angola Education Assistance Fund based in Boston, USA. The start-up activity entailed connecting three schools in Luanda to the Internet and training teachers at these schools in basic ICT skills. The Catholic University was used as its base. The start-up process in this case did not involve setting up SchoolNet Angola as an institution, nor did it support the employment of full-time personnel to run the institution.

Lesotho

The Lesotho project, the "Application of ICTs in Schools and Rural Training Centres," was set up to provide connectivity to a Centre for Rural Business and Community Development in Liphering, providing ICT access to ten schools and four tertiary institutions in the area. The project also targeted four training programmes to train 38 teachers, rural development workers, students and trainers in Liphering and to train teachers near the Institute of Extra-Mural Studies. The project was geared towards creating awareness of the potential of ICT in the schools and the community.

Mozambique

Acacia supported the establishment of an Internet for Schools project in partnership with the Centre for Informatics based at the University Eduardo Mondlane (CIUEM) in Maputo, UNESCO's Southern African Intergovernmental Informatics Programme (IIP), the Ministry of Education and the World Bank's World Links for Development Programme (WorLD). This project targeted ten schools that would receive 11 computers with email and Internet connectivity, content and courseware development and a report on learning and teaching outcomes.

Namibia

Acacia supported the development of a business and strategic plan as part of the process to set up SchoolNet Namibia as a formal institution. SchoolNet Namibia was set up in partnership with a range of education, private sector and government institutions.

Senegal

Acacia supported the Youth Cyber Clubs project, which involved the establishment of 12 cyber youth clubs as part of a national network of youth clubs in schools. The project is an experiment in secondary schools that allows for ongoing dialogue and increased public awareness on adolescent issues, using ICTs, in Senegalese schools. The project was developed in partnership with an NGO called Group pour l'Etude et Enseignment de la Population (GEEP), the Ministry of Education and a Canadian youth group called Club 2/3 Canada.

South Africa

SchoolNet South Africa (SNSA) involved the employment of a full-time executive director and technical director and the establishment of SNSA as an NGO, housed in the IDRC offices in Johannesburg. SNSA's original start-up objective was to provide one to three computers to 48 schools and hold eight educator training workshops.

Uganda

Acacia collaborated with WorLD in the start-up of SchoolNet Uganda. The partnership took the form of regular communication between Acacia and SchoolNet Uganda, which laid the basis for the establishment of CurriculumNet, a project geared towards developing local education content on the Internet. CurriculumNet commenced in December 2000 with support from Acacia.

Zambia

Acacia supported a project that provided the basis for the establishment of a national SchoolNet structure by targeting 14 provincial teacher resource centres situated in each of the nine provinces in Zambia. These centres were already equipped with computers, telephone lines and electricity.

Zimbabwe

Acacia supported the development of a WorLD SchoolNet project, SchoolNet Zimbabwe, by providing financial support for a national workshop on ICT in basic education, the training of trainers and of schools involved in the networking programme, and the development of provincial business plans. The project was organised in partnership with the Computer Society of Zimbabwe, WorLD, the Ministry of Education, the British Council, Peace Corps Zimbabwe and UNESCO.

* * *

Therefore, in some cases where Acacia actively promoted and supported the development of a SchoolNet, while in others it supported start-up activities under the aegis of existing institutions. In the case of both SchoolNet Zimbabwe and SchoolNet Uganda, WorLD played was instrumental in setting up these institutions, whereas Acacia supported two start-up activities in Zimbabwe.

Table 2.1: SchoolNet projects evaluated in this study, late 2000

Country	Project Title	Phase of SchoolNet	Brief Description	Project Value (CAD)	Project Duration
Angola	School Networking in Angola	Early start-up	Connectivity with three urban schools.	31 871	6 months
Lesotho	Application of ICTs in Schools and Rural Training Centres	Early start-up	Introduction of the concept of school networking and providing sites to show how the use of ICTs can be of benefit to education.	27 500	1 year
Mozambique	Introduction of ICTs in Secondary Schools in Mozambique	Start-up	Introduction of computer literacy into secondary education.	437 855	3 years
Namibia	Support to SchoolNet Namibia Implementation	Late start-up/early implementation	Support for the development of business and strategic plans for the establishment of SchoolNet Namibia.	50 000	1 year

Table 2.1: SchoolNet projects evaluated in this study, late 2000 (Continued)

Country	Project Title	Phase of SchoolNet	Brief Description	Project Value (CAD)	Project Duration
Senegal	Youth Cyber Clubs	Early start-up	Using schools in supporting youth access to ICTs.	207 180	2 years
South Africa	Development of SchoolNet SA Programme	Implementation	Establishing SchoolNet SA.	472 000	Initially two years
Uganda	SchoolNet Uganda	Implementation	WorLD project	No funding from Acacia	Initiated in 1996
Zambia	Promotion of Regional School Networks in Southern Africa	Early start-up	Developing school networking projects in Zambia.	29 804	9 months
Zimbabwe	Promotion of Regional School Networks in Southern Africa	Start-up	Developing school networking projects in Zimbabwe.	29 804	6 months

The full range of SchoolNet projects supported by Acacia is incorporated in this study, which allows for a comprehensive overview of the wide range of experiences. Notably the study did not take the form of a comparison between the various SchoolNet projects but, instead, focused on experience with SchoolNet projects in sub-Saharan Africa.

Research questions

The primary evaluation questions for this study were:

1) How have SchoolNet projects been implemented and what have been the effects of IDRC's investment in supporting school networking start-ups?
2) What lessons emerge from the activities and developments of IDRC supported SchoolNet projects?
3) What common themes, trends and lessons emerging from school networking can guide future SchoolNet projects and evaluation activities?
4) What areas require further investigation and what evaluation agenda is proposed for the subsequent phases of IDRC's evaluation and research?

In addition to the primary research questions posed, the following themes were explored – context, infrastructure and connectivity, content development, teacher training, policy, project planning, project activities and implementation, effects of the project and the lessons learnt. There were, however, variations between the country studies, as circumstances demanded. A detailed list of the types of questions posed is included in Appendix 2.

Data-gathering techniques

The following data-gathering techniques were applied:

- **Document reviews:** This included, inter alia, project proposals, progress reports, planning documents, correspondence, annual reports and websites, as well as policy documentation.
- **In-depth interviews (face-to-face and telephone):** Key stakeholders included project staff and committee members, government officials,

41

teachers and students, Acacia staff and other key beneficiaries identified by the evaluation team.

- **Email surveys:** As a data collection technique, the email survey proved
  useful because a number of countries were covered at much lower
  direct research costs, and respondents had time to consult other relevant documents and people when answering the questions. However,
  the limitations with this technique were the lack of control by the research team over the process of completing the questionnaire, delays
  resulting from technical problems, and misinterpretation of questions.
- **Site visits and observation:** Details are provided for each of the case
  studies presented later in this book.
- **Photo documentation,** where available.

Validation of the research results included:

- Interviewing different stakeholders on the same issues in order to obtain a range of views and opinions;
- Conducting site visits and testing observations against the points raised
  in interviews;
- In some of the country studies, researchers tested the computers by
  trying to log on, access the Internet, send email and open other programmes such as MS Word, Excel and PowerPoint. The latest documents on the computers were also checked to find out whether the
  computers had actually been used; and
- A feedback workshop was organised with SchoolNet project managers
  in January 2001. Here the research findings were presented to the
  SchoolNet project managers, evaluators and donor representatives,
  who gave extensive comments on the findings. This workshop included
  a site visit by the entire workshop team to a local school in South Africa
  and tested the findings of the visit against the research findings of the
  SchoolNet study.

Challenges in the research process

A range of factors influenced the outcomes of the research, particularly
during the data collection phase. These included:

- The timing of data collection. The data were collected at a time when students were writing exams, which limited the amount of teacher and student time available. As a result, the number of teachers and students that could be interviewed was very limited.
- As English was the language of communication during the interviews, and the informants from different African countries spoke English as a second language only, this impacted on the quality of the information provided.
- In some countries, the key respondents were not available. In Angola, for example, the researcher only interviewed one respondent. This has major implications for the extent to which one can generalise the findings of this evaluation study.
- A related factor is that some SchoolNet projects had no people employed on a full-time basis. The board and steering committee members were employed elsewhere and their participation in the SchoolNet project was on a voluntary basis, making it difficult to arrange for an interview. Two cases in point were SchoolNet Zambia and SchoolNet Namibia, where the researcher had to spend more days on the site visits than initially planned for, because some of the crucial members of the board were not available.
- A number of the SchoolNet projects had multiple sources of funding and in some cases such as SchoolNet Zimbabwe, Acacia support was minimal. This affected the assessment of the direct impact of Acacia's support in particular.
- Some of the projects did not have a management structure – Lesotho and Zimbabwe are cases in point. This made it difficult, particularly in the case of the start-up projects, to access key players.
- Generally there were poor responses to the email surveys, where these were undertaken.
- The SchoolNet projects were at different levels of development. Some projects (such as the one in Lesotho) had only just started their activities during the time of data collection, which made it difficult for some issues to be probed.

Chapter 3

Emerging Pictures – Lessons Learnt and Recommendations

Tina James

Introduction

Scrutiny of the results of this evaluation study reveals a number of lessons that can be regarded as emerging best practice for developing SchoolNets. This chapter therefore presents the emerging base of lessons that can inform both new and existing projects, as well as guide policy-making processes. It provides suggestions and makes recommendations for future projects, and also lists possible research areas that merit further attention. The outcomes of the study are presented at this early stage in the book so that the reader can relate the specific start-up experiences of country case studies to the broader perspectives that have been consolidated here.

The chapter discusses the following broad areas:

- Conceptualisation of a SchoolNet project;
- Institutionalisation;
- Connectivity and Access;
- Capacity Building and Teacher Training;
- Content Development;
- Policy; and
- Future Research.

Initial conceptualisation and planning of SchoolNet projects

The initial conceptualisation and subsequent planning of SchoolNet projects are crucial milestones in determining whether the eventual implementation will be successful or not. A number of very important lessons emerged during the evaluation – the importance of thinking big and the need to think of sustainability beyond the lifespan of a donor's funding cycle.

Small is beautiful, large is necessary

All the SchoolNet projects in this study were conceptualised and implemented as pilot initiatives, which in some cases were very small-scale ones. This means that they were designed as an experiment and hence their implementation was likely to be fraught with unforeseen difficulties and challenges with unintended and unexpected consequences.

The experience with most pilot initiatives is that they rarely progress beyond the testing phase. While development discourse is permeated with the language of 'sustainability', the conceptualisation of the SchoolNet projects at the design stage did not factor in the possibilities for scaling up and moving beyond the pilot phase, nor was sustainability factored into the original plan. SchoolNet Namibia is perhaps the rare example in this study – it was conceptualised initially as a pilot but then very rapidly proceeded with developing a systemic approach by devising a national strategy for integrating ICTs in all schools in that country.

While this may be the case, there can be little doubt that the major impact of ICTs educationally will be at the macro-systemic level. The reasons for this are twofold:

- Investment in ICTs is being mobilised – in Botswana, Namibia and South Africa at least – in significant enough quantities for their impact to be of serious consequence. (There is sufficient anecdotal evidence to suggest that this level of spending may well spread to other countries in the region); and
- At the macro-systemic level, efficiencies derived from using any particular technology have an impact that far surpasses the use of that technology at the project or microlevel.

At the project level or microlevel, the justification for using ICTs is usually quite easy to establish. Individuals can, with the right focus and skills, deploy technologies to increase their efficiency and productivity significantly. Small projects stand to benefit significantly from intelligently considered integration of ICTs into project management, whether this is to improve communication, to generate project documentation more efficiently, or to harness the power of software applications (desktop publishing, graphics packages, and so on). Likewise, it is possible to construct small-scale educational interventions that demonstrate the educational potential of ICTs.

However, there are associated problems when it comes to scaling up these projects. Most importantly, scaling up a system of any significance does not, by definition, improve the efficiency or productivity of that system. Here, 'efficiency' and 'productivity' are used to describe the two complementary gains that a technology must demonstrate before investment in it can be justified. Either it must demonstrate potential to allow a system to produce at lower cost what it was able to produce without the technology (increased efficiency), and/or it must demonstrate potential to allow a system to produce more – or operate better – than it was able to produce or operate without the technology (increased productivity). Although this may seem a crude generalisation, it is a fundamental rationale behind any technological investment, subversion of which will undermine the system's ability to function over time.

What works well at the microlevel can be disastrous at the macrolevel, because it may require levels of complexity that a large system is unable to accommodate sustainably. More often than not, models of successful ICT use at the microlevel are evolved by dedicated, highly proficient individuals, and depend on these people's personal traits and commitment for ongoing success. Such models do not translate easily or at all to the macro-systemic level. On the contrary, attempts to escalate such models of operation to the systemic level may have a seriously destabilising effect on a large system.

Linked to this problem is the concern about the financial impact of scaling up successful small-scale educational practices. Certain distance education practices provide adequate evidence of this problem. The South African Institute for Distance Education (SAIDE), an NGO based in South Africa, has costed models of distance education developed for use at a very small scale (say, 30 to 250 learners), which are pedagogically sound and sometimes financially sound as well because participating individuals are willing to invest huge amounts of time and energy into their implementation. Taken to scale (i.e. thousands of learners), however, these models would overload the systems in which they operate, as they would place impossible financial demands on them. In one example, a sustained loss of US$ 4 million over ten years was projected for a distance education programme being planned because it attempted to translate the logic of microlevel teaching into a very large programme.

Further, it is much harder at the systemic level to justify the massive levels of investment that would be required in ICTs. At the macrolevel, project planners lose this control, often with serious unintended consequences. If use of ICTs fails in a single university course or at one school, the consequences are relatively easily contained. However, if technology is integrated into mission-critical systems (e.g. deployment of a new, computerised student registration system), failure has much more serious implications.

Ongoing policy research, development, and implementation processes need to be aware of the significant differences between micro- and macromodels of ICT use. By definition, national policies will be primarily interested in models of ICT use that are relevant at the macrolevel, and care should therefore be taken to ensure that these models do not simply draw on successful models of ICT use developed under very specific circumstances at the microlevel.

Given the contextual realities of Africa, this approach has to begin with:

- Strategies for improving basic national infrastructure (roads and telecommunications) and for reducing the costs of using this infrastructure sustainably;
- Building the professional capacity of people and organisations throughout all levels of the system who will, in some way or another, take responsibility for use of ICTs in education; and
- Ensuring financial accountability by integrating expenditure on ICTs into sustainable budgets at national and institutional levels.

Focusing on these basic building blocks in national policies is likely to create the conditions most necessary for successful integration of ICTs into education systems, and thus will ensure that the potential of these technologies is realised in the shortest possible time. Given the challenges facing the region's education systems, this endeavour becomes a matter of some urgency.

Pushing the concept of ICTs or 'ICTs in education'

The evaluation study shows that SchoolNet projects have developed a stronger 'technological' than 'educational' approach, with their activities focused mainly on installing and making accessible the technologies, and less on using them for educational purposes. This has arguably been a necessary first step for SchoolNets, given the problems associated with gaining access to the technologies in the first place. Since the integration of ICTs into educational systems is still largely uncharted territory, it becomes clear that more research is needed on how such integration can be managed, and to support well-planned exploration and develop a system where lessons learned from such exploration are systematically integrated into new projects.

Institutionalisation

Institutionalisation refers to the mechanisms put in place to ensure that a project has the necessary strategies and implementation plans, management structures, staffing, facilities and capacity (financial and human resources) to deliver on its set goals and objectives. Presented below are a number of guidelines that could be followed to ensure that SchoolNet projects are sustainable in this regard.

The realities of contexts need to shape the project

One of the critical decisions that has to be made relates to the scale of implementation. Often ambitious projects do not take sufficient cognisance of the realities. A project is affected by contextual factors such as infrastructure, shortage of ICT skills, geographical location, and lack of a culture of use of technologies. Similarly, the working conditions of employees also affect the chances of successful implementation. When a project is initiated, it is viewed as an opportunity for a job and payment is expected. When such expectations are not met, people become demoralised.

Projects should start by performing an infrastructure and ICT skills audit at the national level. If ICT skills are concentrated in one province or city, then the project should be initiated where there are available skills and resources, or where these are likely to be developed relatively quickly. Expansion to other areas can be considered at a later stage. This will reduce the initial risk of failure and allow project implementation to be undertaken in a less risky environment, thus increasing the likelihood of achieving success. In most of the evaluated projects in this study, informants were adamant that it was access to electricity and telephone lines that should determine the selection of schools to participate in the project.

Simple and clear project objectives are important

Key objectives must be clear. Where a project is being implemented on a long-term basis, specific phases of implementation with clear objectives for each phase need to be determined. Timeframes and measurable deliverables for the completion of project phases must be made clear to all stakeholders. Accountability for deliverables should also be clearly articulated so that there is no confusion as to who will be held responsible for completing tasks and activities. This will make the ongoing monitoring and evaluation of a project easier and ensure that project deliverables have been met; that problems are picked up in time; and that the project is implemented effectively and efficiently. Regular meetings and updates are necessary to keep stakeholders informed of progress on the project.

Dedicated ICT champions: Blessing or curse?

The most successful SchoolNets appear to be the ones that have dedicated champions. A champion who is considered a good leader for a school networking initiative should provide visionary leadership and possess good communication and project management skills. Champions should also have excellent lobbying and negotiating skills and strong networks in both the public and private sectors. Generally champions are characterised by high levels of enthusiasm.

Dedicated champions should not be equated with full-time paid staff. In some cases, the role of a champion can be fulfilled on a part-time or volunteer basis, by a person who is driven by the vision and future potential of the project. This person may be a key stakeholder in government or a community member, and may not even be the project manager, although having the latter fulfil the role of champion does appear to bring many advantages to a SchoolNet project.

Many informants reiterated the role of ICT champions at every level of the organisation, from the level of executive director to the level of individual educators. As illustrated in the case of SchoolNet SA, motivated educators were a powerful force in the realisation of large-scale project implementation, and required little intervention from the national level.

There is the danger, however, of developing a dependency on one or a few individuals. This poses problems for sustainability as projects easily collapse when those individuals move away from the project. Similarly, because an undue amount of their time goes into making the project work, these individuals also find few – if any – opportunities to undertake meaningful succession planning. Thus it is proposed that developing a team of SchoolNet leaders and managers is imperative in order to avoid dependence on individuals. Developing such a team requires effective team building and capacity building in leadership skills, in particular.

Volunteerism may put the project at risk

In countries where incomes are very low, and where there is no culture of volunteerism, it is difficult to sustain the necessary momentum with volunteers only. In most cases, volunteers appear to expect some payment for their services and are unlikely to stay with a project if this is not forthcoming. The difficulties faced by Zambia and Mozambique's SchoolNet projects relate directly to this factor – the pace of project development was affected negatively because people participated on an ad hoc basis, as and when they had the time and inclination.

Using volunteer staff (usually teachers) also presented difficulties when their regular workloads became too heavy to cope with the additional demands of teaching and supporting ICTs at the school level. This was particularly noticeable in cases where schools relied on volunteer teachers for technical support.

Train to sustain scarce management resources

Project management and implementation skills are scarce in Africa, and even more so in rural areas. It is worth noting that this also extends to weak capacity in the private sector, where both ICT skills and entrepreneurial capital are much more limited than in other parts of the world. This makes it significantly more difficult to generate innovative local solutions to educational problems, and also raises the cost of attempting to maintain technology-dependent projects. These realities may explain, in part, why so many of the SchoolNet projects have international links or are initiated by international agencies. Aside from directing resources to capacity building, strategies for dealing with this problem might be to ensure that:

- The project has the support of the key decision makers before it starts;
- There is a formalised 'mentorship' or understudy programme to diffuse skills in-house;
- There is a suitable management structure, with shared knowledge transfer mechanisms in place;
- Support functions are centralised and shared once connectivity is achieved, which allows most maintenance issues to be dealt with online; and
- ICTs are used to retain organisational learning through keeping proper electronic records and data – this will ensure that some of the knowledge and learning in the organisation are not lost when a key staff member or champion leaves.

Create flexible management structures

For a successful start-up phase, there needs to be a flexible management structure, one that allows exploration of different ideas and is very responsive to an environment that requires quick decision making. Because of its inflexible bureaucratic nature, the public sector may therefore not be the optimal structure to run a SchoolNet project, particularly during the start-up phase.

Incubate within an existing organisation

Incubation in existing institutions (whether universities, Ministries of Education or the private sector) has been the appropriate starting point for most SchoolNets. It serves to consolidate partnerships with established education institutions and encourages outreach within universities. From a SchoolNet development perspective, it promotes an awareness of the potential that ICTs hold for the promotion of education.

Set up as an independent NGO

Another essential ingredient for success is the establishment of the SchoolNet initiative as an independent organisational entity. This not only reinforces ownership and control by the SchoolNet governing structures and staff, but also widens the scope for decision making and determining SchoolNet activities and partnerships. While establishing an independent organisation is essential, this has to be coupled with the development of the network through partnerships with government ministries, the private sector and civil society structures. For example, the strength of SchoolNet Namibia lay in its independence from the government and the private sector, although it developed strong partnerships with stakeholders in these sectors. In Zimbabwe, the SchoolNet project interviewees cautioned against a dependency on the Ministry of Education.

Play an advocacy role

In many of the countries under evaluation SchoolNets have played a leading role in raising awareness of the use and importance of ICTs in education. In some cases they are seen as the strategic partners of Ministries of Education (as in Mozambique and South Africa). In others they have played a strong advocacy role in communities and among the youth (e.g. Senegal). In Uganda, SchoolNet's advocacy role to parents has been recognised and suggestions were made that schools should organise workshops to expose parents to the benefits of ICTs and to see what they are paying for. There is also a need for schools to extend their partners beyond the parent community, thus building local partnerships to mobilise resources.

Understand the implications of donor support on financial sustainability

The SchoolNet projects in this study have, in most cases, been exclusively donor funded. This should be distinguished from donor-driven projects where the donor provides the leadership. The research in this study suggests strongly that all the SchoolNets were driven and led by local project leaders and not by the donors.

A number of the SchoolNets have not been able to move beyond donor resource and financial inputs, and hence a dependency has been created, especially because the projects were not planned to generate revenue and support from other sources at the outset. However, there are cases where an embryo of financial sustainability has emerged, particularly in the form of private sector involvement and support for the projects. SchoolNet South Africa and SchoolNet Namibia are cases in point.

Where models of financial sustainability are not encouraged to emerge, the medium- to long-term future of projects is rendered very fragile. This is exacerbated by projects that do not ensure that the prerequisite ownership by intended recipients is in place before proceeding, resulting in these initiatives remaining very much at the margins of social activity and limited in impact. In Zambia, for instance, the process of developing the project proposal for the IDRC was flawed. It was reactive, rather than proactive, in the sense that the project proposal was developed to respond to an IDRC request for a school networking initiative in Zambia to spend US$ 20,000. This resulted in inappropriate activities being included in the proposal, and important aspects being neglected during the process of development. For example, some of the technologies proposed and purchased were very inappropriate for the conditions in Zambia.

The lesson for the IDRC, SchoolNet projects and particularly communities that intend to start up new SchoolNets is that, at the design stage, it is important to factor in the possibilities for moving beyond the pilot phase and to develop a framework for sustainability at the inception stage. From an evaluation perspective, clarity on the research questions is crucial at the outset of the project. These should be clearly stipulated in project agreements and proposed outcomes be identified as deliverables.

Develop a clear partnership strategy

Partnerships with a number of stakeholders are an important criterion for success. They can assume different forms, in terms of both financial support as well as non-financial support, the latter through in-kind contributions. In-kind contributions have been extremely worthwhile in the growth of SchoolNets. In the case of SchoolNet Zimbabwe, for instance, the Ministry of Education provided office space and human resource capacity. For SchoolNet Angola, the local Internet service provider (ISP) offered free Internet access to the schools belonging to the project. In SchoolNet Namibia many private sector companies provided, *inter alia*, incentive mechanisms for the project participants.

This evaluation recommends that SchoolNets consider integrating their activities with national strategies that involve a range of stakeholders:

- The government, to gain support for enabling policies;
- ISPs for cheaper Internet access;

- Telecommunications companies for cheaper telephone access;
- Ministries of Trade for cheaper imports of computers and software; and
- NGOs, such as teacher unions, to foster support among teachers for the SchoolNet initiative.

Locating SchoolNet organisations and activities within a holistic system poses a huge challenge but seems to provide the key to encouraging sustainability. SchoolNet projects should therefore ensure that they develop strategies for managing relations in projects that involve various stakeholders. There should be a clear understanding of how the donors intend managing their projects, and of their expectations regarding project management, implementation and reporting.

Develop innovative models for financial sustainability

Importantly, few government education administrations have acknowledged that innovative financing models will need to be used in the medium to long term if projects seeking to harness the capacity of ICTs in education are to make a meaningful impact. Sharing of ICT resources and connectivity across sectors (e.g. the rural health clinic, school and community), and generating revenues through the provision of public access services to offset costs have yet to be discussed at a national or regional level in Africa. Herein, however, lie the seeds of potential financial sustainability of SchoolNet projects. Sustainability models would have to factor in not only the possibilities for generating revenue but also, very importantly, the development of public-private partnerships where the private sector can be shown the positive effects of partnering with SchoolNets. In Angola, the project provided an opportunity for the private sector to implement some of its social responsibility programmes, which were likely to result in a return on investment. Similarly, in Namibia, a networking model was explored through the SchoolNet, which was made up of different partners with different interests, yet contributing towards the same vision, with the hope that fulfilling this vision would benefit the partners.

Schools could lobby large organisations for donations of ICT equipment, as well as the government to waive taxes on ICTs. SchoolNet Uganda, for instance, could pursue this route but the individual schools should take responsibility for mobilising their own resources.

While most SchoolNets will essentially remain non-profit entities, organising the project on sound business principles has become critical for the longevity and sustainability of the initiative. This involves generating products and services with potential revenue streams and developing aggressive marketing strategies.

Connectivity

The main issue that affected the use of ICTs by various communities was, and continues to be, connectivity and its availability and affordability. The problems of using dial-up connections were highlighted but even schools using wireless connections complained about the low bandwidth. SchoolNets need to explore in detail the various technical options available and affordable to schools so that they can make informed choices in relation to connectivity.

The obstacles faced by all SchoolNets include problems of accessing computers and the high ratios of learners to computers. The cost of telephone calls and Internet access was a key prohibiting factor – a number of schools had their connection terminated due to unpaid bills. A contrary view was expressed that the Internet could be a distraction to new users. Connectivity is very expensive and the suggestion was made that it would be more appropriate to have a single dial-up connection used by a knowledgeable teacher, who could then make the Internet content available offline to other educators and learners.

Broaden available connectivity options

Both wireless and cable connectivity were used in SchoolNet projects. Both Lesotho and SchoolNet Namibia, for instance, have experimented with wireless technologies. The project in Lesotho purchased a portable ground station using low orbit satellite (Pacsats) and solar panels as the schools were based outside of the electricity grid. SchoolNet Namibia recognises that a single communication solution will not be viable due to regulatory issues, limited access to utilities, terrain and issues of location of and distance between schools. It has been experimenting with wireless Ethernet bridges with high-gain antennae to link schools to a central wired node. WiLan Hopper Plus bridges have been tested, with proper antennae where ranges of up to 60 km are possible.

56

New or refurbished computers?

A wide range of computers was found in the various SchoolNet projects – from new Pentium IIIs that were often donations from the private sector or donors, to old computers donated to schools. In some cases, for example SchoolNet Mozambique, the latter proved to be unworkable. Schools generally used Windows 95 operating system and software from Microsoft, with the exception of SchoolNet Namibia, which used a Linux operating system and open source software.

Second-hand computers are useful for demonstration purposes and the teaching of keyboard skills, but mechanisms need to be in place to test the computers before they are dispatched to schools, and for refurbishment and upgrade facilities to be readily available. Refurbished computers are not always cost effective due to high support costs and shorter lifespans. Most of the technical breakdowns and connectivity problems were blamed on the fact that old, slow computers were used. This was exacerbated by the fact that users were frequently new to computer technology.

In view of the technical problems experienced with using old computers, the lesson is that faster and newer computers are needed to access the Internet and download materials. This would also assist in keeping telephone bills low.

In countries where technical support is likely to be scarce in rural areas, a strategy of using refurbished computers is unlikely to work unless a concomitant strategy is put in place to develop local technical support skills.

Access

In the context of exploring ways to enhance universal access to ICTs in Africa, schools were perceived as one entity that services a range of communities. This study has revealed that using schools as an access point for ICTs has been very successful. In a wide range of cases ICTs based in schools have provided, in varying degrees, access not only to different sections of the school community (teachers, learners, principals and administrators), but also to sections of the community outside of the schools (youth and residents within the school's vicinity).

Thus, different models of access have been applied:

- ICTs in schools where the users are only from the school concerned: Here the range of usage varies from only the principal using the one computer available to the school, to learners, educators and principals using computers in a computer lab at a school. At Josina Machel Secondary School in Maputo, Mozambique, the principal, teachers and learners use the computers housed in a computer lab. By contrast, in Katlehong High School in Johannesburg mainly the teachers have access to the computers in the school.

- ICTs in schools where the users are from both the existing school and the surrounding community: This situation exists in a number of communities in almost all the SchoolNet projects. In South Africa, Mafikeng High School in North West province has made its computer laboratory available to youth in the community for training in computer literacy after hours. Similarly, in Nampula, Mozambique, the Industrial Institute allows community members to be trained by teachers who have undergone training themselves. In this way the Institute also generates income.

- ICTs in one school, where the school acts as a hub site for servicing surrounding schools and the community: There are different models of the hub site concept. In some cases, for example Katlehong in South Africa, the hub site is a community resource centre. SchoolNet Zimbabwe also uses the 'school-based telecentre' model, where the school serves as an access point to ICTs for members of the broader community in addition to students.

Capacity building and teacher training

Teacher training in basic ICT skills and, in some cases, using ICTs to enhance teaching, features prominently as a focus activity of a number of SchoolNets. Notably all SchoolNet projects featured teacher training as pilot projects and none factored in ICT training as part of the teacher training system. An exception is the SchoolNet project Internet para as Escolas, which targeted teacher training colleges as sites for teaching computer literacy, and also for computer installations and connectivity to the Internet.

Emphasise the education dimension

Most SchoolNets failed to introduce education content in the first phase of their development. The raison d'être for setting up SchoolNets is to demonstrate the beneficial effects of ICTs on education. For this reason, it becomes imperative to initiate content-based projects. In Uganda, a

CurriculumNet project was developed in partnership with SchoolNet Uganda, which integrates teacher involvement in the development of local education content in a very innovative way. A number of SchoolNet projects can certainly learn from the CurriculumNet experience.

Develop technical troubleshooting skills

The development and growth of support mechanisms for effective connectivity and effectively working computers are very important. The development of local capacity in technical skills, a team of troubleshooters and people capable of upgrading and refurbishing computers, and the setting up of help-desks are particularly necessary. In the case of Senegal, training was noted to be inadequate, often unsuited to users' needs and conducted with little or no regard for concerns related to maintenance. This comment reflects feedback from a number of SchoolNet project managers and educators. Mechanisms for improving technical support, particularly in remote areas, need to be addressed during teacher training, if only to deal with basic troubleshooting skills. More emphasis should be placed on technical training for teachers so that they can undertake their own local first-line technical support.

The idea of training some teachers in schools as laboratory coordinators, responsible for ensuring that the laboratories function properly and that both teachers and learners have locally based support, seemed to work well in Mozambican schools. This also ensured a contact point for SchoolNet staff in the schools. In Namibia, learners from the Polytechnic were provided with on-the-job training, which simultaneously prepared them for the job market. They were referred to as 'flyers' who could 'fly' to schools requiring technical support and assistance. Both may be possible models for emulation in other SchoolNet projects.

Consider longer courses and ongoing training for teachers

An important lesson in teacher training is that teachers who attended ICT training courses complained that persons with varying computer competencies were placed in the same sessions, and that in some cases trainers combined basic computer training with advanced training. Experience also shows that the timeframes for teaching ICT skills is too short and that these crash courses are more successful with teachers who already have some computer knowledge. Educators need time to internalise the training and it is unrealistic to expect people with no previous ICT experience to be up to speed within a few days. Although course materials are valuable, educators need the opportunity to practise their skills until they become comfortable with them. Training cannot be a one-off intervention, but has to be ongoing and followed up. Different levels of training should be considered for teachers at varying levels of competencies. Furthermore, mechanisms are required to provide teachers with continuous ICT support, for example, through help-desks, as in the case of SchoolNet South Africa.

Content development

A strong technology Base for local content development

No single issue stood out as a primary lesson in the area of content and curriculum, probably because this theme area is still being formulated into a coherent form of practice. What was evident is that much of the content available through the Internet was developed elsewhere and not always relevant to the local situation in African countries.

Of all the components of SchoolNet activity, the development of education content online or through the use of ICTs was extremely limited, or was marginalised completely, even though these activities were part of the original SchoolNet design. For example, the early stages of SchoolNet South Africa show an emphasis on connectivity projects, as does the Internet para as Escolas project in Mozambique, which did not manage to develop customised mathematics software at all over the project's three-year existence. The Youth Cyber Clubs in Senegal did, however, show a strong focus on local content development, using information related to family planning and sex education through the use of the Internet.

Apart from the experience in SchoolNet South Africa and the Youth Cyber Clubs, almost no SchoolNets had developed projects on content development. SchoolNet projects commenced with a stronger focus on the technologies and less emphasis was placed on the educational dimensions of school networking. The numerous obstacles and challenges the SchoolNets faced in first achieving the connectivity objective consumed the available human resources, particularly in the start-up phase. This should, however, be seen in a broader context – developed countries such as the USA and Sweden experienced similar problems in the start-up phases of school networking. Familiarising educators and learners with the technology seems to be a necessary step before effective content development can take place.

Integrating ICTs into the curriculum

ICT implementation in education often shows a disjuncture between the ICTs themselves and their use in education. One teacher commented that 'teachers seem motivated to learn about ICT application skills, but less so to explore curriculum applications of ICTs'. This may suggest that SchoolNets should pay more attention in their training to exploring ways in which ICTs can be integrated into the curriculum and thus be used more effectively in the teaching of a wide range of subjects.

The linkages need to be made explicit and this is a potential area for future research. It also suggests close partnering with Departments of Education because of the implications for teacher-based and school-based curriculum-based development models.

Policy

There is significant variance in terms of the range of approaches to establishing national policy frameworks. Countries can be categorised according to the level of policy activity in education as follows:

- **No policy:** There is presently no evidence of policy that attempts to either regulate or stimulate use of ICTs in education (Angola).
- **National ICT policies:** A national ICT policy covers the use of ICTs in education (Mozambique and Namibia).
- **Integration into general education policy:** Policy statements on the use of ICTs are integrated into general policies on education (Swaziland).
- **Broad technology use in education policies:** Broad policies on the use of technologies in education are established, and strategies – at national and provincial levels – for developing specific use of ICTs in education emerge from this broad policy framework (South Africa).
- **Specific ICT in education policies:** Policies are developed that focus specifically on the use of ICTs in education (Namibia).
- **Specific policies on schools and ICT infrastructure:** Specific policies on equipping schools with ICT infrastructure are developed (Botswana).

The general perception, however, is that there are very few policies covering the use of ICTs in education. This was confirmed by interviewees in Angola, Lesotho, Namibia and Zambia. All respondents indicated that there was no policy in place that informs the work of school networking projects, nor are there any country plans underway to develop such policies. Where policies do exist, they tend to remain vague and make little reference to implementation.

For the majority of education systems in sub-Saharan Africa, ICTs do not yet constitute a significant policy or financial priority. There are important shortfalls in local expertise in the field of educational technology that need to be redressed. Several competing priorities – such as budgetary constraints, administrative and management challenges, teacher supply and the impact of HIV/Aids on education – all vie for the attention of local policy makers. ICT-related education policy still needs to establish itself within this set of priorities.

Close working relationships with policy-making entities are important for SchoolNets. The close involvement of policy makers in implementation processes has proved to be the single most enabling factor in the development of policy around the use of ICTs in education. This is borne out by experiences in Mozambique, Namibia and South Africa. In most cases, though, capacity constraints within policy-making entities have been a major constraint – the portfolio is generally understaffed, or staff allocated to the portfolio lack ICT experience or an understanding of the value of integrating ICTs into the broader school curriculum at the national level.

Implications for future research

This study has investigated the experiences with school networking in nine African countries and has only scratched the surface in terms of generating knowledge on this subject. A number of research gaps have, however, emerged during the course of the study, particularly in answer to Research Question #4 – What areas require further investigation and what evaluation agenda is proposed for the subsequent phases of IDRC's evaluation and research?

Acacia's hypothesis that ICTs enhance learning and teaching in Africa has not been proven conclusively. Further research is needed, over a longer period, of the outcomes and effects of ICTs on enhancing learning and teaching in Africa. Overall, three glaring gaps emerged during the study, for which further research is needed:

- Experiences and support with policy development;
- Replicable and sustainable models for SchoolNets; and
- The development of curriculum and content.

Policy development

The role of supportive and enabling policy environments for ICT-enhanced learning and teaching in schools needs to be investigated. This includes taking a closer look at all other existing sectoral policies that inform the process of ICTs in the education environment.

Sustainable SchoolNet models

- A number of SchoolNets in Africa are starting up and will no doubt be able to use the findings of this research in their design process. It would be important to investigate sustainability models that SchoolNets have applied and to establish which models work best. For example, some of the schools are running training programmes for community members during holidays. Depending on the different locations of schools (i.e. urban or rural) and the socio-economic status of the surrounding community, the training of community members – especially in rural areas – is likely to remain more of a community service than an income-generating activity. If a school aims to raise funds through these kinds of initiatives, it is likely to experience some frustrations, especially in areas where people are relatively poor and the demand for computer training is limited. There will also be areas where people cannot afford to pay much for these kinds of services, much as they would like to undergo such training. If the school's aim is to provide a community service, then the training for community members may have to be highly subsidised in most cases. The question, however, remains: subsidised by whom? This raises the question to what extent schools can afford to offer these kinds of services to their surrounding communities and at whose cost the services would be rendered. It also raises the matter of long-term sustainability. Issues such as these require further research.

- Many of the SchoolNet projects are dependent on donor support. However, if they decide to phase out funding for the project, what measures will be taken to replace them? If the state adopted a clear policy on the application of ICTs in schools, the situation would be less problematic and an environment for innovative types of partnerships would be enabled (e.g. public-private partnerships). Even then, what kind of partnership would public authorities propose to promote? Further research on partnership models for SchoolNets would be invaluable for new SchoolNet projects.

- There are as yet no clear answers as to why some SchoolNet projects have been able to move successfully to macrolevels of implementation whereas others have struggled even to survive as small pilot initiatives. This evaluation has highlighted some of the necessary elements, but further research is needed to provide answers that carry higher levels of certainty.

Content and curriculum development

- Research should be conducted to ascertain the usefulness of the myriad educational software available and of online curriculum projects in Africa, and the extent to which these are effective in supporting the learning and teaching process.

- In SchoolNet projects with a strong content focus, such as the Youth Cyber Clubs in Senegal, further research is needed to determine whether the existing content has any effect on school performance or on the management of FLE clubs. In other words, is there a direct relation between student/teacher access to ICTs and positive results in learning/teaching? Certainly, considerable progress has been made if one considers the level of achievement in the implementation of project activities. Nevertheless, to be able to measure this progress against Acacia's underlying objective, it would be interesting to know the extent to which the project has enabled behavioural change.

- Existing online curriculum projects in Africa should be evaluated, as well as the extent to which these are effective in supporting the learning and teaching process.

Connectivity and access

- Alternative low-cost connectivity options need to be investigated, including the use of two-way Internet satellite systems, wireless technologies, radio and cellular telephony.
- The possible reasons why female pupils and teachers tend to use computers less than males could be researched. Reasons for this reluctance are not very clear and need to be understood if the gender imbalance in the use of computers is to be addressed.
- Problems associated with the use of email questionnaires, and possible underlying reasons for low or no response rates in this study, should be investigated.
- The different connectivity options that can be used by different schools should be explored more seriously, keeping in mind the issues of cost, reliability and efficiency. There is a need not only for technical studies, but also for feasibility studies to minimise the kinds of frustrations experienced by schools.

Capacity building and training

- It cannot be assumed that the positive potential changes that can be brought about by the integration of ICTs in education will necessarily be welcomed and embraced by all educators. Some educators may not be interested, or are yet to be convinced. It is therefore important to build a more solid cost-benefit case in support of the use of ICTs in schools and their integration into other parts of the school curriculum.
- Further explorations are needed into ways and means in which ICTs can be popularised and made available to all at a reasonable cost. Questions of equity arising because of the introduction of ICTs in education need to be investigated further.
- The integration of ICTs involves a shift from teacher-centred methodologies to learner-centred approaches. This necessitates a shift not only in methodology, but also in attitudes and, eventually, a shift in the philosophy of education. Educators need to be retrained to think differently about their pedagogical role. Teachers also need to be encouraged to create their own content. Further research is needed to ascertain how this can best be achieved.

- It would be worthwhile investigating the most effective ways to develop teacher training programmes in a systematic way by encouraging the introduction of ICT training in the teacher training system.

Future evaluation research processes

Future pan-African studies should focus more closely in the pre-research phase on the nature of the linkages between the various study components. While there is value in pan-African research, more work needs to be done on the meaning of pan-African research as an approach, as well as on the intended goals of this type of research. The linkages between the studies in the various countries are highly implicit, and more pre-research might have made them clearer and hence easier to focus on in the research process.

Future evaluation projects should be undertaken on a smaller scale in order to facilitate rapid feedback into the projects so that learning can take place. Delayed feedback means that the project management cannot respond quickly enough to the suggestions and incorporate them into project phases or new components.

More specific to Acacia-funded projects, recipients need to be made more aware of the IDRC's role in supporting development research as such. At the time of Acacia's birth in 1997, the idea of applying ICTs for development was a novel one. Acacia projects (including SchoolNets) were therefore inevitably involved in the setting up of new institutions and providing the necessary funding to do so. Consequently, there was proportionately less funding for research, which deviated from the norm for other IDRC projects with their strong research focus. SchoolNet recipients of IDRC support seemed relatively unaware that they were explicitly part of a research process. Data gathering and knowledge generation activities were thus not factored into the project activities at the outset. This should be remedied in future projects.

This study has, as its title suggests, focused on the reality that school networking projects over the past two to three years have very much been an appetite-whetting exercise. Many SchoolNets are not yet ready to move to the 'main course'. Nevertheless, this evaluation consolidates some of the African experiences that will hopefully inform the future of school networking on the continent. We trust that it will also stimulate further interest in research that will broaden the range of options available to African educators on how ICTs can be best used to provide a better education for African children.

Chapter 4

Starting National Schoolnets

Malusi Cele and Shafika Isaacs

Introduction

The African continent has, since the mid-1990s, seen a rapid rise in interest in the use of ICTs in schools. By 2000, more than 23 countries were initiating school networking projects. While many had not yet moved beyond the initial start-up stage, others were already addressing full-scale national implementation. As there are common issues facing most SchoolNet start-ups, it was decided that a section specifically evaluating such start-ups should be included in this volume. Because the SchoolNets in Mozambique, Senegal, South Africa and Uganda are documented as in-depth case studies in Chapters 5 to 8, the evaluation of the start-up experience focuses mainly on the SchoolNets in the remaining five countries: Angola, Lesotho, Namibia, Zambia and Zimbabwe.

This chapter provides a brief overview of the context within which these SchoolNet projects operated, highlighting the poor infrastructure, shortage in human resource capacity and shortcomings in the policy environment by which they were characterised. It also examines the entry points for starting SchoolNet projects in Africa, and the enabling factors needed to support and sustain the initiative. By documenting the difficulties and successes experienced by a cross-section of African countries, it is believed the lessons learnt can inform future school networking start-up endeavours in Africa.

An overview of the various emerging start-up models is provided, followed by a discussion on the experiences in connectivity, teacher training, content and policy development. The start-up evaluation places emphasis on the content, initial planning, conceptualisation and delivery of SchoolNets. The intention was never to conduct detailed impact analyses of beneficiary responses or reactions. Such a focus on project implementation and lessons is the domain of the detailed case studies.

The research methodology outlined in Chapter 1 is adopted here, but is guided by one primary research question being addressed: How have Acacia-supported SchoolNet projects been implemented and what have been the effects of Acacia's investment in supporting school networking in start-up?

The research instruments were piloted with SchoolNet South Africa and the SchoolNet project in Lesotho, following which the data-gathering process was initiated. Thirteen email surveys were sent out, of which eight questionnaires were completed and returned. In-depth interviews were the primary data collection method. In the case of Lesotho, Mozambique, Namibia, Senegal, South Africa, Uganda and Zambia, in-depth and face-to-face interviews were conducted while respondents in Angola and Zimbabwe were interviewed telephonically. In total, 19 interviews were conducted, and seven group discussions were held with a total of 24 participants.

The research on the start-up phase was limited to documenting and understanding the beginnings of each project, and was less extensive in its scope. It nevertheless provided useful snapshot case studies for understanding the context and conceptualisation of the projects in the different countries. Table 4.1 provides an overview of the size and scope of the five start-up SchoolNet projects surveyed.

Findings

Context

Comments from a representative of a leading Zambian information technology company highlighted the following main points. They apply equally well, to varying degrees, to all the countries under study. All are environments of stark contrasts and wide disparities:

- Most schools need significant maintenance;
- Economic conditions of the country are very poor. Most children cannot afford basic learning material such as textbooks;

Table 4.1: Overview of start-up SchoolNets surveyed, 2000

SchoolNet	Organisational Form	Pilot Activities	Targeted Schools	Schools Reached	Partners
Angola	Project supported by the ISP and based at the Catholic University	Installing two school computers Teacher training	3	4	Catholic University Ebonet (ISP) Angola Education Assistance Fund (based in Boston)
Lesotho	In-house project of ISAS at the University of Lesotho		One school and one community centre	One school and one community centre	Institute of Southern African Studies (ISAS), University of Lesotho
Namibia	NGO	Insect@thon – insect database Connecting schools to the Internet Training students in technical skills Project of student volunteers with a reward system	50, plus programme to connect all 1 500 schools in Namibia	31	Ministries of Education Nampower Polytechnic UUNET
Zambia	Voluntary association	Connecting schools with computers to the Internet Teacher training	14 centres	9	Zamnet (ISP)
Zimbabwe	NGO	School-based telecentres Teacher training	30 schools	30	WorLD Ministry of Education

- The management systems of schools are still paper based, and likely to be less efficient than those run through computerised systems;
- The telecommunications infrastructure is inadequate. The installed capacity of telephone lines in Zambia was estimated at 128,000, of which 50 per cent were in Lusaka, with the rest of the country sharing the other 50 per cent of the lines. Teledensity ranged from 1.4 in Lusaka to 0.0002 per cent in other areas of the country. The enormous digital divide between urban and rural typifies the situation in most African countries;
- The policy context was not conducive to guiding and informing school networking in the country. There was a need for an aggressive policy with an ICT agenda attached to it – a policy that would advocate universal access to telecommunications throughout the country;
- The working conditions in the public sector, more specifically within the education sector, are poor. Most of the teachers are earning poor salaries and are not motivated; and
- There is a general state of collapse or "implosion" of institutions in the country, due to the lack of expertise and the necessary skills to run these institutions.

In Angola, schools are generally very poor and have been heavily damaged by the war. As a result, they need rebuilding. The situation is exacerbated by the poor telephone infrastructure in the country, and in schools in particular. The poor state of electrification limits effective implementation. Some of the schools experienced problems with paying teachers' salaries. In some instances, teachers were not paid for three to four months. Furthermore, the country has an unfriendly tariff system, with very high custom duties imposed on imported items, such as computer equipment.

In Namibia, infrastructure in schools was generally very poor, except in the former whites-only institutions. Given the backlog of 2 000 classrooms and the fact that most schools lack toilets, running water and telephones, ICTs are perceived as a luxury. At the time of the evaluation in 2000, there was little interest in developing ICTs in schools. ICTs in education were seen in the context of teaching pupils how to use computers. This was taught as a subject in the formal curriculum, and could be examined and certified.

The context in which the SchoolNets under study were set up is chiefly characterised by poor infrastructure, limited access to basic resources in schools, poor human resource capacity and a serious lack of policy support. If the newness of the SchoolNet concept is considered, the general atmosphere in which SchoolNets are operating is fraught with difficulties and characterised by scarce resources.

The incubation process

Within the contexts described above, a range of start-up models has emerged with different incubation processes. Some have used existing institutions as entry points, while others have established new organisations at the outset.

The SchoolNet in Mozambique was set up in the University's Informatics Department, while in Angola, it was embedded in the university's outreach centre. The support provided by the universities assumed varying forms:

- They provided an established administrative base through which SchoolNet activities could be managed and administered. Donor agencies could channel funding for the SchoolNet projects on the basis of the reputable and credible financial control mechanisms within university-based centres and departments. The Institute for Southern African Studies at the University of Lesotho and the Catholic University in Luanda, Angola, assumed this role, as did the Eduardo Mondlane University in Mozambique;
- They offered resources on which the emerging SchoolNet projects could draw. In the case of SchoolNet Angola, the Catholic University provided premises where a computer room could be established; and
- They provided expertise that the SchoolNet projects could use. At the University of Lesotho, the Institute for Southern African Studies supplied human resource support.

SchoolNet Zambia started out by collaborating with the Provincial Resource Centres (PRCs), which are centres for teacher development based in each of Zambia's nine provinces. Most of the PRCs already had computer rooms with about ten computers on average.

While SchoolNet Namibia had its origins in the Namibian National Museum (through the Insect@thon project which involved young learners capturing insect data on an established database), it set itself up as an independent institution at the outset. By contrast, SchoolNet Zimbabwe forms part of the WorLD programme, whose approach is to set up SchoolNets through the Ministries of Education. Unlike the other SchoolNets, SchoolNet Zimbabwe was formed after the World Bank sent a consultant to the country to conduct a feasibility study. Feasibility studies of this kind had not occurred in any of the other countries covered in this study.

In the cases where SchoolNets used existing institutions as a base for conducting SchoolNet activity, they did not set themselves up as independent organisational entities. Instead, they assumed the organisational form of an outreach project based within an existing legal entity. In the case of Zambia, the SchoolNet used the resources of the PRCs but was not a project within the PRCs. It took the form of a voluntary association supported by Zamnet, the ISP in Zambia.

Given the challenging contexts in which many SchoolNets start up, it is crucial that pre-start-up and start-up activity be located in an established organization because:

- Starting new organisations is often viewed as a long, costly and risky process, particularly with new and innovative agendas that are being piloted or tested out;
- By associating with other organisations, the new institution can be protected and supported within an existing administrative, financial and human resource infrastructure. The success of the project can be monitored and grown as it progresses and overcomes setbacks; and
- Where setbacks are met and changes in initial conceptualisation are needed, these can be accommodated and new projects embarked upon without threatening fragile new structures.

In view of the above, it appears that incubation in existing institutions (whether universities, Ministries of Education or the private sector) is an appropriate starting point for SchoolNets. This process appears to work well in the context of a pilot initiative. It serves to consolidate partnerships with established education institutions, encourages outreach within universities and, from a SchoolNet development perspective, promotes an awareness of the potential that ICTs hold for the promotion of education.

The research reveals, however, that at the conceptualisation stage and as the projects were implemented, challenges involved in moving beyond the support of the institutions were not factored in. This raises the potential risk of continued reliance and dependency on the support institution. The same arguments for incubation within an existing institution can equally be used to argue against prolonged association with a particular institution:

- While starting a new organisation may be a long, costly and potentially risky process, a new organisation may be precisely the vehicle needed to start a new and innovative venture. The end goal of the SchoolNet should be considered from the outset so that choices made in the initial phases are not choices of convenience that have to be undone at a later stage, with further delays and cost implications;
- Protection and support (administrative, financial and infrastructural) can create a false sense of security. This can hide the real costs and capacity implications, and hinder sound business planning and thinking from the outset. By relying on existing systems and processes, the new SchoolNet functions and requirements may be modelled to meet existing and available functions and requirements, rather than developing new ones that may better suit their needs; and
- Location within an existing organisation can prolong establishing a clear focus and tight business objectives, and prevent operations from starting on a sound and sustainable footing from the outset.

While there was evidence of discussions and plans to scale up and evolve into a second phase of development, at the time of the study SchoolNet Angola and the SchoolNet project in Lesotho had not proceeded with operationalising this plan, nor had they considered moving out of their support institutions. That these SchoolNets did not have a full-time coordinator may have been a contributing factor, although further research needs to investigate the causal relationships in greater depth.

Pilot activities versus establishing a national programme

Initial activities in all cases focused on sourcing and installing computers, and linking these to the Internet in selected schools. The approach was based on either arbitrary or pre-established criteria. These activities are broadly referred to as "connectivity" and analysed in more detail later in this chapter. Given the newness of the SchoolNet phenomenon in all countries involved in this study, connectivity was of necessity the principal activity. This compelled the respective SchoolNets to confront obstacles presented by limited infrastructure, high prices and low bandwidth. In view of these problems, all SchoolNets commenced their piloting connectivity activities in schools that were relatively better resourced by way of established infrastructure and where there appeared to be greater receptivity to a new approach.

Four of the five SchoolNets initiated small-scale ICT skills training activities aimed largely at teachers. This was mainly to create awareness of the potential of ICTs and to encourage teachers to utilise ICTs as a resource for enhancing their teaching. In Angola, Lesotho, Zambia and Zimbabwe, teacher training in the use of ICTs featured highly on the priority list of activities. ICT training assumed the form of end-user skills, with a focus on how to use different application packages. However, the skills imparted were not about information technology maintenance and troubleshooting. This deficiency in the training focus had serious implications for the optimal use and maintenance of the ICT resources, particularly in cases where second-hand computers were used and breakdowns were frequent (refer to Section on Capacity building and training).

SchoolNet Namibia stands in contrast to all the other SchoolNet projects in that it made the learner the main focus, rather than the teacher. SchoolNet Namibia's director indicated that the main thrust of its programme is "youth empowerment". The project trains young school-learners and technikon students in ICT skills. SchoolNet Namibia established a volunteer programme to utilise these skills in providing maintenance and technical support to schools.

The scale of activities ranged from very small-scale, pilot project-based activities, such as SchoolNet Angola where three schools were identified for installing computers and providing teacher training, to large-scale national programmes, such as SchoolNet Namibia where a national approach was adopted at the outset and all schools in the country were targeted. At the time of data collection, SchoolNet Namibia had already distributed and connected computers in 50 schools.

Most SchoolNet projects did not start out with pilot activities that were clearly designed as part of a national strategy or programme, nor were they initially intended to progress beyond the pilot stage. SchoolNet Namibia is clearly an exception, as it progressed rapidly towards a national programme, a strategy that was not part of the project's initial design but which became a product of the evolution of the project. The drawback with pilot activities that have not factored in ways to scale up at the design stage is that the longevity and sustainability of the project are hampered. This was one contributing factor in the decline in activities in the case of SchoolNet Zambia.

Selection of schools

The schools targeted by the SchoolNets were all relatively better resourced in that they had access to electricity and basic infrastructure. Schools chosen were located either in relatively well-resourced urban or poor under-resourced rural environments. In the case of SchoolNet Angola, the project focused only on schools in Luanda. Likewise, SchoolNet Zambia focused mainly on the urban centres in the nine provinces. However, the SchoolNets in Lesotho, Namibia and Zimbabwe started out with schools in poor under-resourced and rural environments that had no access to electricity.

Schools were all public, government schools and predominantly secondary schools. SchoolNet Zambia initially focused exclusively on secondary schools, whereas SchoolNet Angola included one primary school among its initial target of three. The SchoolNets in Namibia and Zimbabwe extended their activities to both primary and secondary schools.

Management structures and staffing

All SchoolNet projects were governed by multi-stakeholder steering committees or boards of directors, on which all stakeholder representatives served voluntarily. In all cases, the SchoolNet champion, whether full-time or voluntary, was a member of the governing structure. The voluntary nature of the structures affected the effective governance of the SchoolNets concerned. In the case of SchoolNet Zambia, the steering committee did not meet regularly because individuals on the committee were very busy. The members of SchoolNet Namibia's board of directors were not very active and, as one of the members indicated, the Board was perceived as not playing its role optimally in driving the process. The Board did not meet frequently, and the interaction between the Board and the Director was perceived to be quite informal and unstructured. Similarly, a volunteer worker for SchoolNet Zambia indicated that the management of the project was dependent on the participating individuals' free time. People were not obliged to participate, which delayed the pace of development and rendered the project vulnerable.

All SchoolNets in this study operated with voluntary workers, with the exception of SchoolNet Namibia, which employed a full-time director. The advantages of a full-time director meant that the project progressed far more rapidly than anticipated. The research reveals that in all the other cases the absence of full-time dedicated staff and the reliance on individuals who volunteered their time and services to the SchoolNet project seriously hampered progress. SchoolNet Zambia interviewees all indicated that because the project was run by volunteers, very little follow-up and monitoring were done on the important targets and milestones that the project had set itself. An important caveat to this was that, in the case of Zambia, the prospective champion for the project was sent on a skills training programme with SchoolNet South Africa for six months before he proceeded with setting up the SchoolNet. This proved to be useful and is a recommendation for other SchoolNets to consider.

Clearly, having full-time staff, or at least one dedicated champion, is an important success factor for SchoolNets to consider seriously. Evidently too, a multi-stakeholder governing structure is strategic for the purposes of enhancing partnerships and obtaining widespread support for SchoolNet activities. Having leading figures from private sector and government organisations serve on the governing structures has proven to be worthwhile for SchoolNets in Namibia, Zambia and Zimbabwe. However, encouraging active participation from board or steering committee members who serve largely on a voluntary basis poses a challenge to SchoolNets. It may well be worthwhile to explore various levels of governance and support for the SchoolNet organisation. Several possibilities are worth considering, such as the use of patrons who are public figures and who express support for the SchoolNet; advisory structures consisting of strategic partners; and a group of active supporters who may be paid an honorarium.

Partnerships

All SchoolNet projects partnered with various organisations and institutions from the following sectors:

Government

In the cases of partnerships with the government, they were with Ministries of Education. SchoolNet Namibia and SchoolNet Zimbabwe, for example, had explicit support from their respective Ministries of Education. Here the partnership arrangement assumed the form of human resource provision to the respective SchoolNet projects. In both cases, the Ministry of Education seconded individuals to lead the project. In addition, the Ministry provided office space, electricity, a telephone and, to a lesser extent, transport for the SchoolNet project's work.

In Zimbabwe, the Ministry of Education played a very significant role in supplying human resources for the project. Some 18 to 20 teachers were seconded to work full-time in the WorLD centres. The Ministry paid the salary of these teachers and provided office space. The Ministry further mobilised numerous other resources, such as transport and a mobile unit during the beginning phases of the project.

Local communities

For two of the five SchoolNet projects, local communities were considered partners in the activities. SchoolNet Zimbabwe officials raised funds from local communities and its own coffers, and lobbied neighbourhood residents to be part of the project. This encouraged a sense of community ownership. The community involvement was in addition to the teachers supplied by the Ministry to drive the operations of the programme. This model worked because the SchoolNet was set up in the form of school-based telecentres, which opened them up to community involvement and support. The SchoolNet project in Lesotho also involved community members in its training activities.

Parastatals

Electricity companies and telecommunications companies, where these are parastatals, were notably in support of the SchoolNet project. In the case of SchoolNet Namibia, Telecom Namibia, through its Deputy Chief Executive Officer, and Nampower, through its Marketing Manager, were members of the SchoolNet Board of directors. In addition, Nampower provided placement opportunities for the student trainees of the project.

79

Private sector

Privately owned firms who tended to support SchoolNet projects included local ISPs, computer companies and telecommunications companies. Zamnet in Zambia, Ebonet in Angola, and UUNET in Namibia were all cases of local ISPs playing an instrumental role in promoting SchoolNet projects in their respective countries.

Having corporate leaders serve on the SchoolNet decision-making structures appears to have been a strategic decision adopted by three SchoolNets. In Zambia, Zamnet had its Managing Director serve on the SchoolNet Zambia steering committee. SchoolNet Angola had two members of Ebonet represented on its steering committee and, in the case of SchoolNet Namibia, the board of directors included the Managing Director of UUNET.

Partnership with the private sector benefits SchoolNets in many ways:

- It encourages cheaper Internet access for schools, as was the case in Zambia, where Zamnet offered support. Similarly in Angola, Ebonet agreed to link the four schools to the Internet, using a special rate, which was 30 per cent less than the normal rate;
- It gives SchoolNets access to technical expertise for hardware and software support. For example, Ebonet has offered Internet and technical assistance at no cost since 1998;
- As in the case of some of the parastatals, the private sector provides placement opportunities for trainees, UUNET in Namibia being a case in point;
- The private sector often provides other material support to SchoolNets. For example, different private companies in Namibia participated in various incentive schemes, such as providing pizzas to the volunteer students maintaining the computers.

Private sector involvement is motivated by many factors:

- The need to participate in development through social responsibility programmes (e.g. Ebonet in Angola and UUNET in Namibia);
- The need to create product demand (e.g. UUNET in Namibia); and

- Concern about the lack of high levels of science, mathematics and technical literacy in schools (e.g. Zamnet in Zambia).

Contrary to the above cases, three of the SchoolNets were not able to secure significant partnerships with the private sector. For instance, the coordinator of SchoolNet Zimbabwe explained that the private sector was, in principle, very supportive of the project but that this did not translate into practical or material involvement. He stressed, however, that the private sector was willing to participate but that poor economic conditions in the country made such involvement difficult. Nevertheless, a few private sector companies were able to donate to the project, such as the local business that donated five new computers. Supporting this view, the Managing Director of UUNET pointed out that his company's economic standing in the country made it possible for them to be involved. He noted that UUNET's strategic vision played a significant role in determining whether the company would be involved in non-profit-making projects such as SchoolNet.

Donor agencies

In three of the five cases, the IDRC through its Acacia programme was the dominant donor supporter of the SchoolNet project. The World Bank's WorLD programme was the major donor supporter in Zimbabwe. In Namibia, an agreement was reached with SIDA, which committed about ZAR 50 million to the SchoolNet project.

Education institutions

Three out of the five SchoolNets were actively supported by centres and departments based at universities. In the case of SchoolNet Namibia, the local Polytechnic is a visible partner of the project.

Partnerships with a range of stakeholders are essential for spreading support and increasing the SchoolNet's visibility. Partnerships not only evolve around financial support for the SchoolNets. Also non-financial support in the form of secondments of staff, donations of computers, and lowering the cost of Internet access contributes significantly to the success of the projects. Encouraging the support from the Ministries of Education has proven to be very useful for SchoolNet Namibia and Zimbabwe. Buy-in from other Ministries such as Communications, and Science and Technology is worth exploring, as was the case with SchoolNet South Africa. Private sector buy-in, not only through service on the Boards but also through support in various ways – from placements for graduating students to donations of computers – is an area that requires further research.

Connectivity

Connectivity refers to the installation of computers in schools and connecting the computers to the Internet – this forms the principal activity of all SchoolNets in this study. There has been considerable variance in the connectivity models in the five SchoolNet projects. In general, connectivity activities were characterised by the following:

- Sourcing computers (usually PCs) from firms, or buying them in bulk;
- Transporting computers to the schools;
- Installing computers in the schools and linking them up to a local area network (LAN), usually with the support of electricity;
- Providing telephone line connections;
- Providing Internet service connections; and
- Training a technical support base to assist with computer breakdowns, upgrading and refurbishing.

The SchoolNet projects installed both new and refurbished computers and, in the case of SchoolNet Namibia, Apple Macintoshes were installed. The technological platforms ranged from «connecting a complex that is purely solar system driven» in areas not located within the country's electricity grid, to those schools that had electricity. The project in Lesotho purchased a photovoltaic solar system, to be used for generating energy, as the community skills centre and the secondary school identified for the project were outside the electricity grid. A ground station was donated.

A number of obstacles emerged, some of which could not have been anticipated. As the coordinator of SchoolNet Zambia states:

> In Zambia, the project was hampered by inadequate telephone lines, not having enough computers, and cost-related problems. For one, the telephone line was stolen. As a result, there was no telephone line to use for connecting to the Internet. The other telephone line that could be used was located at the building outside the school. Even in this building, there was only one telephone line and a com-

puter that could be used for Internet access, by both the school and other community members. The latter was used for reading online local newspapers, sending e-mails, etc. Because this line did not belong to the school, there were limitations on using it for Internet connection by students. These limitations included firstly, [the fact that] because there was [only] one computer that could be used, not more than four students at a time could connect to the Internet. Secondly, because of cost implications for being online for extended periods, teachers and pupils could only use this line for a very limited time, that is, not more than one hour. Thirdly, the other alternative was to use the telephone line connected to the principal's office. The limitation to this option was that the line could only be used for connecting after hours, when there was less or no administrative demand for the line. This meant that for most of the day, students were not able to use the facility, because they needed to leave early to commute long distances to their homes. The result of all the above limitations was that since the school was connected some few years ago, only seven students had been exposed to the Internet. Interesting to note, however, was that despite these difficulties in accessing the Internet, and the negligible number of pupils that had been exposed to Internet, some of these pupils participated in Internet-based collaborative projects with other schools.

The problems outlined above resonate with the situation at other SchoolNets. In general, problems associated with limited infrastructure, high telephone costs, inaccessibility of telephone lines, high learner-to-computer ratios, low bandwidth and slow Internet access, especially with older computers, feature significantly in all SchoolNet projects.

Different modalities for providing ICT infrastructure were explored by different SchoolNets. These included a cost-sharing arrangement between businesses and schools, where the business provided Internet connections either free of charge or at a discounted rate (Zambia, and Angola); the transfer of redundant computers to schools to be refurbished and then used for educational purposes (Namibia); and community networking where ICTs in schools were used for learning and teaching during school hours and for providing community education through Internet access to community members after school hours (Zimbabwe).

Capacity building and training

Much of the training and capacity-building activities focused on training people how to use various application systems and how to access information on the Internet. There was less emphasis on the higher technical computer literacy skills, such as developing appropriate programmes for use in education. The training in the use of application systems was not contextualised for education purposes. In Zambia, during the few times when the teacher and a number of learners were able to connect to the Internet, they were taught how to transfer or download files from the Internet, purchase something on the Internet (e-shopping) and write emails (e-communication). Similarly, in Angola, the local ISP Ebonet provided the training for teachers, which included training in Windows and the Internet.

SchoolNet Namibia, as mentioned earlier, focused its attention on students. The training involved more than basic computer literacy and included troubleshooting, upgrading and installing computers.

Content development

The SchoolNets in Namibia, Zambia and Zimbabwe developed websites containing content on local developments, events, news, contact information and links to useful sites. However, none of the projects explicitly developed education content or curriculum material on the Internet for use by learners and teachers. None of the projects took action regarding policy concerns with the development of online curriculum and content.

Policy

All the SchoolNets in the study operated without the support of an explicit national policy framework relating to the use of ICTs in education. In all cases, the development of policy on ICTs in general, and ICTs in education in particular, lagged behind events. In cases where policies were developed, they were not implemented. As one Namibian interviewee stated:

> Policies on their own did not make things happen. SchoolNet Namibia's role was to install computers in as many schools as possible, and the Ministry would be forced to catch up with appropriate policy development or formulation.

In the case of SchoolNet Zimbabwe, for example, there was no visible effect or influence on government strategy on ICTs in any significant way. However, the research did find that reference to ICTs might well exist in policy frameworks relating to different sectors within the policy environment. This suggests that policy coordination with respect to ICTs appears to be lacking and should be addressed.

Effects of SchoolNets

Increasing awareness of ICT potential

One of the key findings of this study is the extent to which the SchoolNet projects raised awareness about the potential of ICTs, even at the government level. In Namibia, for example, the Ministry Board approved a new project aimed at promoting an ICT programme in the education sector, proposed by the Ministry of Science and Technology. SchoolNet Namibia also played a significant role in raising issues about ICTs in schools on the agenda of policy makers, with all the important role players or partners having an opportunity to meet their needs through the SchoolNet initiative. As one key stakeholder stated:

> [The SchoolNet] had created awareness that required the support of appropriate policy development on the part of the government. For example, it brought home the idea of using the Internet in the process of learning and teaching, which then requires guiding and managing through an ICT policy. This was the most important impact of the project.

Similarly, in Zambia, the most important outcome of the project was the extent to which it managed to raise awareness about the benefits that could be accrued by networking different schools in the country. This is despite the fact that the project had failed to produce a significant number of champions to lead the project at school level.

According to a Zambian university lecturer,

> ... it generated national interests and a realisation of the need for and role of ICT in education. As a result of this, for example, schools were increasingly calling for more computer literacy training. Pressure for appropriate developments of ICT in schools was now coming from within. Teachers could now understand and were in fact

using the «ICT lingo», and facilitated links between pupils of different schools. For example, students from different schools were now communicating electronically; they connected the Minister of Education as part of the strategy to lobby support from the Ministry's top officials; and schools were making significant use of connectivity facilities. For example, the Matatele Boys held an exhibition at the District Fair using the Internet service. It changed the attitude of the Ministry of Education towards ICTs in education. This change in attitude is indicated by some reference to ICT in education in various policy documents, for example, the National Policy on Education document and curriculum development documents. Other officials, for example the Permanent Secretary, had strongly expressed a wish for his computer to be connected to email. This change in attitude could be attributed to the work of SNP Zambia, and other pressures, for example external pressures from the Leland project, the visit of the Ministry of Information from London.

In summary, SchoolNets have assisted the process of ICT diffusion into the education sector by raising awareness about the potential of ICTs when integrated into the process of teaching and learning.

Increasing use of the Internet

The significant increase in the use of computers and the Internet by learners and teachers stands out as an important outcome of the work of SchoolNet projects. This was highlighted by one of the Angolan interviewees who indicated that teachers and students in the targeted schools were using the Internet, thereby demonstrating the successful training of a team of 12 core trainers in basic computer skills.

Training materials were developed with training courses suitable for local contexts. Curricula were developed to guide the teaching of computer skills in schools. The main emphasis of these curricula is the use of various application systems in teaching and learning, including skills for surfing the Internet.

Collaborative projects between schools within and outside Angola were another element that was built into the curricula to expand computer usage beyond just computer literacy or programming. There is less emphasis, therefore, on the latter in these curricula. Those schools that were already offering some computer training were involved in developing the curricula, as they already had some experience and expertise in the area of ICT in education.

On the basis of the above example, it is clear that there was some integration of computers as resource tools, thus providing access to information and other resources.

Promoting SchoolNets

The SchoolNets of Namibia and Zambia stand out as having achieved significant visibility among communities in their respective countries. As one interviewee said, "Everyone in Namibia knew the project."

The growing political will and support for ICT application in education in Namibia and the growing international support through pledges from various foreign agencies were considered effects of the strong marketing drive of SchoolNet Namibia. Foreign donor agencies from the USA, Britain, Italy and Sweden pledged support for the project, some of which resulted in financial commitment.

Exposing learners to the world

The SchoolNet projects also facilitated the exposure of students to the outside world through email and the Internet. As the coordinator of SchoolNet Zimbabwe indicated:

> For students, the project provided an opportunity for interaction with the global world through, for example, the international collaborative projects in which the students were participating. Communities saw the project as providing supportive resources and enhancing their own development. Through these centres, community members were able to print their curriculum vitae, and community organisations were able to print their proposals and business plans.

Increasing the skills base

Evidently the base of technical skills has increased, albeit slightly in cases where there was a strong focus on skill development. Through the activities of the SchoolNet Namibia project, students learnt how to fix computers, set up Internet connections, assist at the help-desk, develop websites and, lastly, how to work as a team. This resulted in an increase in technical skills among the project's student volunteers and placements for 23 students with different companies, parastatal organisations and government departments. This will undoubtedly increase the eventual marketability of students in the job market. The Director of SchoolNet Namibia suggested that the training of students and the arrangement of job placements in companies meant that SchoolNet Namibia was slowly becoming a labour broker for the information technology companies and ISPs.

Similarly, in Zimbabwe, the project benefited teachers, pupils, rural communities and the private sector. Teachers and pupils received application-orientated training in the use of ICTs, and technical training that enabled them to manage and maintain centres independently. Because of this technical ability, schools could support each other, including those schools not part of the programme. One of the unintended consequences of the high technical capabilities of the programme was demonstrated in a region where the WorLD teacher served as a regional ICT consultant for schools. Teachers wanting to take up new ICT posts were being referred to the WorLD centre to prove their suitability. The programme was therefore offering some accredited support on behalf of the government, albeit unofficially. Another benefit was that teachers who were pursuing their part-time studies through academic institutions such as the Open University were able to use the centres.

Conclusion

This study has broadly captured the experiences of five African SchoolNet start-ups and highlighted that probably the biggest challenge facing all of them involves establishing connectivity. Current obstacles (having few available telephone lines, the high associated costs, and a lack of human resources for computer maintenance) are formidable and likely to hamper future efforts to bring the Internet to schools. Despite these obstacles, however, it emerges that a culture change regarding ICTS has been introduced by these pilot projects and that the groundwork has been laid for introducing computers into schools on a more extensive basis.

Chapter 5

Internet para as Escolas in Mozambique

Ephraim Siluma, Daniel Browde and Nicky Roberts

Country context

Socio-political background

The wars and their effects

Between 1964 and 1974, Mozambicans were engaged in an armed war against Portuguese colonialists, which led to their declared independence on 25 June 1975. This was followed by a protracted civil war between the two parties, FRELIMO and RENAMO. The wars left the country's infrastructure in ruins and devastated ordinary citizens. Many buildings and roads in the cities of Beira, Maputo, Nampula and Quelimane bear evidence of years of neglect. Services such as electricity, telephones and water supply are still unreliable.

Education was also heavily disrupted. As education reflected the political and ideological line (socialism) of FRELIMO, schools were major targets of destabilisation by RENAMO. The report of the Central Committee of FRELIMO to the Fifth Congress in 1989 indicates that more than 2,655 schools, amounting to 45 per cent of the whole primary school network, had been closed or destroyed by then. At the lower primary schooling level – the most disrupted by the war – 807,926 pupils and 12,515 teachers were affected between 1982 and 1989. The war drove thousands of people from the countryside to the cities, which further affected schooling in the cities. Between 1983 and 1992, approximately 60 per cent of the junior primary school infrastructure catering for 1,414,222 pupils and 18 per cent of senior primary school infrastructure catering for 13,266 pupils were disrupted by the war (Ibid.).

The civil war ended in 1992 and the first multi-party elections were held in 1994. By the end of the war, Mozambique was classified as the poorest country in the world. However, it soon became a country with the highest economic growth rate in Africa. It is estimated that Mozambique's economy is the fastest growing one on the continent, at the rate of 10 per cent per annum. But the country remains extremely poor. About 50 per cent of its public expenditure is covered by aid and loans. The education budget in 1999 was 14 per cent of state budget, of which 26 per cent went to higher education (Ibid.).

Floods

The floods that hit large parts of the country in late 1999 and early 2000 badly affected the lives of the people of Mozambique and undoubtedly set back development. The INGC Situation Report of 2 August 2000, showed that the floods affected 760,000 people either directly or indirectly; over 534,900 people were displaced and 132,600 families left homeless. It was also mentioned in the report that:

> 'In qualitative terms, the destruction did not spare public infrastructure, notably access to roads, water supply, sanitation and drainage systems, protection dykes and other equipment' *(NGC Situation Report).*

A number of schools in various provinces were badly affected. For example, the report received on 31 July 2000 from Gaza showed that 245 schools were damaged, affecting 74,830 pupils and 1,031 teachers. In the same province, two boarding schools for 958 pupils were destroyed, while 46 literacy centres with 2,786 learners were also unusable (*NGC Situation Report*). In Sofala province, 98 schools in the Buzi, Chibabava and Machanga districts were destroyed. These included 57 schools built of conventional materials and 41 built of mud and wattle. The total number persons affected in these schools at the time was 24,067 pupils and 329 teachers (Ibid.).

The floods may not have directly impacted the SchoolNet project, but had the potential to divert government attention from supporting projects such as the *Internet para as Escolas,* to taking care of the emergency of relocating the displaced victims of the floods.

Box 1: Mozambique in brief

Area: 799 330 sq km

Provinces: 10

Capital: Maputo

Population: 17.5 m (est. 2001)

Age: 46% of population <15 yrs

Urbanisation: 71% rural

Illiteracy: 60.5% of adult population

Life Expectancy: 42 years; Male: 41, Female: 44

Active Labour: 36% of population

Official Language: Portuguese

Telecommunications: Landlines: 78,072; Mobiles: 101,000
No. of Schoolchildren, 1994–97:
    Primary: 60% of schoolgoing age
    Secondary: 7% of schoolgoing age

Evaluation Survey Sample Size:
  No. of Schools: four secondary pre-university schools and two
  industrial institutes
  No. of Interviews/questionnaires: 27 (12 completed questionnaires)

Period of Evaluation: October to December 2000 Project Information
Name of Project: *Internet para as Escolas*
  Duration: 1998 to 2001
  IDRC Contribution: CAD 437,855
  Implementing Agency: Centre for Informatics, University of Eduardo
  Mondlane (CIUEM), Maputo, Mozambique
  Partners: IDRC and World Bank (WorLD Links for Development),
  Netherlands Government, ICEIDA
  Beneficiaries: 350 teachers and 4,680 learners
  Source Cross, M. (2000). *Education in Mozambique.*
  Mozambique Commission for Information and Communication
  Technology Policy. (2000). *Draft Policy for Information and Communi-
  cation.* As approved by the Council of Ministers on 30 May 2000 and
  in a national debate between 18 June and 28 July, 2000,

Sources: http://www.onfopol.mz; Cross (2000); BMI-Techknowledge. (2001);
Cellular statistics-Africa, http://www.cellular.co.za/stats/stats-africa.htm; World
Bank, based on UNESCO figures. http://www4.worldbank.org/afr/stats/adi2000/
default.cfm

Educational background

The period between 1962 and 1974 is paraded as the one that laid foundations for a new education system and pedagogy in Mozambique (Cross 2000). During that period, areas under the control of FRELIMO became known as 'liberated zones'. It was mainly through experiences in these zones that FRELIMO came up with new concepts and principles, which formed the basis for an alternative curriculum of socialist orientation and a new pedagogy. Methods and programmes in the alternative curriculum were geared towards replacing a colonial-capitalist, individualistic and competitive mentality with a revolutionary mentality based on the practice of collective work and study, democratic participation and the working out of new kinds of social relations between people.

Educational transformation in Mozambique was also heavily influenced by the Beira Seminar held in January 1975. Following the Seminar, preliminary changes were made to school curricula. These included the abolition of religion as a school subject; replacement of the history of Portugal with the history of Mozambique as a compulsory subject in 1975 for all levels of schooling; extension and standardisation of physical education to include girls; suspension of most colonial textbooks; the training of new teachers, the monitores (teachers without formal teaching qualifications), and improvisation of new teaching methods. According to Cross (2000), most of the educational policy changes adopted at the Seminar were based on political grounds. There was no research undertaken, nor was there a consideration of environmental factors, materials and human resources. As a result, attempts to implement the changes were problematic.

The nationalisation of schools in 1975 led to a number of positive and negative experiences. On the positive side, there was an increase in the school population. On the other hand, there was a sharp drop in numbers of qualified teachers, mainly because of the massive emigration of Portuguese settlers (Cross 2000). For example, the number of learners in primary schools increased from 695,885 in 1974/75 to 1,276,500 in 1976, while the number of teachers increased from 10,281 to 15,000, which corresponded to a teacher/pupil ratio of 1:85 in 1976 from 1:67 in 1975. Staff shortages led to the recruitment of foreigners from various countries. This created its own problems because large sections of highly assimilated Mozambican elite saw the status of those cooperantes (cooperators) as economically and socially more desirable than their own status as citizens of the country. Consequently, skilled and semi-skilled Mozambicans renounced their citizenship and adopted Portuguese citizenship to be employed as *cooperantes*. The government retaliated by expelling them from the country, which in turn exacerbated the shortage of skilled people.

The period between 1988 and 1990 saw education in Mozambique being seriously disrupted by the war. The numbers of children in schools declined. It was estimated that 59 per cent of children between the ages of seven and ten years were not in school. The quality of education also declined, as the number of learning hours decreased. As more people fled the countryside to the urban centres, education institutions, including the Ministry of Education and provincial departments, could not contain the problem. Their activities became limited to the main centres of Beira, Cabo Delgado, Inhambane, Lichinga, Maputo, Nampula, Quelimane, Tete and Xai-Xai. Rural areas became depopulated as people migrated to the urban centres (Cross 2000).

In 1987, the World Bank introduced a Structural Adjustment Programme (SAP) in Mozambique. The effects of SAPs in various developing countries have been well documented. In Mozambique, the programme led to the abolition of a number of socialist strategies to give way to private initiatives. It privileged the expansion of basic education and selective expansion of post-secondary schooling. It also led to the devaluation of the meticais (Mozambican currency). This had an effect on the working conditions of teachers, which was exacerbated by the fact that the education budget had been decreasing since about 1980. Salaries of teachers declined along with their motivation. The dissatisfaction in the teaching profession led to nationwide protests and strikes of teachers in early 1990 (Cross 2000).

Following the 1990 conference on Education for All in Jontiem, Thailand, the Mozambican government started a national review of the education sector and established a forum for dialogue with donors to look into ways of streamlining the aid programmes and ensuring that they operated within the national programme. In 1992, the structure of the national education system was spelt out. The education system would be structured around three bands:

- Preschool education for children under the age of six;

- School education, including general, professional, technical and higher education; and
- Extra-school education, covering educational activities that take place outside the context of formal education.

In this way the process of rebuilding the education system commenced. Some of the priorities included expanding the school infrastructure, which had been badly affected by the war, and improving the nation's capacity for strategic planning and management.

Portuguese is the official language of instruction, although it is the mother tongue of less than 6.5 per cent of the population, despite the fact that many Mozambicans, including people in rural areas, are able to communicate in the language. At secondary schools, English and French are taught as subjects, and English is increasingly gaining prominence since Mozambique joined the Commonwealth. There are about 13 African languages spoken in Mozambique. The Ministry of Education recently decided to introduce the use of the mother tongue in initial grades on an optional and selective basis.

ICT infrastructure and policy

Mozambique has, for a long time, experienced limited penetration of ICTs, mainly because of its poor infrastructure. According to an Acacia document,[1] the private sector and the state were the main consumers of information technology. Computers were not used in schools. For a long time, the Centre for Informatics at the University of Eduardo Mondlane (CIUEM) remained the key ICT organisation in Mozambique, providing access both to the Internet and an email service to NGOs, business, the government and members of the international community. With a large user base, the volume of email occupied much available bandwidth. Full Internet access was made available to dial-up users but access to international websites was slow. There were also problems due to the lack of additional lines to host the numerous simultaneous dial-up connections required by users of a full Internet service. At the time of the study, most of these problems were being attended to in various ways and the number of ISPs was increasing in the country.

The telecommunications sector in Mozambique was growing considerably – between 1995 and 1998, there was an increase from 65,606 to 75,354 lines for subscribers and cellphone users increased from 2,500 to 6,725 (IDRC 1997). However, it was also conceded that with a teledensity of 0.46

per cent, Mozambique had one of the lowest rates of national telephonic coverage. Despite many problems and financial, infrastructural and technical limitations facing the country, access to and use of the Internet was increasing rapidly. In 1995, the country had only one ISP and fewer than 100 Internet users. By 2001, the figures had risen to eight major ISPs and estimates of between 6,000 and 12,000 Internet users (James and Hesselmark 2001). The increase in Internet use occurred despite the relatively high cost of access – Internet cafes in Maputo charged about US$3 an hour for access and dial-ups cost about US$ 30. Most Internet users (about 75 per cent) were found in Maputo. However, there were plans to roll out information and communication infrastructure to rural areas (Cross 2000).

The success achieved in Mozambique in setting up infrastructure to facilitate access to and use of the Internet can be attributed to commitment from the government in setting up an enabling environment. Despite the fact that the country did not have any formal policy on ICTs until the draft policy was released in 2000, government officials, including the President and the Prime Minister, recognised the development potential of the Internet and insisted that Mozambique link to the global information highway. It was for this reason that the government set up a high-level working group to define a national information policy (IDRC 1997).

The Commission for ICT Policy produced a national policy that was approved by the Council of Ministers in December 2000. The policy's objectives were to:

- Increase national consciousness about the role and potential of ICTs for the sustainable development of Mozambique;
- Expand and develop training in information science in the national system of education;
- Encourage and support the training of government authorities, community leaders, women, youth and children in computer usage;
- Eliminate absolute poverty and the improvement of standards of living for Mozambicans;
- Increase efficiency in the public and private sectors;
- Provide universal access to information for all citizens in order to improve their level and productivity in education, science and technology, health, culture and entertainment, and in other activities;
- Create a favourable climate for industry, business and investment in ICTs;

95

- Create a favourable climate for industry, business and investment in ICTs;
- Facilitate Mozambique's integration into and participation in the local and global economy and in the global information society;
- Ensure that all development plans and projects in every sector have ICT components;
- Help reduce and eventually eliminate all regional asymmetries and differences between urban and rural areas, and between the various segments of society, as regards access to development opportunities;
- Create a proper environment for cooperation and partnerships in ICTs, between the public and private sector, and between all interested parties at the national, regional and international levels; and
- Help Mozambique become a producer, not a mere consumer of ICTs (MCIC 2000).

The policy states that, since Mozambique does not have a strong national private sector, the government would have to play a meaningful role in raising and channelling resources for investment in an infrastructure to support ICTs. At the same time, it acknowledges that the government will be facing serious challenges, which include the general absence of a culture and tradition of using ICTs, and the limited human resources (including technicians and financiers) available to stimulate the sector's development.

Project background

Conceptualising and launching of the project

The *Internet para as Escolas* project was officially launched in Maputo on 4 September 1998 by the Prime Minister, Dr Pascal Mocumbi, in the presence of representatives of the government, the IDRC, the World Bank and teachers and learners from the ten pre-university schools chosen for the project (MCIC 1998).

The project was conceived following a series of workshops and seminars organised to create awareness of the use of computers in secondary and primary schools in southern Africa. During the workshop entitled, "Towards an Information Society" (IDRC), the education working group recommended that the CIUEM and the Ministry of Education jointly develop a project to connect pre-university schools, teacher training colleges, and technical institutions and the Ministry of Education (CIUEM). The purpose of the project would be to improve the exchange of experience and information in the education sector and to pilot the use of Internet-based education tools. Subsequent to the recommendation, the CIUEM, working with the Ministry of Education, submitted a joint proposal to both the World Bank and the IDRC.

Project objectives

In broad terms, it was envisaged that the project would allow the introduction of ICTs in pre-university secondary schools. By doing so, it would make a valuable contribution to the general curriculum in Mozambique and reduce inequalities of access to information between students in Maputo and those in the provinces. The project was also seen as a valuable investment in the sense that computing skills are some of the requisites demanded in the labour market (Abridged activity appraisal document). The project would also encourage the sharing of information and communication among students, teachers and educational departments using email and the Internet. It was seen as a major stepping stone towards introducing computer literacy, as well as integrating computers into the teaching of different subjects benefiting students and teachers from secondary pre-university schools.

The following specific objectives of the project were articulated:

- Sensitise educators, researchers, policy makers and communities to the need to change existing concepts of education and learning in view of today's requirements for lifelong learning and, in particular, the potential role teacher training colleges can play in this context;
- Promote the introduction of computer literacy, and develop an ICT culture in secondary education where technology is integrated into teaching processes;
- Stimulate the enhancement of the schools in question to become centres of sharing of information and communication in the education sectors;
- Provide training opportunities for teachers, students, researchers and policy makers in the effective use of email and Internet applications in the context of improving teaching and learning towards the creation of a national school network;

- Promote the use of email and the Internet by secondary pre-university schools, medium-level technical institutes and teachers training colleges and partners for:
  o The professional development of teachers;
  o Collaborative research and learning activities, including joint projects developed by pupils from different schools;
  o Creation of school homepages;
  o Development of locally adapted and produced learning materials and curricula;
  o Community-based learning activities benefiting surrounding schools;
  o Participatory education policy development and implementation; and
- Promote the exchange of experiences of the project within the southern African region and create awareness of the use of computers in education (EMUCI 1998).

According to the proposal, the project would commence by providing connectivity to five secondary pre-university schools, two medium-level technical colleges and commercial schools, and three teacher training colleges.

Project beneficiaries

Initially, the project was meant to benefit 24 educational institutions. Ten of these (five secondary pre-university schools, two medium-level institutes and three teacher training colleges) would be covered in the first phase of the project. They would be drawn from Beira, Maputo City, Matola, Nampula and Quelimane. The average number of teachers and learners to benefit from the project in the first ten institutions was estimated at around 5,000 (EMUCI 1998). New pre-university schools, medium-level institutions and teacher training colleges would join the project as funds became available. It was also envisaged that each institution would receive 11 computers for the computer laboratories and one for email and Internet connections.

Management structures and staffing[2]

From the outset, the project considered hiring personnel to ensure its effective implementation, but it did not have any full-time staff members. Management structures were established, each of which had clearly articulated responsibilities. These included:

- A **steering committee,** which was to preside over all decisions at policy level, oversee the implementation of the project and help in raising funds. As the highest decision-making structure, the steering committee comprised members from key stakeholders such as the CIUEM, Ministry of Education, World Bank, IDRC, Telecommunication Company of Mozambique (TDM) and the private sector;
- The **national project coordinator**, who would be responsible for coordinating all activities of the project at both the levels of policy and implementation in order to provide teachers and students participating in the project with ongoing technical and pedagogical support;
- An **operational project manager** who would, amongst other things, be responsible for providing face-to-face and online technical and pedagogical training and support to schools; facilitating teacher access to collaborative projects; distributing materials produced by WorLD and other international education exchange programmes; and
- A **school system manager** who would be responsible for the training of fellow teachers; carrying out curriculum-based Internet research; developing collaborative projects; supervising students and doing technical troubleshooting. This person would be the primary contact point for the operational project manager.

Of these structures, the steering committee appears to have been the most crucial in decision making.

Project activities

Pre-start-up and start-up phase (Year one)

Following an awareness-raising campaign with the national and provincial Directorates of Education, the project was launched in September 1998. The first year saw the establishment of school networking in three schools. This included site preparation and the installation of the necessary hardware and software, computer literacy training in four provinces, as well as the training of trainers in Maputo. A SchoolNet users forum was set up and, finally, a project evaluation methodology was designed. In the initial phase, the project invested heavily in the refurbishing of computer equipment and the purchase of auxiliary equipment to enable the computers to function.

Second phase (Years two and three)

Several activities were planned for the second phase of the project, some key players believe the project never moved beyond the start-up phase, mainly due to management problems. The second phase was planned to address the consolidation of computer literacy training and courseware into the school curricula; to initiate business strategies in three schools; to review training needs; to expand capacities for creating learning content; and to adapt software using authoring tools. In addition, an impact study was planned for students, teachers and the community, with a concomitant refinement of indicators.

Partnerships

The project received resources from various partners:

- The Netherlands Embassy financed equipment, training and the connectivity of two institutions in Nampula;
- The Government of Mozambique was responsible for supplying furniture, air conditioning and other necessary equipment for connectivity;
- The Icelandic International Development Assistance Agency (ICEIDA) bought computers for the Escola Secundaria Francisco Manyanga in Maputo. The organisation sent a teacher from the school to a conference in England, and arranged for a teacher from Iceland to visit the school; and
- The World Bank and the IDRC were the two major funders of the project. The funds were used to facilitate training, purchase and deliver equipment, provide connectivity and cover the operational costs of the project.

Research process

The generic research process is dealt with in more detail in Chapter 2. In the case of Mozambique, the approach involved the use of interviews, questionnaires and site visits. A total of 27 people were interviewed, of which 13 were principals and teachers from the schools visited. These persons were interviewed mainly in groups for the purpose of compiling school case studies, and for understanding how the computers in their schools were used. Twelve questionnaires were completed. Because most of the computer laboratories were empty during the site visits to Mozambique, email question-naires were sent to a number of schools. None responded.

Fourteen of the interviewees were key informants, such as project managers, government officials from the Ministry of Education, and repre-sentatives from funding agencies. Six sites – four secondary pre-university schools and two industrial institutes – were visited. Schools were selected for the project site case studies based on the following criteria:

- The eventual group of schools had to be located in at least three differ-ent provinces;
- The evaluation sites had to be selected from the ten established schools that started with the project;
- There had to be some representation of urban/rural and poor/rich con-ditions; and
- There was to be varied representation of different institutions – sec-ondary schools, technical colleges and teacher training institutions.

Table 5.1 Schools evaluated in Mozambique

Name of School	Type of School	Location Province	City
Escola Secundaria Josina Machel	Pre-university secondary	Maputo City	Maputo
Instituto Industrial de Maputo	Medium-level technical college	Maputo City	Maputo
Escola Secundaria de Nampula	Pre-university secondary	Nampula	Nampula
Instituto Industrial de Nampulat	Medium-level technical college	Nampula	Nampula
Escola Secundaria 25 Setembro	Pre-university secondary	Zambezia	Quelimane
Escola Secundaria Samora Machel	Pre-university secondary	Sofala	Beira

Teacher training colleges were originally included in the site visits. The re-search team later learned they were not participating fully in the project because of an instruction from the Ministry of Education that they were not to receive computers as these would be supplied by the Ministry. One teacher training college in Quelimane had received only two computers from the project, and despite the furniture that had been supplied through the project, their computer laboratory stood virtually empty.

Research findings

Context

The *Internet para as Escolas* project was implemented in an environment characterised by poor infrastructure, lack of capacity and skills in ICTs, and no culture of using ICTs. All these factors had an impact on the project. Three key areas, in particular, hampered the project in achieving its goals:

- **Management issues:** The fact that the project did not have full-time managers was identified as a major problem. In addition, some of the people involved in the project were not paid for their time, which resulted in low morale and commitment;
- **Equipment:** The use of second-hand computers hindered the attainment of project goals; and
- **Lack of technical capacity in the provinces:** Schools experienced constant computer breakdowns related to the use of old computers, a costly exercise as assistance had to be sourced from Maputo.

A more detailed discussion of some of the major obstacles and constraints experienced during the study follows.

Connectivity and access

Telecommunications penetration remains low, despite the rapid growth of the sector. According to Telmina Paixão, the Vice-Minister of Education in Mozambique, the slow expansion of these services to rural areas was likely to impede the expansion of the *Internet para as Escolas* project. Despite these infrastructural problems, there were indications that ICTs were slowly expanding into areas where they did not exist before.

Electricity

There have been reports of cases (e.g. in Nampula) where there were constant power failures in the whole city. Such breakdowns clearly affected the use of computers in the schools. In some of the schools participating in the project, telephone lines and the supply of electricity had been cut and had to be reinstalled. The buildings of some needed to be reconstructed and prepared for the project.

A member of the Project Steering Committee stated:

> The implementation of the project was actually based on nothing. The environment was not functional enough for the project to operate as expected. People in Mozambique had not been exposed to technology ... schools were not ready. When the directors were called to meetings, they did not know how they were going to fit into the project ... Conditions in schools were also not prepared because there were telephone lines that did not work; other schools had only one line used by the director of the school and additional lines were needed. Rooms had to be refurbished as some needed roofing, security, etc.

The Ministry of Education, through its construction wing, *Gabinete Técnico de Gestão de Projectos Educacionais* (GEPE), had to ensure that rooms were well prepared for housing the computers. GEPE had to paint the rooms, install doors and security gates, and install special electrification with separate wiring for computers, lights and air conditioning.

Internet Service Providers (ISPs)

A shortage of ISPs, particularly in the provinces, was one of the major difficulties experienced. Until 1995, the CIUEM was the only educational institution making use of ICTs in order to assist and enhance its pedagogical capacity. When the *Internet para as Escolas* project was first conceptualised, the CIUEM was the only point of presence (POP) in the country. This resulted in the project being centralised and implemented through the CIUEM in Maputo. The CIUEM became the POP even for schools in the provinces, an expensive arrangement for Internet access.

Shortage of ICT skills

There was a shortage of skilled people in ICTs, mainly in the provinces, as well as an absence of a culture of using ICTs. Whenever schools in the provinces experienced technical problems, technicians from the CIUEM had to fly from Maputo to the schools, often for minor problems. This proved very costly. When the project was introduced into the schools:

> ... there wasn't a demand for ICTs. It was clear that ICTs did not fit into their day-to-day running of the schools and the project came like a strange animal for which they were not prepared.[3]

ICT Policy

When the project started, Mozambique did not have a policy on the use of ICTs in education. However, this was not seen as a problem because the project enjoyed strong support from key government officials, including the President and the Prime Minister. This culminated in the establishment of a high-level working group responsible for defining a national information policy.

Project planning and management

A notable feature of the conceptualisation process was that at the outset, the project plan considered potential obstacles to the success of the project, with the intention of identifying solutions.

Planning strategies to address potential problem areas

Several potential problem areas were identified during the planning stages:

- It was felt that the Ministry of Education might respond too slowly to its responsibility to renovate the classrooms prior to the installation of computers, which would have implications for the training plans;
- The project's planning team was aware that technical training and support were critical in remote areas where capacity was limited. For this reason, the project took the following approach:
  - o The ten institutions that had the best chances for success were connected. These included institutions that already had some access to basic connectivity requirements, such as electricity and telephone lines;

o The project identified the need to find local people who did maintenance of computer equipment in provinces and to encourage them to support the schools; and

o Teachers who were interested in informatics in schools were earmarked to be trained to support the project in their various schools. It was also thought that incentives could be created for such teachers. However, the training of teachers whose responsibility would be to train other teachers and learners in their schools and develop collaborative web-based projects for the school, also raised concerns. There were fears that these teachers might leave the schools for higher-paying jobs before transferring their skills to others in the school. Consequently, some mechanism of retaining staff had to be considered. To address the problem it was suggested that the Ministry of Education would be called upon to assist with arranging contracts that would encourage the retention of such teachers at schools.

- Choosing better-resourced schools was clearly a crucial issue. These had to be schools that were ready to adopt that type of technology. The regional spread of schools was seen by some as of political significance, but ultimately the conditions in schools and the levels of "technology readiness" were far more important. In this case, readiness was defined mainly in terms of having access to electricity and telephone lines.

- The project planners were also aware that the success of the project depended on the quality and cost of communication lines. The budget that schools received from the government for their running costs would not be sufficient, especially if schools would have to carry the recurrent costs for the Internet and email connections, electricity, phone connections and consumables. In order to help schools, it was necessary to negotiate with funders such as the IDRC and the Community Development Foundation of Graca Machel to obtain financial support. A second strategy was to invite TDM, the telecommunications company in Mozambique, to sit on the steering committee. This would enable the committee to put pressure on the company if the quality of service was not up to standard (CIUEM 1998).

- While the CIUEM provided free access to the Internet for the schools, schools still needed to make long-distance phone calls from the provinces to Maputo to access the Internet, which was expensive. To address the problem, it was suggested that schools could be transformed into local resource learning centres as a means to generate funds for the recurrent costs. Project leaders later had a meeting with Teledata, a private company co-owned by TDM and Portugal Telecom. The purpose of the meeting was to persuade Teledata to support the connections of schools in the provinces because the company had ISPs in all provincial capitals and it could offer Internet services.

Monitoring and evaluation framework

The design stage was characterised by the inclusion of an evaluation framework that dealt with input, outcome and impact indicators against which the project's performance would be assessed at a later stage. That the *Internet para as Escolas* developed an evaluation framework in the planning stages of the project, rendered this project unique – many other SchoolNets only developed a form of evaluation after the implementation phase of the project(CIUEM 1998).

Institutional Structures and Staffing

The evaluation found that, for various reasons, the steering committee did not function as expected. When the project started, most of the members showed commitment towards the project but, as time went by, absenteeism became a problem. Eventually the steering committee meetings were no longer held regularly and did not start on time, all of which led to frustrations among some members. The quality of meetings deteriorated as no proper reporting was taking place and finances were not properly accounted for. All these problems affected the morale of committed members. A reason for this state of affairs may be that members of the committee were not rewarded for their time and efforts. Because salaries are generally low in Mozambique, it is normal practice for people to take one or two extra jobs to supplement their income. There was therefore the expectation of some form of remuneration.

As the SchoolNet project coordinator asserted:

> When you speak of a project, people expect money and from that point, the project was badly planned. People who designed the telecentre project in Mozambique were paid while those who designed the Internet for Schools Project were not. The steering committee

members were not paid for the amount of time that they spent on the project. They did not even get petrol or per diem allowances for their contribution. That affected the morale and people started prioritising other commitments than the project. People who were paid, for example the operational manager and technical and pedagogical coordinators, at times ridiculed steering committee members who were not paid. They sometimes even absented themselves from the steering committee meetings without apologies.

Another problem was that the steering committee was comprised of members drawn from different organisations with varying commitments and attitudes to the project. As the Executive Secretary explained,

> In having brought together a range of players, each of whom had different lines of accountability, it had been difficult to drive or steer the project forward. Not all participants had the same vision for the project and as none were directly accountable to each other, when there was dissension or disagreement on the course of action, these tensions had been difficult to resolve. Clear allocation of leadership and lines of accountability within the steering committee were necessary to ensure good and efficient management of the project. A smaller team with a clear mandate might have been more effective.

Problems within the steering committee affected the overall management of and communication in the project. Some of the steering committee members were no longer being informed about what was happening in the project as they no longer received email updates.

The project did not have permanent staff members and therefore lacked continuity. For instance, pedagogical coordinators were replaced after one year. This resulted in confusion, in that teachers did not know who was responsible for the project.

Beneficiaries

In addition to providing benefits to learners and educators, all the schools visited were attempting to develop basic computer skills courses for community members. These courses included word processing, spreadsheets, email and the Internet, and were offered to community members at a low cost. The income was used for maintaining computers and paying electricity and telephone bills. Some of these initiatives have not been successful.

According to teachers at the Instituto Industrial de Nampula and Escola Secundaria de Nampula, reasons given were:

- Some people did not have money to pay for the courses;
- Others were not interested, mainly because the culture of using computers had not yet taken root; and
- Those who were interested in the course were only really interested in the Internet. When the telephone lines were cut, learners and teachers as well as community members tended to lose interest.

Partnerships

The IDRC and the World Bank were the two major donor agencies that worked closely with the CIUEM, the implementing agency. The collaborative effort was officially formalised in January 1998, with a memorandum of understanding signed between the two organisations. Within the IDRC, the memorandum of understanding resulted in a project known as the "Introduction of ICTs into Mozambican Schools". While this *Internet para as Escolas* project emerged as a joint venture, the feeling among some stakeholders was that the World Bank treated the project as its own:

> Even the publicity of the project in the press stated very clearly that it was a World Bank project and that it was a WorLD Links initiative. The role of the IDRC in the project was never mentioned.[4]

> The World Bank still calls this the WorLD Links for Development Programme but because the CIUEM brought in other stakeholders and donors to finance the linking of schools, the Bank had to compromise, hence the project is called SchoolNet.

On the other hand, local stakeholders who played a significant role in the conceptualisation and design of the project perceived this as a Mozambican project. Hence they appreciated the manner in which the IDRC conducted itself, allowing the Mozambicans to lead and shape the project:

> At times people from the World Bank would skip ... the overall project coordinator and work with the operational manager and pedagogical coordinators whom they paid through WorLD. The World Bank would also tell them that they were more important than the overall coordinator, but when they experienced problems they would come back to the project coordinator.

The perception of key stakeholders is that the World Bank differed from the IDRC in that it made clear what it wanted and expected to be done, and in the process angered some of the project managers. For example, the fact that the World Bank pushed for the project to be handed over to the Ministry of Education was not well received by some of the project managers. They felt that the Ministry lacked the capacity to take over a project of such magnitude:

> The decision to make the transition to the Ministry of Education was made by the World Bank as it was funding the Ministry through a scheme called capacity building. It was therefore more convenient for the World Bank to have this project located within the Ministry. This was not a correct move because it was driven from outside. There should be a natural maturing process from the inside, with gradual involvement of people from the Ministry. Such a slow hand-over process would ensure quality of the project and avoid the need to stop the project's progress at schools.

Others felt that the IDRC had contributed to some of the project difficulties by not being present hands on in terms of constantly monitoring the project and thus ensuring accountability. For example, before this evaluation was done, the IDRC programme officer had never visited the project in Mozambique to ensure that project managers were held accountable.

The Ministry of Education played a significant role as a partner in the project. Through its construction unit, GEPE, the Ministry was responsible for refurbishing at least one classroom where the computers were to be housed in schools, and for delivering computers to schools.

Private ICT companies such as ICL Mozambique Ltd were involved in the project and assisted, where necessary, with the configuration of computers.

Several problems related to funds and financial accountability to the donors. Different organisations funded different activities, and some of the funds tended to arrive late, causing cash flow problems for the project. As a result, funds that arrived on time were used in activities for which they were not intended. This, together with the lack of a full-time accountant, led to problems with financial accountability. To compound the situation, some of the project funds were kept in the CIUEM account. Consequently, project funds assigned to the project were sometimes used for other purposes.

Connectivity and access

Selection of schools

The schools visited during the evaluation were fairly well resourced as they had libraries and separate laboratories for physical science, chemistry and biology. Some also had technological resources such as photocopiers.

In some institutions, such as the Instituto Industrial de Maputo, there were already computers in place before the project commenced – these were used mainly for administration. The Institute in Maputo had seven fairly outdated computers for the use of teachers only. These were used to type assignments and tests for learners.

Preparation of school sites

In some of the selected schools, services such as electricity and telephone lines had been cut, while others had only one telephone line used by the school director. The refurbishing process run by the Ministry of Education included installing security doors, special electrification, telephone lines and air conditioning, painting the rooms and providing computer desks and chairs. Generally, GEPE's involvement was seen to be free of problems.

Computer installations and technical support

The World Bank donated about 125 second-hand 486 computers. Approximately 100 of these computers worked but were not compatible with the latest available software. These computers had to be reconfigured and software such as Windows, Microsoft Office and antivirus programs installed. Four of the schools that were visited – Escola Secundaria Josina Machel in Maputo, the Instituto Industrial de Maputo, Escola Secundaria 25 de Setembro in Quelimane and Escola Secundaria Samora Machel in Beira – had received second-hand 486 computers donated by the World Bank.

The IDRC provided money to purchase two new computers per school and the World Bank provided funds for purchasing an additional new computer. The Dutch Embassy provided funds for new computers for Escola Secundaria de Nampula and the Instituto Industrial de Nampula. Most of the schools visited had received about 12 computers each (including the server), except for Josina Machel, which had 16 computers.

The training of teachers included basic training in how to deal with minor technical issues. It was only when teachers experienced problems that they could not deal with that the CIUEM was called.

Schools that were visited reported that computers consistently broke down. Some of their problems had been attended to while others had not. Additional problems were mentioned:

- The Industrial Institute of Maputo had two computers with motherboard problems and one with electrical supply problems. Only the latter computer would be repaired but those with motherboard problems would not be able to be repaired at the CIUEM;
- Francisco Manyanga Secondary School had two faulty universal power supplies, while Samora Machel had connectivity problems with its new Compaq computer. According to the report, the computer had been configured and tested by the CIUEM and had been found to be functional. The conclusion drawn was that the problem was caused by lack of experience;
- At Escola Secundaria 25 de Setembro there were four faulty computers and no Internet connection, four computers had no suitable antivirus programs, and six universal power supplies and three network boards were faulty. Attempts to address connectivity problems included the installation of new high-performance SUN systems and Compaq computers in schools. These were to be used as servers.
- At the Escola Secundaria Samora Machel, a faulty electrical installation caused constant electricity breakdowns with resultant computer failure. This problem had since been solved;
- The refurbished 486s consistently broke down and key informants felt this was one of the main factors that hindered the attainment of project goals;
- Technical problems were aggravated by the fact that the users had no knowledge of using computers. For example, according to the laboratory coordinator at Escola Secundaria 25 de Setembro, the breakdown of six of their computers was blamed on learners who, when shutting down the computers, did not follow instructions and had simply switched off the computer;
- Schools complained that technical support from the CIUEM was slow. At Josina Machel, the computer laboratory coordinator said that they

had problems accessing their homepage and that they had been waiting for about three months for the CIUEM to help them. Some schools (e.g. Escola Secundaria Samora Machel in Beira) had been told that technicians could not be sent to attend to their problems because the project could not pay for their services. This frustrated schools and laboratory coordinators, who sometimes had to use their school fees to fix computers.

Contrary to other informants' arguments that the old computers donated by the World Bank were hindering the project in attaining its objectives, the Bank's representative on the project steering committee argued that stakeholders in the project knew that the World Bank was donating second-hand computers. The World Bank had refurbished those computers to perform at least the function for which they were required, and the donated computers had been working well when they were removed from the desks of World Bank officials to be shipped to Maputo. As far as the World Bank was concerned, there was no doubt that it was possible to upgrade the machines to enable students to send and receive messages and access the Internet. The technical problems listed above confirm WorLD's evaluation of the same project, which identified the major barriers experienced by teachers as the lack of good working computers (only 53 per cent are functional), insufficient computer memory (only 59 per cent are reliable), and problems with Internet access (about 65 per cent have it) (WorLD 2000).

Project managers fully acknowledged that their response to problems in schools had not been always quick enough:

> The second major weakness of the project was related to the first one [referring to the use of old computers]. There had been many problems with computers and the distance to the provinces made maintaining the computer network difficult. This was especially so in Nampula. When schools called us it was not easy to diagnose the problem and we always have to fly there to help. This meant that there were limits to how fast we could respond to the need for assistance.

While it is clear that schools experienced many technical problems, some of which remained unresolved, it emerged that some of those problems were expected. Whether the mechanisms put in place to minimise these problems were adequate and sufficient, remains to be answered.

112

Connectivity

Two of the primary objectives of the project were to facilitate communication both within and between schools and to encourage students to engage in collaborative projects. Both these objectives required an email service. We found that most of the schools visited had problems with their email, in particular, the Instituto Industrial de Maputo where most of the computers did not have access to the local server, and Escola Secondaria Samora Machel in Beira, where the server was extremely slow. According to the school director and the laboratory coordinator at Escola Secondaria Samora Machel, emails could take as long as three months to arrive. Due to disconnected telephone lines on account of non-payment, the two institutions in Nampula had no email access.

Another important issue related to the sustainability of the project is the cost of telephone calls. Some schools in the project no longer had access to the Internet mainly because they had had their telephone lines cut for failure to pay their bills. According to Cossa, when the project started, they had budgeted about US$ 50 to assist each school in paying its telephone bills at the end of the month. This money was budgeted on the understanding that users would not be spending too much time on the Internet but rather that they would login to download information that they needed and access their email. Unfortunately, users overspent their limited time on the Internet and schools found themselves with huge bills that they could not pay.

One of the school directors stated:

> There needed to be a clear explanation of how the project would work because in most cases when schools have problems they do not know whom to contact. The ownership of the project and who is funding it must be clearly defined. Schools should not have been expected to pay for the costs of the project. When schools are told that there is no money to send technicians to fix the computers and to help them pay for their telephone bills, the question is, whose project is it?

High bills in schools were further caused by the fact that all schools, including those as far as Nampula up in the north, were connected to the Internet through dial-up modems using landlines, and their POP was the University of Eduardo Mondlane in Maputo. This, coupled with the fact that the computers were themselves slow to open up pages, meant that users spent a great deal of time on the computers to download what they wanted. Even

113

though TDM, the local telecommunications company, was represented on the project steering committee, attempts to get the company to offer lower rates to schools in the project failed. With the project being taken over by the Ministry of Education, its budget would possibly cover the schools' telephone bills.

Several ideas were put forward to address the problem of high telephone bills. These included the use of wireless systems for accessing the Internet, or connecting schools through local POPs. While the former issue was still under discussion, some schools, for example Escola Secundaria 25 de Setembro, had already negotiated to connect through its local Internet provider, Teledata. Schools in Nampula and Beira were also negotiating with Teledata for the same service. Follow-up evaluations of the project should assess developments in this area.

Use of the computers

Computer use differed from school to school. In some schools, such as Escola Secundaria Josina Machel, the computers were used with enthusiasm, while in other schools it was hard to find evidence that the computers were being used at all.[5]

Contrary to the observations of this study, WorLD's evaluation found that although there was an average of 218 learners per computer in Mozambique, teachers and learners were reported to have spent considerable amounts of time using ICT. According to its report,

> Eleven of 15 teachers indicated that learners spent two to three hours or more weekly using computers. The use of computers is concentrated in computer science, word processing, English and Portuguese. Eight of 16 teachers said that students used email one to three times weekly or once or more weekly (WorLD 2000).

Informants in schools gave a number of reasons why computer laboratories stood empty for most of the time. In both institutions in Nampula, the poor turnout of learners in the computer laboratories was blamed on the fact that they did not have access to the Internet.

The computer laboratory coordinator at Escola Secundaria Samora Machel said that since they did not have access to the Internet, they divided their Grade 11 and 12 learners into three groups and offered them a basic computer course. The course focused on switching the computer on and off properly, and using a word processor and spreadsheets. The course had been completed for the year 2000, hence there were no learners in the laboratory.[6]

The computer laboratory coordinator at Escola Secundaria 25 de Setembro allocated different time slots for the training of learners, teachers and community members registered for computer lessons. The timetable also showed special times set aside for teachers visit the laboratory if they needed individual help. Teachers were further allocated a slot twice a week to practise on their own. During the evaluation visit, no learners came to use the computers despite the fact that it was their turn in terms of the timetable. However, according to the laboratory coordinator, learners were no longer using the laboratory because they were preparing for their examinations.

Other schools indicated that they had similar timetables that made provision for different groups to use the computer laboratory. There was no evidence of such use during the evaluation visits.

Capacity building and training

Teacher training became one of the important issues that had to be attended to in the start-up phase. Analysis of the monthly project reports showed that teacher training generally proceeded very well. Various forms of training were organised from time to time, both at national and provincial levels, with most of the national training sessions taking place in Maputo. A total of 136 teachers were trained by the coordinators between September 1998 and June 1999.

Teachers participating in the training sessions were expected to train other teachers and learners in turn. The reports show that many schools had allocated special times in their timetables to the training of teachers and learners. More than 384 teachers, 57 other workers and 2,818 learners were trained between January and August 2000.

Participants in the pedagogical workshop held at the CIUEM in April 1999 (CIUEM 1999) were trained to:

- Use email as their main way of exchanging written messages and education material used in teaching and in the students' collaborative projects;
- Identify the main characteristics of a project-based learning situation. Amongst other things, they were invited to design projects aimed at solving a particular problem related to the content being taught, the

curriculum, students' assessment or achievements, or to the school management;

- Use different ways of engaging their fellow teachers and students in collaborative school activities; and
- Get access to some exemplary collaborative projects and educational material available on the Internet.

Training was offered for one week and the content was based on the outcomes of a questionnaire that teachers had to complete in their schools before attending the workshop. Issues that teachers had shown interest in but which were not covered in the training, included:

- Creating an address book;
- Removing users who are no longer on a particular LAN; and
- Attaching files to an email.

The sessions were evaluated to ascertain the extent to which they had met the needs of teachers. The report is nevertheless silent on teachers' perceptions of the quality of materials and facilitators used for the training.

During site visits, teachers confirmed that they received two types of training:

- **Pedagogical training:** This included the use of email, using computers to support teaching and learning, and designing collaborative projects; and
- **Technical training:** This focused on enabling teachers to attend to minor technical problems that they might experience with computers, including how to install software. Training sessions were organised at three levels:
  o National training sessions were held in Maputo and targeted teachers convened there;
  o For regional sessions, a team of three – the pedagogical director and two technicians – travelled to provinces, and
    teachers in that region were expected to convene at one of the schools in the area; and
  o There were also school-level training sessions, organised and facilitated by laboratory coordinators in each school.

Project managers were generally satisfied with the manner in which the training of teachers had been undertaken. The project coordinator stated:

> Teachers who attended training are able to do many things on the computers, more than just computer literacy. They can download information from the Internet, can use technology to find information for the subjects that they teach, and can communicate by email.

Teachers who were interviewed, however, had mixed feelings about the training sessions. On the positive side, all 13 teachers who were interviewed felt that they had learned how to use a computer and that the training was relevant. They were also impressed that they had received training manuals and software that they could use to learn on their own. On the negative side, they were concerned that training sessions were short and too intensive. According to one schoolteacher,

> Sessions were often homogeneous and did not take into account the fact that there were many different people taking part who were at different stages of knowledge.

Supporting this assertion, teachers at Escola Secundaria de Nampula added that participants were expected to learn basic skills plus some finer details of a computer in one session. Sessions therefore only "scratched the surface".

According to the National Director of Teacher Training, there were as yet no plans in the Ministry to incorporate ICTs in teacher training. This was confirmed by the Director of Planning in the Ministry of Education during October 2000:

> The problem is that at this stage we are not prepared to train teachers in ICTs because most of the teachers are trained in colleges and at university where they receive training in various subjects. The training of teachers in ICTs has not been introduced because the Ministry of Education has not looked at what impact the training of teachers in ICTs would have in schools. In our understanding, before you introduce a discipline, you need to train people who will train others in that discipline. Currently, even in our teacher training colleges we do not have people with ICT skills to train others.

There was optimism that, as there was a process of rethinking the curriculum with the objective of including ICTs in senior secondary schools, the curriculum for teacher training would have to follow suit.

Curriculum and content development

School computer laboratories were used mainly for training teachers and learners in using MS Office (in particular, MS Word, Excel and PowerPoint), sending and receiving email, surfing the Internet, participating in collaborative projects and writing newsletters. The reviewed project reports are silent on whether the computers had made any difference in teaching and learning.

There were problems with the availability of educational software. On the other hand, project managers acknowledged that "the success of the entire project relies on using the appropriate educational courseware", and that "supplying schools with computers without appropriate educational courseware would be disastrous for the project".

The only educational software referred to was Sergo, a mathematical course developed in South Africa for school use. The courseware was thought to be ideal because it was linked to the concept of outcomes-based education and it had already been translated into Portuguese. Suggestions were put forward that the software should be bought and distributed to schools participating in the project, while other appropriate educational software was sought elsewhere. However, the reports are silent on whether the courseware was ever used and, if it was used, what difference it made in the schools.

According to the project coordinator, the SchoolNet project had not made any major differences in curriculum and content. This was because no educational software had been installed, although they had hoped to have done so before the project was handed over to the Ministry. In terms of the project objectives it was also envisaged that teachers and learners would develop locally adapted curriculum content. Most informants felt that this objective had either been partly met or not met at all.

Most teachers indicated that the computers had a positive impact on their teaching only in so far as they were able to type notes and tests for their learners.

As one teacher said,

> Before receiving computers, teachers wrote notes and tests on the chalkboard but now they are able to type their tests and notes.

Another teacher opined,

> Before we got computers, we used to use typewriters, as a result, the flow of documents was slow. With computers we are able to work faster.

Where computers were connected to the Internet, some teachers gave their learners assignments requiring them to search for information on the Web. For example, during the visit to Escola Secundaria Josina Machel, some learners were searching for information on the Internet for their assignment titled, "Location of Mineral Resources and Industries in Mozambique".

During interviews, some of the informants spoke more about the potential computers had in changing classroom practices than about what they were actually doing with their computers. This in itself was positive, because it showed that teachers had been sensitised to new ways of teaching.

Teachers and school directors also indicated that the computers had had a positive impact on administration. In some schools the computers were used for doing school accounts and for developing various administration forms, such as class lists, timetables and reports.

Policy

The process of formulating the ICT policy started at the same time as the conceptualisation of the *Internet para as Escolas* project – both emerged from the joint workshop held in Maputo in February 1997. For this reason it was difficult to determine the extent to which the policy might have been influenced by the project. However, according to Venancio Massingue, the *Internet para as Escolas* project was taking place within the context of that policy framework, as some of the people involved in project management were also members of the commission tasked to develop the national policy. His argument supported the assertion that Acacia-based projects derived mutual benefit from each other.

Effects of the project

This section presents the findings from 12 questionnaires that were completed on whether the original objectives of the project had been met or not. The questionnaire asked the informants to indicate whether each objective had been met fully, partly or not at all. Whether these objectives were communicated to and understood by all participants, particularly schools, was not clear from the evaluation study. Some stakeholders also pointed out that the project was still in its infancy. The project was only intended to whet the appetite of the Mozambican teachers and learners, and to give them a taste of what had been possible with new technologies. In this, the project had been successful. Most of the respondents were fairly positive about the outcomes of the project, but remained neutral when asked to commit on specific sub-objectives.

Overall, the evaluation study confirmed that the *Internet para as Escolas* project is still very much in the first phase, and that most of the schools have not truly moved beyond using computers for basic functions. It was also clear that some of the objectives would take longer to achieve.

Achievement of project goals and objectives

Most respondents felt that the introduction of computers in schools, and teaching teachers and learners how to use the computers had been very successful. The introduction of computers as such rather than the Internet and email was seen as the main focus of the project's objectives. This view needs to be questioned, as it may have emerged from the realisation that the project was not meeting its initial objectives.

For some, getting computers up and running in schools was in itself a remarkable achievement, whether those computers were being used optimally or not. Other achievements mentioned were the following:

- The project had generated interest in computers;
- Teachers and learners in the schools involved in the project under-stood what a computer is and what it can do;
- Some learners had demonstrated clear interest by volunteering to as-sist in the laboratories;
- Teachers were able to communicate using email; and
- Teachers were able to download and use information from the Internet.

Sensitising stakeholders to the need to change their existing understanding of education

Most respondents (83 per cent) were positive that the project had managed to sensitise educators, researchers and policy makers and communities to the need to change existing concepts of education and learning.

According to the IDRC's Liaison Officer in Mozambique,

The project is taking place within the Acacia framework. As such, several of the Acacia projects derive mutual benefit from each other. For example, the policy process has benefited from the experiences of the Internet for Schools project, and the Internet for Schools project has made use of provincial seminars conducted for the information technology policy project.

Government officials also showed an awareness of the possibilities provided by access to the Internet:

This is more important in our case since we do not have enough textbooks. The project has enabled teachers and learners to access information on, for example, science and has helped both teachers and learners to be part of the global village by enabling them to interact with others within and outside the country.

Moreover, policy makers were thinking of introducing informatics as a subject in higher secondary schools and to use ICTs in distance education courses for teachers. According to the Vice-Minister of Education:

In higher secondary education, the government wants to introduce informatics as a subject area. Not all schools have computers, however, and this project has been successful in at least getting computers into some schools. This new commitment to introducing Informatics as a subject is a factor in favour of continuing the project.

Some educators also showed an understanding of the need to change current concepts of teaching and learning:

I would like to involve computers more and more in the daily running of the institute. Worldwide, traditional lessons are disappearing. I would like to use computers to escape from the dull cycle of lessons and tests.

Promoting computer literacy and integratingICTs into the teaching process

The respondents felt that this objective was ambiguous and that it needed to be divided into two parts. Most responses suggested that the project had managed to introduce computers in schools, but that the integration of the computers into teaching and learning had not happened fully. This is not surprising, considering that no special software for teaching and learning purposes had been installed.

Sharing of information and communication in schools

Just over half of the respondents felt this objective had been only partly met. There were attempts to make schools centres of sharing information, and all the schools that were visited claimed that they had designed courses that were offered at a fee for members of communities around the schools. This was evident at Escola Secundaria 25 de Setembro, where the researcher found 11 members of the broader community attending a course in computer literacy. Notwithstanding the positive responses to this objective, it is questionable whether there was any sharing of information and communication within a school or between schools, as access to the Internet was not operational in most cases.

Training opportunities for teachers and students

While most respondents felt the project provided teachers and learners with an opportunity to be trained in the use of email and the Internet, some questioned its effectiveness. For example:

> The opportunities have been provided but this is not yet "effective use". Effective use means exploiting all chances given by the Internet, including publishing materials and information about a school and its achievements using other sites and linking to these.

Professional development of teachers to promote the use of Email

A third of the respondents felt that the use of email and the Internet for professional development had been fully promoted. Half the respondents felt that this had been done partly, whereas the rest did not know. According to the project manager, teachers received ongoing training support via email after the completion of their course. Teachers in schools were unable to confirm this, because in most cases the email and Internet services were not operational.

Promoting collaborative research and learning activities

Judged from general comments, most of the respondents understood the involvement of participating schools in collaborative projects to be one of the key objectives of the project. However, four of the six schools visited indicated that they were not involved in such a project. At the Escola

Secundaria Josina Machel, a group of learners were involved in developing a joint presentation on "Getting married early", which was placed on the school's website.

During a visit to the Josina Machel School, researchers found one learner responding to an email from a learner in Brazil, who wanted some information about Mozambique and about the school. In their evaluation, WorLD found that 10 of 17 teachers had not participated in collaborative learning projects with their students, either within or between schools (WorLD 2000).

The creation of school homepages

Two of the twelve respondents felt that the use of email and the Internet for the creation of homepages had been fully promoted. Four respondents said the objective had been met partly, while two felt it had not been met at all. Three respondents did not know, while one declined to comment.

From the general responses, teachers indicated that one of the areas that they received training in was creating homepages. However, it seems that most schools had problems accessing their homepages. Assistance was required from the CIUEM to do so, and this had been slow in being rendered.

Developing locally adapted and produced learning materials and curricula

Of the 12 respondents, 42 per cent indicated that this objective had not been met at all; one said that it had been fully met. Clearly, few people were positive about the extent to which the objective had been achieved. Computer laboratory coordinators indicated that teachers used the computers to design and type tests and assignments. However, the perception was that schools were not at the stage where they could develop locally adapted materials.

Delivering community-based learning activities benefiting surrounding schools

Community involvement was limited, although some schools did attempt to design learning activities for the benefit of surrounding schools. For instance, learners from three schools neighbouring Escola Secundaria 25 de Setembro were allowed to use the computer laboratory. Working with those schools, they had also designed a project to encourage girls to do mathematics and science. In this project, a group of female learners from the four high schools worked on the computers to produce a common science test, which was then sent to all female learners in the four schools. They were expected to complete the test and return it for marking. All female learners from participating schools would then gather at Escola Secundaria 25 de Setembro on a particular day where learners who did extremely well in the test would present how they worked out the answers.

Participating in education policy development and implementation

From the general responses, there were no indications that teachers and learners participated in policy development processes. Apparently such participation only occurred at the level of the steering committee.

Promoting and sharing experiences within Southern Africa

Five of the 12 respondents felt that the project did meet this objective, whereas four stated that it had not been met at all. Knowledge about the project was shared mainly through participation in conferences on the use of technology in education in southern Africa.

Conclusions and recommendations

The evaluation led to a number of recommendations that can be made re-garding the *Internet para as Escolas* project:

- The project needs a clear, effective management strategy with clear lines of accountability and regular meetings. In addition, it is important to ensure that full-time, dedicated and paid staff are allocated to the project to ensure that its momentum is maintained. There is an obvious need for a champion to drive the process forward.
- The severe constraints placed on the project by the lack of resources and capacity in the provinces should be addressed. It is recommended that future ICT projects undertake a skills audit so that projects are initiated in areas that have a greater chance of success because of available infrastructure and human skills.

- Project objectives were ambiguous and open to misinterpretation. Future project objectives should be simple, with clear implementation targets and timeframes. This will assist in the monitoring and evaluation of the project.
- The government should play a greater role in promoting projects of this nature to ensure that the types of connectivity problems experienced in the project do not recur. The need for lowered telecommunications costs in schools is imperative.
- A clear partnership strategy is needed to ensure coordination of donor approaches and activities.
- A clear plan for post-donor sustainability is required to ensure that projects do not collapse after donor funding has been terminated.

Notes

1   International Development Research Centre (IDRC). Acacia National Strategies: Mozambique-IDRC Study/Acacia Initiative in preparation for the workshop entitled "Towards the Information Society", convened in Maputo in February 1997 and sponsored by both the IDRC and the World Bank, http://www.idrc.ca.acacia./outputs/op-mozam.htm
2   This section draws on Eduardo Mondlane University Centre of Informatics (1998), p. 20–22. ·
3   Project steering committee member.
4   Sources of quotations have been protected for the sake of confidentiality.
5   A reason for this may be that, at the time of the visit, the school year was ending and learners were busy with their examinations.
6   In running a quick search on files created or modified in the last month, documents created on the previous day were found.
7   International Development Research Centre (IDRC). Acacia National Strategies: Mozambique-IDRC Study/Acacia Initiative in preparation for the workshop entitled "Towards the Information Society", convened in Maputo in February 1997 and sponsored by both the IDRC and the World Bank, http://www.idrc.ca.acacia./outputs/op-mozam.htm
8   This section draws on Eduardo Mondlane University Centre of Informatics (1998), p. 20–22.
9   Project steering committee member.

10 Sources of quotations have been protected for the sake of confidenti-
     ality.
11 A reason for this may be that, at the time of the visit, the school year
     was ending and learners were busy with their examinations.
12 In running a quick search on files created or modified in the last month,
     documents created on the previous day were found.

Chapter 6

Youth Cyber Clubs in Senegal

Ramata Molo Aw Thioune and El Hadj Habib Camara

Country context

Introduction

Senegal is a Sahelian country situated at the extreme western tip of the African continent, with a surface area of 196,722 km². It is bordered by Mauritania to the north, Mali to the east and Guinea and Guinea Bissau to the south. The Gambia lies completely within Senegal to the south.

With a population of 9,582,542 (December 2000), Senegal has a population density of 35 habitants/km². It has a growth rate of about 2.9 per cent and 85 per cent of its population consists of people younger than 20 years. Women comprise about 51 per cent of the total population, more than half of whom live in rural areas. Muslims make up 94 per cent of the population and there are the following main ethnic groups: Balante, Bassari, Diola, Mandingo, Peul, Seereer, Toucouleur and Wolof.

Economic growth is sustained by the secondary and tertiary sectors. The primary sector, dominated by agriculture, constituted 17.8 per cent of the gross domestic product (GDP) in 1998. The principal products include groundnuts, fish products and phosphate. The transport and telecommunications sectors contributed 62 per cent of the GDP in 1998.

Box 1 : Senegal in Brief

Area: 196 190 sq km
Location: Sahel, West Africa
Capital: Dakar
Population: 10.3 m (July 2001 est.)
Age: 0–14 years: 44.07%; 15–64 years: 52.88% ; 65 years+: 3.05%
Iliteracy: 33.1% (M: 43; F: 23.2)
Life Expectancy: 52 years (1997)
Active Labour: n/a, 40% youth

Official Language: French

Telecommunications: Landlines: 165 874 (1999)
Mobiles: 165 000 (2000)

School Enrolments: Primary: 71% of schoolgoing age
Secondary: 16% of schoolgoing age

Evaluation Survey
Sample Size:
No. of Cyber Clubs: 7
No. of Interviews/questionnaires: 113 questionnaires (94% students);
129 interviews (67% students)

Period of Evaluation: November 2000 Project Information
Name of Project:
Expérimentation d'espaces Cyber Jeunes dans l'enseignement moyen et secondaire au Sénégal
Duration: 1998 to 2002 (two-year project officially terminated in 2002)
IDRC Contribution: 71% of total project costs (FCFA 76 660 000)
Implementing Agency: *Groupe pour l'Etude et l'Enseignement de la Population* (GEEP), Dakar, Senegal
Partners: IDRC/WorLD, UNFPA, Club 2/3 (Canada), GEEP, Ministry of Health (Senegal), School Online
Beneficiaries: Secondary school students (13–21 years) and teachers

Sources: Central Intelligence Agency, *CIA – The World Factbook; Handbook 2001;* African Development Bank, *http://www.afdb.org;* BMI-TechKnowledge. (2001), *Communication Technologies Handbook 2001;* World Bank, http://www4.worldbank.org/Afr/stats/adi2002/default.cfm

The Education System in Senegal

The Constitution of Senegal states that the state is responsible for the country's educational and training policy. This policy is defined and implemented by the Ministry of National Education, Technical Learning and Professional Training (MEN).

Through its Orientation Law (Loi d'Orientation) no. 91–22 of 16 February 1991, the state has to ensure that an appropriate and efficient education and training system is implemented. The state sets the norms, and enables and promotes the full and equitable participation of diverse players, including individual and collective private sector initiatives.

The education system is divided into a formal and non-formal sector. The formal sector is made up of the following:

- A basic education cycle with:
  i) Preschooler cycle education, which is divided into three levels – the lower, medium and higher sections;
  ii) Elementary school divided into six levels; and
  iii) Medium school with four levels;
- General high school with three levels, of which the curriculum generally concentrates on science and literature. At the end of this cycle students receive a baccalaureate diploma and may enter a university;
- Technical education and professional training delivered in specialised schools;
- Higher (university) level; and
- Special education targeting marginalised people, such as people with disabilities.

The national education sector is organised around three sub-Ministries:

- The Ministry of Higher Education and Scientific Research (Enseignement supérieur et la Recherche Scientifique);
- The Ministry of National Education, Technical Learning and Professional Training (MEN); and
- The Ministry of Literacy and Vernacular Languages.

There are ten academic Inspectorates (Inspecteurs d'Académie) in the regions, which are responsible for coordinating education activities. Within each subregion, there is a separate department responsible for the execution of education policy at the local level.

The non-formal sector consists of a functional literacy programme, basic community schools, and street schools.

- The Functional Literacy Programme targets youths up to 15 years of age. This national programme was established in 1993 and although coordinated by the MEN, NGOs, the private sector and other partners were invited to participate.
- Basic community schools constitute an innovation for exploring alternative models of education. These schools target young students from 9 to 14 years of age, uneducated youths or school dropouts. These students are provided with a four-year basic education programme that includes a technical component either in French or in the vernacular. Normally, these students can find an occupation after having completed the programme cycle.
- Street schools are schools that do not fall into any of the above categories and are run by non-formal or non-standardised agencies. The official system provides some form of coordination for these initiatives.

Because of Senegal's decentralisation policy, education is one of the sectors managed at the local level. The project under discussion in this chapter, the Groupe pour l'Etude et l'Enseignement de la Population (GEEP), is such an example.

Education and literacy

The national illiteracy rate is very high among individuals over 15 years: 82 per cent of women and 63 per cent of men are illiterate. The cumulative percentage of children in full-time education (preschool and primary) is approximately 84.2 per cent. There are 5,793 general and vocational education schools, with a total student population of 1,393,730. Schools are unequally distributed throughout the country, with the Dakar region showing the highest number – 900 educational institutions from the preschool to the university level. Dakar also hosts the biggest university of the country, University Cheikh Anta Diop, with more than 20,000 students. The literacy rate in the Dakar region is close to 89 per cent, which is much higher than the national rate (MF 1999).

130

Nevertheless, if preschool and elementary levels are combined, the national literacy rate for full-time learners is estimated at 84.2 per cent. This means that if the trend is maintained, adult literacy will improve with the present and future generations.

ICT context and infrastructure

Over the last ten years, Senegal's progress in the field of communications technology has been remarkable thanks to SONATEL, one of the subregion's most efficient telecommunications companies and also one of the very few on the West African stock exchange BRVM (Bourse régionale des valeurs mobilières). SONATEL has successfully increased the number of telephone subscribers from 23,000 in 1985 to 200,000 in 2000, and the teledensity from 0.5 lines to 2.5 lines per 100 inhabitants.

SONATEL has positioned itself as a major Internet access provider through the SENTOO web access facilities delivered by Telecom-plus. SONATEL has also set up the Sentranet network that provides Internet, Intranet and Extranet facilities to companies. SONATEL offers data transfer services that allow clients quick access and interchangeable operations between different technologies, and has instituted a policy to enhance the quality of services and the management of information transfer.

To implement these innovative projects, SONATEL forged a partnership with CISCO systems through the CISCO Powered Network, becoming the second operator in Africa after UUNET (South Africa) to be a part of CISCO's programme. Nevertheless, SONATEL is not the only large national and international ISP in Senegal. Others include Metissacana, Refer, and Sud Information.

There is no comprehensive and integrated ICT policy in the country, and none that addresses the education system in particular. The technological climate in Senegal is, however, conducive to the spread of ICTs, and extending such technologies to schools is simply a matter of time. Some discrete initiatives have already been undertaken to introduce ICT in schools.

Public authorities launched the LOGO programme at the primary school level. This government initiative funded by the Ministry of Finance aimed to introduce ICTs into primary schools. However, it ended rather abruptly due to lack of resources. At the higher level, other ICT-supported initiatives were underway to promote distance learning, such as the UVA (Université Virtuelle Africaine) initiative at the Université Cheikh Anta Diop de Dakar (UCAD), and CAERENAD (Centre d'application, d'études et de ressources en apprentissage à distance), a collaborative distance education project involving universities in the following countries: Brazil, Canada, Chile, Costa Rica, Mauritius and Senegal. However, as these initiatives are not seeking to integrate ICTs into the curriculum, a more holistic and integrated ICT policy, driven by the state, is needed for the country and for schools in particular.

Project background

Context and project initiation

Like many other developing countries, Senegal's population growth (2.7 per cent per year) is a major problem – fertility rates are high, while the mortality rate is dropping. As a result, the country has registered skyrocketing population growth rates – 3.2 million inhabitants in 1960 as against 8.5 million in 1996, with about 16.9 million predicted for 2015 (United Nations' projects). Senegal's population has doubled in 25 years, with young people making up the bulk of the population. According to the GEEP (1995) Survey on Adolescent Sexuality Among Students, the number of school-age youth (7–19 years) has increased from 580,000 in 1960 to 2,605,559 in 1992 (1,247,693 of them are between 12 and 21 years).

Besides rapid population growth, Senegal's second major problem is the endemic environmental degradation resulting from drought and population pressure in urban and rural areas.

Due to persistent economic crises, in particular unemployment, most young Senegalese are not able to enjoy moral and material fulfilment in adulthood. Many resort to delinquency, prostitution and drugs. They indulge in early sex, putting themselves at risk of early births, sexually transmitted diseases (STDs) and HIV/Aids. Surveys on adolescent sexuality suggest that over half of the school-age youth indulge in sex without prior knowledge of the risks involved. A high proportion of these young people have expressed the need for information on reproductive health and family life, and 83 per cent of them agree that sex education should be introduced in schools (GEEP 1995).

Adolescents' reproductive health and their desire to organise themselves to preserve the environment have only recently become issues of concern for agencies implementing electoral and advocacy activities. It is felt that, in view of their role and contribution to economic, social and cultural spheres, youth should be at the centre of education, training and social mobilisation strategies. The problems they are facing at present and the challenges of tomorrow will then be negotiated most effectively.

In an attempt to address this matter, the Ministry of National Education and GEEP, an NGO for population, environmental and development-related education and awareness raising, launched a youth education programme on population issues to promote environmental and family life education at the intermediate and secondary school levels. This initiative was meant to raise awareness and enhance behaviour change among youth in line with the provisions and principles of the Education Ministry's framework Act, No. 91.22 of 16 February 1999 (Sections 1 and 3).

It is in this respect that GEEP has been drawing on the burgeoning growth of telecommunications at the national level to strengthen and improve the quality of its interventions in the school setting.

Two major initiatives in Senegal deal with ICTs in schools and for the youth. The first is the subject of this evaluation study, the GEEP Youth Cyber Clubs; and the other is the World Bank's WorLD programme, which is also supported by the Ministry of Education. The projects differ in several significant ways:

- The "Cyber Youth Clubs in Senegal's School Setting" project was designed to run for two years. Like the WorLD project, GEEP's project aims to facilitate connectivity and pedagogical applications of ICTS. Nevertheless, it goes beyond that and seeks to improve Family Life Education (FLE) club management;
- GEEP's project differs from the WorLD project in its content and approaches to delivery;
- Youth Cyber Clubs do more than improve teaching and learning. GEEP's FLE activities are meant to upgrade youth's knowledge, decision making and leadership skills. They are vehicles for behaviour change among youth and the wider community;
- GEEP provides target schools with one computer workstation, while the WorLD project generally supplies ten (including furniture);
- GEEP has set up its Youth Cyber Clubs in urban, remote and rural areas for youth who, once trained, can adopt and replicate a community-based approach to training enabling members of the community to access and benefit from the Cyber Clubs; and

133

- From lessons learned in this project, GEEP seeks to provide references for policy makers when introducing ICTs into schools.

In addition, the Ministry of National Education has established the "Quality Education for All" programme, which seeks to expand and intensify the use of Internet-based computer-assisted teaching methods, and to ensure subsequent nationwide coverage for ICTs. Progressively, ICT trial programmes are being institutionalised in school curricula. This change in direction is expected to help formalise the training of trainers. In other words, trainers will be hired to train or initiate other teachers or trainers and students progressively in the use of ICTs in school curricula (as a cross-cutting discipline) and during initial training at the Ecole Normale Supérieure de Dakar (ENS).

In Senegal, the IDRC has been collaborating closely with GEEP to establish in-school Youth Cyber Clubs (Cyber Jeunes) at the intermediate and secondary levels. This school networking initiative falls within efforts envisaged by national education authorities to revitalise the education system. Shortly after the initiative was launched, it drew support from public departments such as the Directorate for General Intermediate and Secondary Education, and long-standing technical and funding partners such as Club 2/3 Canada, the Health Ministry's Programme de développement intégré de la santé (PDIS) and Schools Online.

It is felt that, at a time when all sectors of society are concerned with globalisation and related issues, excluding players in the education sector would be an unpardonable offence. Though youth are presented as the adults of tomorrow and as future decision makers, trainers, businesspeople, politicians, or simply key players, little is done to help them grow to fulfil that hope. Youth need to be prepared early enough to address the challenges of today and, more importantly, the problems of tomorrow when they will be living in an information society.

This initiative therefore expected the use of ICTs for youth in schools to yield concrete benefits in teaching and learning, and to improve the quality of education by contributing towards universal access to the Internet and computer technology.

Conceptualising and launching of the project

When GEEP launched this project in February 1999, it already had a 130-club membership in the FLE network. The project has made it possible for GEEP to decentralise the management of FLE activities and initiate 11 pilot youth centres for information and counselling (youth forums).

Since 1990, GEEP has been working closely with government authorities to give students a leading role in awareness raising, training and research on population and environmental issues. GEEP's main targets in this initiative are secondary school students (13–21 years) and teachers.

In 1994, GEEP took a bold step forward that lent formal recognition to its initiatives in the school setting. It launched a project for promoting family life education at the intermediate and secondary levels in Senegal, implemented with support from the United Nations Population Fund (UNFPA). The project was structured around the following components:

- Setting up FLE clubs;
- Introducing an innovative approach for reviewing methodologies for teaching and learning on population issues and phenomena;
- Undertaking initiatives to improve environmental management based on recycling waste for greener school environments;[1]
- Enhancing the administrative management in the context of better ownership of computer technology and the computerisation of school data;
- Organising the first festival of FLE clubs (1995), as well as youth holiday camps (1995–96), FLE regional reflection days (1996–97), and the annual population and development contest;
- Developing teaching materials to improve teaching and learning on population issues;
- Conducting surveys on adolescent sexuality in the school setting (1995); and
- Providing over half the FLE clubs with audio-visual equipment (45 FLE clubs out of a total of 74 were equipped in 1996).

The project aimed to promote access to ICTs and improve the quality of education by:

- Training teachers;
- Building skills;

135

- Providing relevant and up-to-date teaching and learning mediums;
- Consolidating the Youth Cyber Club network; and
- Bringing significant changes into the school setting and making ICTs more accessible to youth, as the Acacia project is helping to do.

This project also aimed to enhance administrative management by encouraging improved ownership of computer technology and the computerisation of school data.

Setting up FLE clubs has been a challenging, yet satisfying task. By December 1996, GEEP had established 45 FLE clubs, 15 more than the 30 planned initially. After a year, there were 71 member clubs in the national FLE network. The rising numbers in the national territory have, however, made it difficult for the Dakar-based GEEP to communicate directly with all of the clubs. High costs and the difficulty of travelling present major challenges when organising national or even regional events. FLE clubs also experience difficulties in communicating with each other. By virtue of their close partnership with Canada's Club 2/3, GEEP FLE club members find it increasingly necessary to communicate directly with youth in Club 2/3. This is not always possible due to the lack of adequate infrastructure.

The lack of resources, especially materials for teaching and learning, strongly hinders GEEP's work. For example, it is difficult to replicate innovative models such as interdisciplinary population education and FLE clubs. Communication with the wider world is difficult, and teachers as well as students lack the tools to express their creativity more widely.

At the second national festival on FLE clubs, organised with support from the IDRC as part of Acacia's strategy for Senegal, there were various activities, notably those of Youth Cyber Clubs. These were an eloquent testimony to the fact that young people were not only creative and innovative, but also had a great capacity for assimilating new experiences.

The youth in FLE clubs, as well as their supervisors and some parents, requested that the pilot initiative continue, expand and be decentralised after the festival. The ensuing project lasted for two years, from November 1998 to October 2000.

The pilot Youth Cyber Clubs project is part of the Acacia programme in Senegal. Launched in 1997 for a period of two years, the project is a part of global initiatives designed to support Africans in their efforts to develop infrastructure and communication services to connect them to the global information highway.

The IDRC's Acacia programme has provided GEEP with support in the form of:

- Grant funding for equipping the Youth Cyber Clubs;
- Training for students and teachers responsible for providing oversight;
- Hiring of a computer expert and consultants;
- Launching the research programme; and
- Providing documents and tools for facilitation.

Project objectives

The general objective of this project was to:

> Improve the FLE club model for teaching, facilitating and raising awareness of population, environmental and sustainable development issues by introducing ICTs and opening Youth Cyber Clubs in Senegal's schools.

GEEP therefore conceived a comprehensive programme targeting young people. The programme aimed to:

- Build a body of knowledge on issues related to populations;
- Promote new behaviour regarding reproductive and sexual health;
- Promote the introduction of environmental issues in school curricula;
- Develop leadership among youth through education on citizenship and the promotion of human rights; and
- Create an interschool and an international network, sharing knowledge and thinking on sustainable development issues.

Specific objectives were to:

- Open 12 Youth Cyber Clubs through Senegal's national FLE club network. Each club would be equipped with a multimedia computer, a modem, an energy back-up source and a laser printer, and would receive grants for office rental;
- Promote and capitalise on achievements of FLE clubs, and set up a network for exchange between FLE clubs and Club 2/3 in Canada;

137

- Build the skills of youth and their supervisors by training 60 trainers in using ICTs, including 40 youth leaders and 20 teachers serving as technical relays, to enable clubs to be more open to the community;
- Sensitise 10,000 students, 150 teachers and 50 school administrators to the importance of ICTs;
- Improve students' school performance, teachers' teaching methods and the resources available in school resource centres;
- Promote the interdisciplinary model on population teaching and learning;
- Sensitise community members to and train them in ICTs; and
- Study the impact of access to ICTs on the activities of FLE clubs and the performance of children at school.

The project's key education targets were:

- FLE club facilitation;
- FLE club management;
- Population education through the interdisciplinary model on GEEP's website;
- Reinforcing the teaching of social sciences, natural sciences and technology; and
- Promoting discussion forums.

In addition, the project targeted the strengthening and development of research capacity in the FLE clubs. Certain research issues were studied, such as:

- The impact of ICTs on the knowledge, attitudes and practices of student leaders and facilitators in reproductive health and environmental concerns;
- Experiences from rural Youth Cyber Clubs during GEEP's summer holiday camps (e.g. Ndiebel in 1999 and Mboro in 2000). These experiences seek, inter alia, to demonstrate the potential of ICTs; to show rural inhabitants, using concrete examples from their setting, how they can get the best out of their activities through the use of ICTs; and to give those without access to computers the opportunity to understand and familiarise themselves with ICTs.

New activities that were planned included:

- Services to end the isolation of certain localities and to enable them to communicate with the wider world through the Internet;
- Creation of databases in different areas for easy consultation and at low cost; and
- Creation of a computer training centre (for word processing and Internet access), a counselling centre for youth, an intercommunity and intercyber production and exchange centre, and a research centre.

Beneficiaries

The primary project beneficiaries were students (13–21 years old) and teachers involved in GEEP activities, such as FLE clubs. The first beneficiaries were 60 adolescents and teachers who attended a train-the-trainer course. It is worth noting that the actual number of beneficiaries was definitely higher. In effect, the 60 primary beneficiaries in turn trained many other beneficiaries. They extended their reach beyond the school setting to grassroots communities – through awareness raising and the organisation of events such as conferences, public events and cyber holiday camps.

Institutional background

GEEP works as a network of human resources that aims to be a driving force for bringing about positive changes in the Senegalese education system. Through its actions and activities, GEEP promotes FLE for students, learners and teachers while attempting to raise awareness in schools and at universities on the relationship between population issues, the environment, citizenship and sustainable development. Because of the expertise of its members, GEEP is regularly solicited for advice on various issues.

Project management structures and staffing

The project is under the management of GEEP, an NGO constituted by researchers, teachers and professionals interested in population issues, the environment, citizenship and sustainable development. GEEP is led by a national coordinator and team, with regional and local teams throughout the country. The national coordination team is located in Dakar and has an administrative and organisational function. Each project site has its own local management team and a steering committee for the Youth Cyber Club.

Each local management team comprises a teacher and at least one student, with at least one team member being female. The management team plays the role of technical facilitator and is in charge of training, first-level equipment maintenance, and support to users. The steering committee plays an advisory role and includes the school administration and occasionally a few members of the student-parent associations. It also plays a role in controlling the budget and finances. These two bodies are the link between the FLE and the national project coordination team. Periodically, team meetings are held in one location to discuss problems and achievements and to share lessons learnt.

Each Youth Cyber Club received a budget to cover a portion of its telecommunications costs and other running costs such as ink and paper. Some costs are recovered from the services supplied (word processing, computer training, etc.) or from donations. Schools provide the physical facilities as well as water and electricity for each of the Youth Cyber Clubs.

Project activities

Pre-start-up

The first activity was the selection of sites for Youth Cyber Clubs. This was based on how well they could:

- Foster decentralisation of FLE management by hosting Youth Cyber Clubs in a school or structure selected as a regional focal point for youth forums. This would make it possible to endow the host structure with information tools for improving FLE activity management at the regional focal point;
- Enable certain FLE clubs to bridge their isolation in remote areas or to overcome the handicap of distance and improve communication with the executive team; and
- Encourage a number of promising and consistent FLE clubs by giving them incentives, and through their example, promote excellence within the FLE network.

Start-up (Piloting)

At the time of the study, the project was still in the pilot stage, having set up 22 Youth Cyber Clubs in the country. These were provided with computer training and with reading material for students, teachers and school community members.

Several activities were undertaken during the project's life. For instance, cyber youth camps were held each year within the country and in Kenya in 2001. They were held in remote areas, outside of the normal school activities. The purpose of these camps was to enable participants to share their experiences with each other; to create opportunities for deciding on matters to be undertaken for the following year (programmatic meetings); to disseminate project results among the project team and others; to demonstrate the usefulness of computers in school and, most importantly, to be close to the actual developmental issues at the community level.

Several national and local workshops have been organised involving teachers, students, parents, school administrations and policy makers. One of the main influences of these workshops is the adoption of the Youth Cyber Club strategy and approach by the Ministry of Education for introducing ICTs in schools.

Partnerships

GEEP has worked together with, and received support from, other partners to implement the activities of the project. As part of its programme of assistance to Senegal (1998-99), UNFPA committed to supporting GEEP to set up five Youth Cyber Clubs in youth information and counselling centres at Cheikh Anta Diop University and in four counselling offices in high schools with active FLE clubs.

Club 2/3 is a cooperation and development agency that supports GEEP in conducting a three-year experimental programme on environmental education called "Greening Schools and Schools' Environments". This initiative for environmental protection and preservation is expected to open three Youth Cyber Clubs in some pilot schools at the rate of one club per year.

In addition, the Ministry of Health has agreed, as part of a package for assistance, to support GEEP in executing a programme on awareness raising for the prevention of Aids. The Ministry provides institutional support and covers monitoring missions through an endowment.

Finally, Schools Online is providing assistance by upgrading equipment and setting up a new Youth Cyber Club at the Collège d'Enseignement Moyen (CEM), Banque Islamique in Guédiawaye.

Table 6.1 indicates the total estimated costs of the Cyber Jeunes project, and the financial and in-kind contributions made by the various partners.

Table 6.1: Budgetary estimates on Youth Cyber Clubs

Item	Cost (FCFA)
IDRC contribution (71%)	
Equipment (computers/modems)	23 160 000
Logistics, communication and consumables	21 600 000
Training, technical assistance, documentation and facilitation	21 900 000
Research	10 000 000
Total	76 660 000
Other contributions (29%)	
UNFPA 10.44%	11 275 000
Club 2/3 (Canada) 5.55%	6 000 000
Health Ministry 3.70%	4 000 000
GEEP 9.26% (in-kind contribution)	10 000 000
TOTAL COSTS (including GEEP contribution)	117 935 000
Additional contribution:	
Schools Online – Grant to set up a new Youth Cyber Club and upgrade the equipment in two others	US$ 20 000

In addition to the formal partners already discussed above, informal partners of host schools are making a worthy contribution by equipping or strengthening the capacity of the Youth Cyber Clubs. They include small and medium enterprises that deal in computers: solution 2000, informatique pour tous (computers for all), génération informatique (computer generation); communities and schools based abroad that support local initiatives within the framework of overseas cooperation: communities in France, such as Voree and Rieupeyroux, Collège Français de Chatel Guyon; NGOs such as Intercultural Dimensions of Boston, USA; and benevolent individuals, notably former students of CEM Ababacar Sy in Tivaouane, who are currently based in Canada.

Some of these partners have supplied the project with computers. Others make provision for the maintenance of equipment and/or take charge of running costs such as telephone bills. These informal partnerships are worthy of interest. It is difficult to say for how long they will continue, especially as the state is not directly involved in initiatives at the local level.

Research process

Data gathering

The research methodology was based on the research questions outlined in Chapter 2. The following five tools were used to collect data:

- An individual student questionnaire;
- A focus group interview guide;
- A document reading grid for user logs and documents describing the use of services at the Youth Cyber Clubs;
- A questionnaire for the local project team at each site; and
- An interview guide for the local coordinator.

These tools were field-tested at the Youth Cyber Club in CEM Samba Gueye in Dakar. Non-random sampling of schools was undertaken. Interviews were conducted with the national project director as well as with the local project manager, teachers, students, administrative authorities and other users.

The background documents included the project design document, the Ministry of Education framework law, the national ICT policy workshop report, training reports, Youth Cyber Club ICT reports, management tools and products, and photographs of the clubs.

Students represent the bulk of the respondents to questionnaires and interviews (80 per cent) and make up 94 per cent of the questionnaire respondents.

Table 6.2: Questionnaire and Interview Respondents

Site	Responses to Student Questionnaire	Responses to Local Project Team Questionnaire	Number of Interview Participants					Total
			Students		External Users	Teachers	Admin.	
			M	F				
Delafosse	17	1	1	6		3	1	29
Dioffior	15	1	7	6		11	–	40
Kaffrine	15	1	5	1		3	1	25
Kolda	14	1	12	6	3	4	–	40
Oussouye	15	1	2	3	3	3	2	29
Saint-Louis	15	1	5	7		3	1	34
Tivaouane	15	1	16	10		3	1	45
TOTAL	106	7	48	39	6	30	6	242

Site visits

The evaluation study covered seven Youth Cyber Clubs:

- Four Cyber Clubs funded by the IDRC as part of the Acacia programme:
  - o Collège d'Enseignement Moyen (CEM) Ababacar Sy in Tivaouane (Thiès region);
  - o Lycée Babacar Cobar Ndaw in Kaffrine (Kaolack region);
  - o Lycée Charles De Gaulle in Saint-Louis (Saint-Louis region); and
  - o Lycée Aline Sitoe Diatta in Oussouye (Ziguinchor region);
- CEM (Kolda Region) – one youth Cyber Club funded by UNFPA;
- Lycée Delafosse in Dakar (Dakar region) – one Youth Cyber Club funded by Club 2/3 Canada; and
- CEM in Dioffior (Fatick region) – one Youth Cyber Club funded by partners of the school.

These Youth Cyber Clubs are located in schools with populations between 700 and 1,400. Each school is different from the other by virtue of its geographical location and administrative status. Two Youth Cyber Clubs, Kolda and Oussouye, are particularly difficult to reach as they are far from Dakar, very remote, and located in the war-torn southern part of the country. In contrast, the clubs in Dakar and Saint-Louis are located in two of Senegal's urban centres where cyber culture is booming, both in people's homes and in public places. The schools that house the Youth Cyber Clubs in Kaffrine and Tivaouane are situated along the highway. They are the only such facilities in the area. The Youth Cyber Club in Dioffior is located in a rural setting.

All the Youth Cyber Clubs, except in Dakar, serve as meeting points for schools with FLE clubs in their areas. Some of the clubs, for example Kolda and Saint-Louis, serve as regional rallying points for FLE clubs, and as reproductive health resource and counselling centres for youth.

Factors influencing the research

There were a few constraints in the project's methodology, specifically concerning use of the reading grid, the way in which the study team conducted interviews, and in the sampling methods. Yet, the purpose of this study was not to extrapolate the results of the analysis throughout the country. Therefore, despite some of the methodological constraints, the information gathered did assist in responding to the study questions and objectives.

- The team did not make judicious use of the reading grid due to the lack of appropriate tools (monitoring records and an activity register). This limited use of the grid to only a few interviews;
- The study team found it difficult to obtain reliable data on their activities because some clubs lack management tools (such as user logs) or use them in an inappropriate manner;
- During interviews at Youth Cyber Clubs in Delafosse, Kaffrine and Kolda, each member of the study team jotted down information gathered in the form of notes. When they compared their notes later to draft a joint report, they realised that some of the information was either missing or misrepresented. Additional efforts were made to fill the information gaps. In subsequent visits, the team selected one "note-taker" to ensure that feedback was faithful, coordinated and exhaustive;
- Whenever teachers and students were put together in a focus group for discussion, the students were careful in their answers or shy to express their views. To prevent this, the team decided to form separate groups. In Delafosse, Dioffior and Tivaouane, where the team organised student focus groups in the presence of teachers, the teachers did not intervene directly but their presence may have had an influence on the discussion; and
- A targeted (and limited) choice of sites was investigated. Generalising results should therefore be approached with caution. Site selection was based on location (Dakar and several regional locations) and on donor weight, with the IDRC/Acacia dominating (four sites were equipped by the IDRC, one by UNFPA, one by 2/3 Canada, and one by local partners of the school community).

Research findings

Connectivity

REFER and SONATEL are the main Internet access and service providers to the Youth Cyber Clubs. Users appeared to have difficulty connecting to the Internet during office hours (08:00–12:00 and 15:00–18:00) when using the REFER server, because the server was saturated at these times. GEEP's last report on ICTs already highlighted this problem:

> Users of the REFER server have to wait for longer periods of time ...
> They choose REFER as their Internet access provider *because the*
> *annual rate of subscription is low.*

In the case where the Youth Cyber Club uses the same telephone line as the school administrative authorities, as in Dioffior, the club can only be connected after office hours, even if the server is accessible. Consequently, access to servers is easier on days when offices are closed and on working days after 18:00 and between 24:00 and 02:00, when administrative staff are not on duty.

The constraints identified in this area include:

- Difficulties in connecting to servers;
- Lack of equipment (between 120 and 1 000 students per computer, depending on the Youth Cyber Club);
- Lack of trainers specialised in computer technology – judging from the duration of training they receive, Youth Cyber Club facilitators do not have the required level of training;
- Facilitators lack sufficient time for training, given their commitments in other areas;
- The number of facilitators available is low, compared with the number of students who need training (100 facilitators for 500 students);
- The use of ICTs has not been institutionalised in school curricula;
- Lack of equipment for training, especially when it comes to training large groups with just one machine; and
- Some clubs have limited space e.g. the Dioffior and Kolda Cyber Clubs measure 15 m² and 25 m² respectively.

Access and use of services

By setting up Youth Cyber Clubs in schools the project has created a strong demand for training and Internet services that is often difficult to satisfy. This is due mainly to:

- The lack of Intranet facilities in some of the Youth Cyber Clubs with a sufficient number of workstations;
- The insufficient number of workstations in most of the Youth Cyber Clubs;

147

- The lack of skilled trainers in ICTs in the clubs; and
- The frequent breakdowns resulting from poor maintenance or poor manipulation of equipment.

Available equipment includes workstations (computer and peripheral equipment) as indicated in Table 6.3. All computers, except those in Dioffior, are Pentiums. The clubs in Tivaouane and Dioffior have several computers, but due to a lack of funds only one of these is connected.

The Cyber Clubs at Delafosse and Dioffior have scanners and digital cameras. All the clubs have direct telephone lines, except Dioffior, which uses the line belonging to the Collège d'Enseignement Moyen (CEM).

The infrastructure has been placed in rooms that were provided by the school authorities with support from GEEP. The rooms vary in size between 15 m² and 30 m². None of the rooms is air-conditioned.

Where school authorities show strong commitment to the cyber initiative, the Youth Cyber Clubs are endowed with more equipment, as in Dioffior, Oussouye and Tivaouane. The equipment audit also shows the high ratio of computers to students. In comparison, the WorLD programme, launched in 2000, donates an average of ten computers per Youth Cyber Club. Most of these clubs are based in urban schools. It is important, however, to note that, unlike the WorLD project, GEEP is an action-research project. Computers are introduced as a means to test conditions under which ICTs may play a role in schools. The lessons learnt can then inform education policy makers. Some Youth Cyber Clubs have taken full advantage of decentralised cooperation (via their communes) or opportunities at the local level to upgrade their equipment. As mentioned, difficulty in accessing servers during office hours is one of the major problems facing the clubs.

At all Youth Cyber Clubs, users can access equipment only when they are:

- FLE club members or pay an annual contribution for training at a rate that corresponds with the user's status – student, teacher, outside user; or
- Clients who pay each time they use the club's Internet services on a minute-by-minute or an hourly basis.

Certain Youth Cyber Clubs (Kolda, Oussouye, Saint-Louis and Tivaouane) request that users commit to the following before they link to the Internet:

- Follow internal rules and regulations; and
- Fill in a logbook each time they use services at the Youth Cyber Club (user name, type of service, duration and amount paid). This is used to monitor users.

In order to ensure efficient use of those Youth Cyber Clubs with a lack of adequate equipment, there is a need to institute good management practices and make sure that users adhere to laid-down rules and regulations.

Pricing

The rates charged depend on the profile of the different Youth Cyber Clubs. Tivaouane charges FCFA 1,000 per student and FCFA 2,000 per adult for training. Elsewhere, the prices vary between FCFA 300 and FCFA 500.

Internet services cost FCFA 25-35 per minute, except in Dioffior, where the charge is FCFA 15 per minute. Even though these rates are lower than those charged by private for-profit outfits, not many students can afford them, especially in the rural setting where incomes are low.

The prices Youth Cyber Clubs charge for connectivity are far lower than those charged by SONATEL (FCFA 60 per minute). As a result, the clubs are constantly subject to shortfalls. Partner grants have to be used each time to clear these shortfalls to make it possible for the clubs to function.

Teachers protested about the fact that they paid out of their own pockets for students to conduct documentary research, key in data or print documents, even though they acknowledge the need for the Youth Cyber Clubs to operate smoothly. On this issue, one teacher in Saint-Louis said:

> We are going to continue offering our services to earn income … The school authorities have withdrawn completely from the management of the Youth Cyber Club … We need money to maintain machines and buy consumables … In fact, the funds we get are not substantial. We shall call in college clubs to key their cards … The school authorities too must pay to process report cards, exam papers, etc. They could allocate a proportion of their budget to us. We need to discuss this at the college managers' meeting, because the room has rendered a great deal of service to the college.

149

Table 6.3: ICT equipment in Youth Cyber Clubs

Cyber Club	PCs	Power Back-up	Printer	Scanner	Modem	Digital Camera	Telephone	Students per PC
Delafosse	3	1	1	1	1	1	1	457
Dioffior	6	–	1	1	1	1	1	126
							(CEM line)	
Kaffrine	6	1	1	–	1	–	1	1,434
Kolda	6	1	1	–	1	–	1	700
Oussouye	6	1	1	–	1	–	1	170
Saint-Louis	6	1	1	–	1	–	1	1,371
Tivaouane	11	1	1	–	1	–	1	131
TOTAL	44	6	7	2	7	2	7	

Similarly, students in Tivaouane request their class- and schoolmates to pay FCFA 25 for documentary research and keyboarding to contribute towards operational costs.

Hours of operation

The Youth Cyber Clubs are generally open on:

- Wednesday afternoons and Saturday afternoons when the public schools are closed;
- From 18:00 each day, and infrequently between 12:00 and 14:00, as well as times when the Youth Cyber Club facilitators are available; and
- Occasionally during holidays, as managers (especially teachers) generally have to travel from another location.

Considering that ICTs are not part of the school curriculum, it is easy to understand the nature of this schedule and especially the motivation of users who find the time to visit the Youth Cyber Clubs at such hours.

Patterns of use

Close to 41.5 per cent of student respondents use the computer more than once a week and 37.7 per cent do so once a week.

Table 6.4: Frequency of computer use by learners

Frequency	Learners	%
More than once a day	5	4.7
More than once a week	44	41.5
Once a week	40	37.7
Once a month	3	2.8
Less than once a month	2	1.9
No response	12	11.3
TOTAL	106	100

Data from the semi-structured interviews and user logs show that between five and ten users on average visit the Youth Cyber Clubs each working day, with a record high of 27 users registered in Oussouye.

Records suggest that Wednesday and Saturday afternoons are the busiest, which are days when students do not have classes. User turnout is high just before exams. Users spend 30–60 minutes on average in the facility. A teacher said:

> When we the trainers go to teach, the room is closed most of the time because there are no permanent staff assigned to the facility ... The room is used in an irrational manner ... Many more users turn out on Wednesday afternoon ... Towards the end of last academic year, just before the baccalaureate, the facility registered high demand, especially from students who were in search of information on admission to universities abroad.

The Youth Cyber Clubs are mainly frequented by students, teachers and school authorities. Other users not directly related to host schools include primary school teachers, veterinary doctors, businessmen, Liberian refugees and Economic Interest Group (EIG) members. Some Youth Cyber Clubs fail to record the profile of all visitors they receive due to the lack of appropriate management tools. Others list only the services they provide to the various users.

Initially these services were offered free of charge for teachers and students. To remain sustainable, the clubs were then opened to the general public, who were charged for services offered. From June 2000 all users were charged as the project approached its closure.

Table 6.5 shows that the Youth Cyber Clubs in Kolda, Oussouye and Saint-Louis had the highest number of service requests. The users were mainly adults, especially teachers. In all the clubs, the bulk of users came from the school setting. In Kaffrine, Saint-Louis and Tivaouane, the predominance of in-school users was even more pronounced. Respondents indicated that even the "out-of-school" users came mostly from other schools. In Dioffior, Kolda and Oussouye, the Youth Cyber Clubs were more open to community-based users, most of whom were professionals from other sectors.

Table 6.5: Number of users for services[1] requested,
Dec. 1999–July/Aug. 2000

Localities	Students	Teachers	Admin.	Others	Total
Delafosse[2]	–	–	–	–	–
Dioffior	–	–	–	–	92
Kaffrine	8	20	2	4	34
Kolda	–	–	–	–	219
Oussouye	52	92	14	46	204
Saint-Louis	34	173	2	–	209
Tivaouane	21	49	5	16	91

Notes: [1] Excludes computer training; [2]Delafosse did not keep a service delivery logbook for the period covered.

Using the GEEP website and resources

The Youth Cyber Clubs have information on certain subjects that they have succeeded in downloading through documentary research, or information that has been prepared by teachers in a diverse range of areas such as history of art, philosophy, French philosophers of the 19th century, malaria, cloning issues, environmental topics, exercises in maths and science, gardening, famine, immigration, Aids in Africa, and so on. These data were compiled in part by teachers in schools hosting Youth Cyber Clubs. While respondents affirmed that they regularly visited GEEP's website, this could not be verified.

Respondents mentioned that students had conducted documentary research on subjects that were not mentioned at all, such as history and geography (33 per cent), French (13.2 per cent), graphics and art, as well as English language, civic education, natural sciences, applied sciences, maths and economics.

The most frequently used search engines were:

- Education issues: Yahoo (26.2 per cent), Francité (21.2 per cent), Nomad (14.3 per cent), Hotmail (11.9 per cent) and Altavista (11.9 per cent).
- Reproductive health issues: Francité (21.2 per cent), Nomad (18.2 per cent), Yahoo (18.4 per cent) and Hotmail (18.2 per cent).
- Environmental issues: Francité (26.7 per cent), Nomad (20 per cent), Yahoo (20 per cent) and Altavista (20 per cent).

Reasons for using ICTs

Some 73 per cent of student respondents used ICTs for schoolwork and FLE club activities, whereas 24.3 per cent of them used ICTs for personal business. A teacher said:

> Following the institution of new curricula, our colleagues of the history and geography departments engaged in documentary research on curricula themes ... We who are in the science department have not yet done so, even though we plan to consult the French site called: "examens et concours de la semaine" (this week's exams and tests). But, I see a problem with that, for if the science department engages in documentary research we will spend plenty of time on the Internet and I just wonder who is going to pay the bills.

In addition to teachers and students who use ICTs for teaching and learning, other uses include:

- Personnel management and school mail (school administration);
- Keying in work-related documents and seeking contact with business partners (professional business); and
- Personal activities, such as email and seeking personal contacts (private users).

A teacher in Dioffior:

> The Youth Cyber Club enables me to better prepare my lessons, to have more up-to-date information on science, and to progress more quickly with my school programme.

154

A telecentre operator in Kolda:

> Going to the Youth Cyber Club enables me to familiarise myself with the Internet. This would be of great service to me when I transform my telecentre into a private for-profit cyber cafe.

A veterinary doctor in Kolda:

> The Youth Cyber Club enables me to collaborate with other partners who are not based here. I submitted an offer from here, in response to a call for offers, and was selected.

The manager of the Oussouye Youth Cyber Club:

> Our Youth Cyber Club welcomes people from the local community, in particular women and petty traders in Economic Interest Groups (EIG). Let me relate just two interesting anecdotes in relation to this. A woman who is a member of a women's association asked us to create a page for her where she could advertise her products (palm oil, smoked fish, fruits, etc.). Later on, she received very many requests. A trader who came to learn about the Internet stumbled upon the Paris International Trade Fair. He requested more information about the fair through the Internet, and ended up having an invitation to attend.

Table 6.6: Most frequently used products and services
in Youth Cyber Clubs

Item	Number	%
Word processing	34	32.1
Search engines	41	38.7
Games	5	4.7
Email	17	16.0
No response	9	8.5
TOTAL	106	100

About 70 per cent of student respondents said that they use the computer mainly for:

- Word processing and documentary research, and specifically for school-work (typing exercises, tests and assignments, and doing research to prepare for or improve in certain lessons);
- FLE club activities (club reports, and documentary research to prepare for presentations and conferences); and
- Office administration (class lists and staff lists, memos, and computer-ising school files).

Some other activities observed in a few rare cases relate to schoolwork or private affairs, and include email (for personal and official purposes), sub-scription for admission in schools abroad, and discussion groups.

Some 46 per cent of student respondents had an email address and read national and international daily newspapers.

Respondents most frequently used the search engines Yahoo (36 per cent), Francité (15.2 per cent) and Nomad (10.6 per cent). Others included Altavista, caramail, dromadaire, Francimel, Hotmail, lockase, MSN and Toile du Quebec.

The manager of the Kolda Cyber Club stated:

> Youth in our area are in contact with young Belgians. Through these contacts they are able to organise group discussions on a range of different issues: health, education, the rights of the child, environment, politics, democracy … Last year, one of our students received an invitation from a group of young people who submitted the 'World Claims' from youth (April 2000).

Levels of activity

The results obtained from the different Youth Cyber Clubs suggest that all the clubs are operational in spite of the obstacles they face. However, they do not all have the same level of dynamism. The Dakar and Kaffrine clubs, for example, appear to be less dynamic than the others. This may be because the Dakar club was opened later (April 2000) and students in Kaffrine were persistently on strike between February, March and April.

The other Youth Cyber Clubs seem to have been well accepted by and integrated into the activities of the host schools. However, the results obtained on Internet training and students' requests for services show that the students are not the main users of the facility. Instead, it is mainly the teachers who use the Youth Cyber Clubs, while students benefit from the work they do.

The Youth Cyber Clubs in Dioffior, Kolda and Oussouye and, to a lesser extent, Tivaouane, are inclined towards community-based users. This is probably because of their geographical location and administrative status, and the lack of private for-profit cyber outfits in these localities.

Obstacles and constraints regarding connectivity and access

Close to half of the student respondents acknowledged that Youth Cyber Clubs were more accessible to students than to outside users. However, some students maintained that teachers most often monopolised workstations once they got access to them. While this may be due to teachers' position of authority, teachers also appeared more inclined to use the Internet than students.

Over 70 per cent of student respondents felt that access to these facilities was difficult due to the following:

- Lack of computers – the computer/student ratio varies from 1:120 to 1:1,400, depending on the school size;
- High cost of services – this is due to the high cost of telephone bills, which include value-added tax (VAT). As a result, lines are often cut if the bills are not paid;
- Lack of time;
- Short time period for students' training, e.g. one hour per week in Dioffior and two Wednesdays per month in Saint-Louis;
- Lack of permanent trainers in the Youth Cyber Clubs – teachers who offer training in these facilities still have to cope with their normal workload;
- Equipment in the clubs is frequently out of order due to weather conditions (lightening and thunder), lack of air conditioning and incorrect use;
- Difficulty in accessing the Internet during office hours;
- Youth Cyber Club trainers are not well qualified;
- Voltage capacity drops frequently, which is exacerbated by the lack of a universal power supply source; and
- The long wait before users actually get to use the computers. A student said: "The room is always so full and there is only one machine con-

nected ... sometimes one has to wait for one or even two hours to access the workstations."

These constraints not only hamper activities at the Youth Cyber Clubs, but may also considerably curtail the success of the programme.

The first major challenge is to ensure that all Youth Cyber Clubs function correctly and are connected to the Internet at all times. Some facilitators have suggested that the Ministry of Education should provide a server exclusively for schools, as is the case in France.

In other areas (Kaffrine, Kolda and Oussouye), there is a need for better maintenance of equipment and qualified technicians for repairs, as none were available at the time of study.

Capacity building and training

Training sites

For students and many other users, the school setting is the ultimate site for initiation in the use of ICTs. In certain areas (Dioffior, Kaffrine, Kolda and Oussouye), the Youth Cyber Clubs are the only institutions with computers for public use. Because income levels and the standard of living are low, people cannot afford their own PCs at home.

In Dakar and Saint-Louis, for example, there are private for-profit cyber cafes and some parents can afford computers at home. Nevertheless, the school setting is the only area with easy access to ICTs, given the high costs charged by private for-profit institutions. As a result, 78.3 per cent of respondents received their training in the school setting, compared with 4.7 per cent at home and 2.8 per cent who received it elsewhere.

Trainers' profiles

Training for trainers in Youth Cyber Clubs is done by teachers hired by the WorLD project or by GEEP's team of managers. Users are initiated in the use of ICTs by training facilitators (student leaders and technical facilitators), or by partners of the respective schools (experts in computer science).

Type and duration of training

The training of technical facilitators was organised in five-day sessions. GEEP conducted three of the five sessions between March 1999 and October 2000. In all, 100 training facilitators took part.

Initiation for users at the Youth Cyber Clubs is conducted according to schedule – one day per week in Dioffior, one Wednesday two or three times a month in Saint-Louis, every Wednesday in Tivaouane and Kolda, and every day after 18:00 pm in Oussouye and at Delafosse.

In certain Youth Cyber Clubs, facilitators offer training every day (to adults especially), depending on their availability. They meet with teachers during off-peak hours and with out-of-school users after 18:00.

Training content

Training programmes include the following elements:

* Windows and keyboarding skills;
* Services available on the Internet;
* Internet exploration tools and pedagogical applications; and
* Using email.

Training materials

The first two sessions for the training of trainers in March 1999 were based exclusively on work with computers. In the third session, however, trainers used a video projector and a giant screen in addition to the computers, because they considered this approach more practical. In the Youth Cyber Clubs, the facilitators initiate learners mainly through work on the computers. This is neither practical nor convenient for training students, particularly in situations where there is only one workstation. Some trainers (e.g. those in Dioffior) recommended the use of video projectors with large screens as one way to address needs in the school setting.

Profile and number of trainees

Table 6.7 gives a breakdown of the number of users trained between December 1999 and June 2000 – note that far more people received computer

159

Table 6.7: Number and percentage of trained users

Cyber Clubs	Students	Teachers	Type of Training							
			computer training (%)				Internet Training (%)			
			Students	Teachers	Admin	Others	Students	Teachers	Admin	Others
Delafosse	1,300	–	87 (6.6)	6	0	–	45 (3.4)	4	0	–
Dioffior	719	16	300 (41.7)	30 (187)	6	8	2 (0.2)	25 (187)	2	4
Kaffrine	1,383	51	26 (1.8)	12 (24)	5	–	15 (1.1)	5 (24)	2	–
Kolda	700	–	72 (10.2)	–	–	–	12 (2.5)	–	–	–
Oussouye	1,032	50	205 (19.8)	12 (24)	7	13	51 (4.9)	12 (24)	7	9
Saint-Louis	1,300	72	135 (10.4)	18 (25)	3	28	10 (0.7)	18 (25)	1	–
Tivaouane	1,400	45	200 (11.1)	15 (33)	1	–	60 (4.2)	15 (33)	1	–

Note: The number of teachers in Delafosse was not provided; the figures in the first two columns of the table were derived from secondary sources (school statistics or documents, etc.). Each Youth Cyber Club may train teachers from other schools, hence the high number of teachers trained at Dioffior.

training than Internet training. This may be due to the difficulty in accessing servers and/or the high cost of using the Internet.

Whatever the case, the number of trained users is far too low, considering the number of teachers and students in the host schools. For example, 81 per cent of student respondents said they were not sufficiently skilled in using ICTs, while 82 per cent acknowledged that they needed help in using the computer.

In view of the constraints identified, the lack of training is a problem that certainly needs to be addressed. It is also worth noting that the facilitators in the Youth Cyber Clubs lend a helping hand to student users to ensure that they do not mishandle equipment or venture onto restricted sites.

Content development

Within the framework of GEEP's project, the Youth Cyber Clubs launched several new activities. These include:

- Designing teaching materials (in the form of guidelines) to make up for the lack of textbooks;
- Setting up databanks (for science subjects);
- Producing cards of various sorts (membership cards, greeting cards, fancy calendars, school newsletters);
- Producing school journals;
- Producing receipt books for traders;
- Producing comic strips conveying information on early pregnancy; and
- Seeking admission to universities abroad through the Internet.

For students in FLE clubs and for teachers, especially those active in population and environmental issues (e.g. geography, social and family economics, and natural sciences), GEEP has designed useful material that can be accessed easily on its website (www.refer.sn/sngal_ct/rec/geep). This includes:

- FLE club management tools;
- An interdisciplinary model for population and environmental education developed with support from UNFPA; and
- A peer education model designed in collaboration with UNESCO.

The website also contains information on the group itself – how it is organised, its activities and partners. At the time of the study, some of GEEP's key publications were not on its website, for example the newsletter "La Lettre du GEEP", and two publications on environment and reproductive health respectively.

The Youth Cyber Clubs have also compiled and stored data on the Internet about discussion forums they initiated. These include:

- "ICTs in our day-to-day lives", initiated by the Oussouye-based Youth Cyber Club;
- "Why students drop out of school at the intermediate level", initiated by the Tivaouane Youth Cyber Club; and
- "ICTs in development", initiated by Delafosse.

While several other Youth Cyber Clubs did participate in the first two forums, only the Kolda Youth Cyber Club participated in the last discussion forum.

Policy

At the time of the study, no formal ICT policy nor education policy dealt with the use of ICTs in schools. Senegal had not yet institutionalised the use of ICTs in schools, while some public institutions and NGOs already used them. The Ministry of Education's ten-year education and training programme (2000–2010, "Quality Education for All")[2] aims to intensify the use of ICTs by introducing them to half of all colleges. The programme is therefore mainly concerned with connecting and equipping colleges, as well as training teachers. At the end of the programme, students all over Senegal will have access to ICTs and to quality education. There is therefore government commitment to driving ICTs in educational institutions but not yet at the school level. The Minister of Education's support to the WorLD programme and the Youth Cyber Clubs indicates that this is an area likely to receive more attention in the future.

Effects of the project

It is difficult to measure the real impact that the ICT project has had on the activities of schools, given the duration of the pilot phase (less than two years) and the constraints that were encountered. Using the initial objectives of the project as an entry point, this study attempts to measure progress (i.e. what has been done against what was planned) and to indicate whether the resulting trend has been mainly one of success or failure. Working from a set of indicators as indicated below, this section of the study seeks to determine the level of progress for the various activities of the Youth Cyber Clubs.

Successful establishment of Cyber Clubs

Indicator #1:

Twelve Youth Cyber Clubs have been established as part of a system (network) for electronic communication in the school setting

This network boasts 22 clubs at present, thanks to the project's diverse partner base. The project has therefore exceeded expectations in terms of its original objectives.

Level of Internet activity by Cyber Clubs

Indicator #2:

The e-network is used to improve and intensify information flow within the network of FLE clubs, between the network and GEEP's team of managers, and between the clubs and external partners

- Each Youth Cyber Club has an email address and five of the seven clubs under study were designing their own websites (Delafosse, Dioffior, Kolda, Oussouye and Tivaouane). There is evidence of communication via email between the clubs themselves and between the clubs and GEEP's team of managers (reports and email).
- Three target Youth Cyber Clubs (Delafosse, Oussouye and Tivaouane) engaged in discussion forums that focused on ICTs in development, ICTs in day-to-day life, and school dropouts.
- Through their FLE clubs, the Dioffior and Kolda Youth Cyber Clubs correspond with young people in France (Dioffior), Egypt and Pakistan (Kolda). Kolda's members were admitted to a discussion group with young Belgians for the exchange of ideas on such themes as health, environment, the rights of the child, and education.
- Since May 2000, the national network of FLE clubs has been sharing experiences on environmental issues, youth activities, anti-personnel

landmines and globalisation with youth from Burkina Faso, Chile, Paraguay and Quebec on Club 2/3 Canada's site (through RIJ 2/3, the International Youth 2/3 Network).

Building the skills of the youth

Indicator #3:

Build the skills of the youth and their supervisors by training 60 trainers in the use of ICTs.

Three training sessions were organised for over 100 Youth Cyber Club facilitators. The level of progress has, therefore, exceeded expectations.

Training in ICT skills

Indicator #4:

Sensitising 10,000 students, 150 teachers and 50 administrative officers to the importance of ICTs.

Data that emerged during the study show the following levels of progress:

- Students received training in commonly used computer applications (1,025, or 10 per cent of the target group), and on how to use the Internet (195 or 0.19 per cent);
- Teachers received training in the same: 93 (62 per cent) and 79 (52 per cent) respectively; and
- Administrators also received training in the same: nine (18 per cent) and four (8 per cent) respectively.

These figures do not include all teachers and administrative officers who have received training, as some Youth Cyber Clubs had no logbooks on service delivery, while some had not been keeping their books well enough to provide reliable data. If one considers only those who have received training on how to use the Internet, for example, the partial results from the seven clubs under study show a clear bias in favour of teachers. The discrepancy in levels of progress for teachers and administrative officers shows that there were difficulties at that stage.

The five-day training delivered in one stretch to Youth Cyber Club facilitators does not provide them with the necessary skills to implement and oversee training in a satisfactory manner. Training in the Youth Cyber Clubs is hindered in large part due to the:

- Lack of workstations (computers and ancillary equipment);
- Lack of appropriate material for training (e.g. group training); and
- Unavailability of trainers because of tight schedules in their respective areas of activity.

Some Youth Cyber Clubs have forged partnerships with small and medium-sized computer suppliers to improve the quality of training they offer. The cost of training in Youth Cyber Clubs is lower than in the private for-profit sector, yet most students in the rural setting are often unable to afford training even at low cost. As ICT training had not been institutionalised in schools at the time of the study, it was not considered a part of the curriculum and appeared instead as extra work for Youth Cyber Club facilitators.

Training is probably the project's weakest component – it has been noted to be inadequate, often unsuited to users' needs and conducted with little or no regard for concerns related to maintenance. The Cyber Club facilitators themselves have frequently expressed these inadequacies.

Training places yet another burden on facilitators and students who already have heavy workloads and tight schedules. Mechanisms for institutionalisation are needed, i.e. a training curriculum that combines current school curricula, and activities by GEEP should become part of the school timetable.

Improved performance in ICT users

Indicator #5:

Improved school performance by students, teaching methods for teachers and documentation for the school authorities.

Results show that 70.8 per cent of students believed that their performance had improved, 9.4 per cent did not see any improvement and 19.8 per cent did not know. Comments from several teachers, administrators and students indicate that there was an improvement:

> Last year, the history, geography and science teachers used the Youth Cyber Club quite a lot. Incidentally, the school obtained particularly satisfactory results on these subjects during the baccalaureate *(school authority in Saint-Louis).*

165

Last year I used documents from the Monde Diplomatique on the Internet to prepare for the public exam on Population and Development, and I passed *(student from Saint-Louis)*.

The change in students comes from the fact that they can now access maps, data and notes on interesting pieces of information and use them to improve their performance at school *(teacher)*.

Last year while I was in the Lower Sixth form, our programme dealt with development and underdevelopment. We sought documentation from the Monde Diplomatique, and found out that we had information that was richer than what our teachers had given us. We used this information together and did very well in the exam *(student from Kaffrine)*.

Students use ICTs to seek information through documentary research and complement the information they receive in class. They feel this information is more complete and up-to-date than what they receive from their teachers. Usually, students from the same class or level share the cost of undertaking documentary research on a theme via the Internet, including the cost of printing documents. This helps them to reduce costs and makes it easier for them to have access to these services.

Teachers who use ICTs for teaching and learning have the tendency to:

* Key in their exercises, notes and exam questions all by themselves (this helps to cut down on information leaks before the examination);
* Provide their students with more up-to-date maps, graphics, notes and other data; and
* Encourage their students to undertake preparatory documentary research on the Internet even before they deal with topics in class.

Here is what a number of teachers had to say in this regard:

We can key in information, surf on the Internet and expect to improve the ways in which we teach. We can make amendments to our material using documentary research if need be. I try to update my material each time I come across more current data *(teacher from Dioffior)*.

We have observed a clear improvement in the quality of documents. We used to work under very difficult conditions, using stencils or pens to draw diagrams. When we needed notes, secretaries who were not familiar with technical terms would type some of the material and produce unreadable work. Since I began keying in material by myself, I produce more presentable documents. A lot has changed for students, for they can now access maps, statistical data and other material of interest to them. This certainly has a positive impact on their performance at school *(teacher from Saint-Louis).*

Access to documents

GEEP has deployed a considerable amount of energy to develop content for its activities and tailor it to the needs of students and teachers at the local level. Students and teachers can thus adapt material from other sources to their specific educational needs.

Youth Cyber Clubs produce a varied range of material, most of which is on schoolwork or FLE club activities. It is published by GEEP, downloaded or produced by teachers and sometimes by students themselves.

Students can design guidelines (as in Kaffrine, Saint-Louis and Tivaouane), set up databanks for given exercises (at Saint-Louis and Tivaouane) or download material for exercises from other websites (all the Youth Cyber Clubs).

School administration

Gains in time, efficiency and energy spent on specific tasks have been the key changes ICTs have brought to this area, notably in:

- Transmitting administrative documents, including letters, to superiors (the school inspectorate, Ministry officials) via email;
- Keying in and printing various documents (notebooks, report cards, registers, etc.), which formerly meant hiring the services of a private printer; and
- Setting up databanks (lists of staff and students, memos).

In view of the above indicators, the overall trend is a positive one and one can rightly say the ground has been prepared for good results. Meanwhile, there is a need to exercise caution, as the major constraints that have been identified could reverse the trend.

This study on Youth Cyber Clubs highlights the diverse range of activities conducted for interpersonal communication (via email), data collection, team work (teachers and students), use of professional services (in the school and out-of-school settings), publications on the Internet, and self-learning.

These activities can open up new prospects for the school and community settings in certain cases, considering the positive impact they have already had on students and other users.

Policy

The project on Youth Cyber Clubs contributes meaningfully to efforts by Senegal's education authorities to extend the use of ICTs through the PDEF's WorLD project. The project's positive results can be used to inform decision making among education authorities in Senegal before they embark on introducing ICTs in schools. The Director of Intermediate and Secondary Education in Senegal echoed this wish at the School Networking Africa Workshop held in Okahandja, Namibia from 17–20 July 2000.

Conclusions and recommendations

Perpetuating the experience of Youth Cyber Clubs will be a logical next step, a desire strongly expressed by users, club managers and the authorities of host schools. Through its findings, this study shows that introducing ICTs in schools and grassroots communities in Africa is a useful and feasible endeavour. Other partners have understood the key importance of this initiative and are already taking concrete steps to replicate the Acacia programme. A case in point is the programme by School Online, an American NGO whose initiative builds on the lessons learnt from the pilot project on Youth Cyber Clubs. Recently, a new club was set up in CEM Banque Islamique with six workstations, while the clubs in Lycée Blaise Diagne (Dakar) and CEM Kolda (Kolda) both received two workstations to upgrade their equipment.

The students and teachers who will be using the new equipment in these Youth Cyber Clubs will certainly commit more to producing teaching materials suited to the history, institutions, culture and geography of their regions and country. This material could then be published on the Internet.

A number of recommendations were made by stakeholders and researchers, which are indicated below according to the four theme areas of this evaluation.

Connectivity and access

- Because of the difficulties in connecting to servers, it would be interesting to look into the possibility of using other providers, even if this is more costly. It would be essential to know beforehand the running costs of the Youth Cyber Clubs (i.e. the cost of connection, consumables and repairs) and in what proportion these costs can be covered;
- The Youth Cyber Clubs need to consider ways in which the existing schedules could be reconciled with the possibility of giving each user unlimited access to the cyber facility;
- The state could set up a dedicated server for schools; and
- The project could also:
  o Network all computers in each Youth Cyber Club;
  o Upgrade technical equipment by forging meaningful partnerships, while inviting contributions from the parents' associations (a quota on school fees) and the host schools (part of the administrative department's budget should be allocated to the Youth Cyber Clubs);
  o Recruit an expert on ICTs for each Youth Cyber Club or, failing this, see to it that teachers or supervisors can give more time to the clubs; and
  o Negotiate with SONATEL the possibility of suppressing VAT from bills sent to the clubs.

Capacity building and training

- The state should institute refresher courses for Youth Cyber Club facilitators and trainers;
- School authorities should include training as a curricular activity, use video projectors and giant screens to deliver group training, and use curriculum subjects, as much as possible, as media for training students in the use of ICTs; and
- Education authorities should include ICTs in the preservice training curricula of teachers' training institutions.

Content and Curriculum Development

- The state should encourage the design and development of content adapted to the local education system and the national policy for education and training; and
- The project should set up a committee for content development and validation at the local level, encourage the exchange of content among Youth Cyber Clubs, and promote service delivery at the local level.

Policy

At the policy level, it would be possible to work with public authorities on designing possible national strategies that would draw from the experience of this ICT initiative. These national strategies could then help formulate national policy on the application of ICTs in schools. In fact, because of the involvement of policy makers in the GEEP project activities, the Ministry of Education has expressed its intent of using the project approach and strategies to introduce ICTs in schools at the national level.

Partnerships and sustainability

- Partnerships, a fundamental dimension of this project in terms of durability and sustainability, should be given further attention. The bulk of funding for this project comes from development partners. However, if partners were to decide to phase out funding for the project, it is unknown what measures would be taken to replace them. If the state adopted a clear policy on the application of ICTs in schools, the situation would be less problematic and an environment for innovative types of partnerships would be enabled (e.g. public-private partnerships). Even then, what kind of partnership would public authorities propose to promote?
- The state should:
  - o Coordinate initiatives by GEEP and MEN through installing a common network of Youth Cyber Clubs and WorLD Links;
  - o Ensure that all material and equipment for the school networking initiatives are tax free;
  - o Encourage private donors to promote school networking initiatives; and

o   Enable Youth Cyber Clubs to take full advantage of the facilities offered by SONATEL to WorLD (i.e. tax exemption, free installation of telephone lines and connection fees less than FCFA 50,000 every two months).

Notes

1   Club 2/3 funded this last component and UNFPA assisted with funds for several other initiatives.

2   As stated in the *Programme décennal pour l'éducation et la formation (PDEF)*, Component 2: Improving the quality of teaching/learning.

Chapter 7

SchoolNet South Africa

Edward Holcroft

Country context

South Africa is unique in terms of Africa for several reasons. Having only recently emerged from its apartheid history, South Africa has, in a sense, its own domestic digital divide. There exists a paradoxical situation in that the best commercial, business and technological practices live within a social system also characterised by widespread illiteracy, poverty, unemployment, crime and disease. Confirming the paradox are the significant successes that have been achieved in building a new national education system and the policies associated with it, in contrast to the chronic shortages of resources, including ICTs in schools.

Socio-economic background

After a protracted struggle for political rights and the abolition of the system of apartheid, the country held its first, non-racial elections and installed a democratically elected government in 1994. In June 1999, South Africa successfully held its second democratic elections, marking the official start of the post-Mandela era. Some positive aspects of the new South Africa include the promise of normalisation of the country's external relations and the intended economic empowerment of once disadvantaged communities.

Given the country's mineral and marine wealth, infrastructural networks, financial services, manpower and market, South Africa is one of Africa's economic giants. Agriculture, mining, manufacturing and a tourist infrastructure constitute the core pillars of the economy. However, South Africa's

173

Box 1: South Africa in Brief

Area: 1,219,912 sq km
Capital: Pretoria
Population: 43 586 097 (CIA July 2001 est.)[1]
Age: *0–14 years:* 32.01%; *15–64 years:* 63.11%; *65+ years:* 4.88%
(2001 est.)
Urbanisation: 54% urban (WPB 2001)[2]
Literacy: 81.8% (persons aged 15+ years)
Life Expectancy: 48.9 years (2001 est.)
Unemployment: 30% (2000 est.)
Official Language: 11 languages
Telecommunications:
Landlines: 5.85 million (2001 est.)[3]
Mobiles: 9.4 million (Cellular Statistics Nov. 2001)[4]
Internet: 2.85 million (BMI-TechKnowledge 2001)[5]
No. of Schoolchildren[6]
Primary: 133% of schoolgoing age
Secondary: 94% of schoolgoing age [7]

Evaluation Survey
  Sample Size:
  No. of Schools: 10 (two in five provinces)
  No. of Learner Questionnaires: 102
  No. of Educator Questionnaires: 17
  No. of Partner Responses: 2
Period of Evaluation: October 2000 to May 2001
Project Information
  Name of Project: SchoolNet South Africa
  Duration: November 1997 to the present
  IDRC Contribution: CAD 472,000 (Phase 1)
  Implementing Agency: SchoolNet South Africa
  Partners: IDRC, National/provincial Departments of Education, Telkom,
  Nortel, WorLD, IICD, Open Society Foundation SA, Netcorps, VSO
  Canada
  Beneficiaries: Learners and teachers, Departments of Education
  (national and provincial)

economy also displays several features characteristic of the continent as a whole. These include a high population growth rate, heavy dependence on the export of primary products and income distribution inequalities. Approximately 50 per cent of South African households earn less than US$ 34 per adult per month. While the country's performance in education and health is above the average for sub-Saharan Africa, there remains a considerable backlog in the provision of social services. In particular, a high degree of divergence is reflected amongst the different races and regions, a legacy of the apartheid era. A major challenge for the future remains managing and sustaining a fragile democracy in a culturally diverse society and rejuvenating the economy, which is still suffering from years of isolation and inward trade and investment policies.

Educational background

The education system in South Africa is undergoing major restructuring under the democratic government. The system inherited by the government of 1994 was characterised by high rates of repeaters, poor learning outcomes and substandard education offered to black South Africans, with the consequence that there is a high rate of adult illiteracy and innumeracy. It is estimated that only one out of three learners in South Africa obtains a high school pass (matric) and that 29 per cent of the teachers did not pass matric.

According to the 1996 *Schools Register of Needs*,[8] South Africa had about 27 000 schools serving the needs of just over 12 million learners with about 380 000 educators. Only 59 per cent had grid electricity, 59 per cent had exchange telephone lines and only 15 per cent had two or more computers. One in four schools had no water within walking distance, less than half (43 per cent) had electricity, 73 per cent had no learning equipment and 51 per cent did not have adequate textbooks (Mutume 2000).

A consolidation of the statistics shows that only 15 per cent of schools possessed telecommunications potential by meeting the three basic prerequisites to connectivity, namely grid electricity, exchange telephone lines and two or more computers. Some provinces were worse off than others. For example, Northern Province showed only a 1 per cent telecommunications potential, compared with 38 per cent in the Western Cape. SchoolNet SA conducted a school connectivity review of its own in 1996 and the findings were similar to those of the Schools Register. The research showed that about 1 per cent of South African schools had any form of Internet access. Internet access in this case meant any form of access – it may have been a single modem on a single computer. It did not imply that the learners in the school had access to the Internet, nor that the access was being used in an educationally meaningful way.

In September 1994, the publication of a Draft White Paper on Education and Training sparked public debate about the possibilities of a a new non-racial, non-sexist and democratic education system. The main points highlighted in the paper were as follows:

- The government would provide funds to schools on an equitable basis in order to ensure an acceptable quality of education;
- Uniform national school models would replace previous models, such as the Model C,[9] farm schools and others; and Equity of access to educational institutions, as enshrined in the South African Bill of Rights, would be pursued.

Formal education is categorised into public ordinary school education (Grades R-3 as the Foundation Phase, Grades 4–7 as the intermediate phases, and high school from Grades 8–12), teacher training, technikon and university training.

In 1998, Curriculum 2005 was introduced in Grade 1 as the new national curriculum framework for schools based on the outcomes-based education (OBE) system. OBE regards learning as essentially an interactive process between educators and learners, with the learner at the centre of the process and the teacher as a facilitator. Curriculum 2005 has its foundation in the establishment of the National Qualifications Framework and the South African Qualifications Authority. Both were established in accordance with Act No. 58 of 1995, with the intention of giving structural weight to efforts to transform education at school level by moving from content-based to outcomes-based education. Key objectives of Curriculum 2005 are to shift radically from traditional approaches to teaching towards more active learning approaches; examination-driven to ongoing assessment and, finally, from rote learning to critical thinking, reasoning, reflection and action.

Educator training

Educator training in South Africa is provided through two institutional mechanisms:

- Traditional universities provide a degree programme linked to a post-graduate Diploma in Education aimed at preparing students for a career in teaching. Typically, this consists of a three-year degree followed by a one-year full-time diploma. Some universities offer a combined four-year professional degree to the same end; and
- Alternatively, prospective teachers can attend a teacher training college, culminating in a teaching diploma (also four years of full-time study).

Content and curriculum development

Curriculum and content development in the government education system in South Africa is a function of specialist divisions within the Departments of Education. The National Department of Education assumes responsibility for development of the core curriculum, Curriculum 2005. This, in turn, is interpreted and implemented at provincial level by the various provincial Departments of Education. The selection of learning materials and examinable content is shared between individual schools and provincial Departments. Schools assume a primary responsibility in this regard at the General Education and Training (GET) level, and provincial Departments of Education are responsible for the Further Education and Training (FET) level, in particular at matriculation level. Examinable education outcomes at provincial level are directly informed by the national core curriculum.

Curriculum 2005 does not exclude the integration of ICTs into the curriculum; in fact, it welcomes their use where they may be appropriate to achieving educational outcomes. However, it does not make special provision for the use of ICTs, nor does it offer specific guidelines on the use of ICTs in the core curriculum. Furthermore, the outcomes have not been designed in such a way that they require the use of ICTs in meeting them.

Major landmarks of ICTs in education in South Africa[10]

In South Africa, the use of technology in education has been on the policy agenda since late 1995. As the country emerged from apartheid rule, the first democratic government was faced with a plethora of educational problems. Both within and beyond policy circles, several people began to turn greater attention to the possibility of using a range of information, communication and broadcasting technologies to find solutions to these problems.

177

This interest brought with it a proliferation of technology vendors marketing technological 'one-size-fits-all' solutions, particularly to the national Department of Education.

In response, the Ministry of Education and the Department of Education initiated the Technology-Enhanced Learning Investigation (TELI), in order to establish a clear policy framework for the effective use of technologies in education. In 1996, the Minister of Education published a call for nominations of persons to serve on an investigating committee relating to the development of a national framework and a strategic plan for technology-enhanced learning. This led to a series of policy processes, which are listed below. These included the development of educational television and radio television channels, and the creation of the Centre for Educational Technology and Distance Education. It also laid the foundation for school networking initiatives in a number of South African provinces.

Key educational technology milestones in South Africa since 1995 include:

- **November 1995:** The Department of Education workshop identifies the need for the TELI process.
- **July 1996:** The TELI discussion document is completed.
- **September 1996:** The Department of Education establishes an agreement with the South African Broadcasting Corporation (SABC).
- **January 1997:** A draft policy position is written, but is not enacted or gazetted.
- **April 1997:** The TELI strategic plan is competed, and includes plans for 14 projects.
- **December 1997:** SchoolNet SA is launched.
- **December 1998:** The TELI decision-making framework is finalised.
- **February 1999:** The SABC/Department of Education Broadcasting Conference reintroduces the idea of a dedicated educational channel.
- **August 1999:** The Department of Communication's first-phase report on a dedicated educational channel is released.
- **November 1999:** A joint Department of Communication/Department of Education report on the feasibility of a dedicated educational channel is released, which proposes a converged educational network.
- **2000:** Planning for the Khanya project begins in the Western Cape.

- **March 2000:** The Department of Education releases the value chain framework.
- **February 2001:** Gauteng Online.com is launched in Gauteng province.
- **March 2001:** The National ICT Forum is established to guide national ICT strategy.

The TELI framework and its role in addressing ICTs in the South African education system

TELI establishes a clear commitment to using technologies in education and training. It stresses the importance of examining teaching and learning environments in depth before choosing which technologies to integrate into those environments. It also considers the need to identify strengths and weaknesses of different technological options, and uses these to inform decisions. The TELI framework stresses the danger of allowing technology choices to drive educational decisions about how to integrate technology use into teaching and learning environments.

It offers a decision-making framework as a strategy for overcoming this problem. The aim is to fit appropriate technological choices with the educational contexts in which they are needed to make sure scarce resources are used as effectively as possible. The framework contained in the TELI discussion document poses challenges implementing and planning a technology-enhanced learning strategy, and provides a starting point for an investigation of different technologies to support education and training. The intention of this approach is to guard against technologically driven educational projects, which do not always provide effective or sustainable educational solutions.

Centre for Educational Technology and Distance Education (CETDE)

The CETDE was established in early 1997 as a subdirectorate of the Ministry of Education, and was a direct outcome of the TELI process. Its mandate was to "promote open and lifelong learning through the use of media, educational technology, libraries and distance education" (SADE). The centre set out policy guidelines for the educational sector, supported the use of technology through research, coordinated initiatives and organised partnerships between the government and the private sector.

In South Africa, education is a provincial matter. The CETDE therefore did not have direct authority over the implementation of initiatives at school level. However, it was instrumental in many initiatives at the national level, which have had indirect effects on the use of ICTs in education. For example, the CETDE, together with the IDRC, played an important part in the founding of the national SchoolNet SA initiative, set up in November 1997.

The original TELI documents outlined 19 related projects, of which six were identified as lead projects undertaken by the CETDE:

- Doing an audit of ICTs in South African schools;
- Carrying out research and producing a report on the role of technologies in supporting the development and provision of education and training through multi-purpose community learning centres;
- Developing technical standards and protocols for educational technologies;
- Establishing a clearing house of information – a tender for the design and development of a website of information relating to technology-enhanced learning initiatives in South Africa was awarded. A printed version of aspects of the information available on the website was made available, and distributed quarterly as part of *The Teacher*;
- Coordinating school library services, which included investigating the future of library services and norms and standards for school libraries; and
- Working with the SABC to produce comprehensive reports relating to a school-based educational broadcasting service for South Africa, and educational broadcasting interventions in the fields of adult education and youth development.

The CETDE also developed a framework of quality standards for distance education. This was important, because it contained value statements that could be used to measure the quality of a technology-enhanced learning project.

South African broadcasting policy

Various broadcasting policy processes in the 1990s have given attention to its relevance and role in the dissemination of educational content. In April 1998, the public broadcaster SABC and the national Department of Education produced a report, *A School-Based Educational Broadcasting Service for South Africa – Strategic Plan Developed for the South African Broadcasting Corporation.* The aim was to prepare for the phased implementation of a school-based educational broadcasting service that would support teaching, learning and whole school development. The report describes a strategic plan that will ensure educational relevance and financial sustainability, and its significance lies therein that the public broadcaster had an educational mandate to fulfil. Consequently, these plans focused on the role that a broadcasting service could play in assisting school education in terms of curriculum support, the professional development of teachers and the governance, management and administration of schools. The school-based educational broadcasting service was launched early in 1999 and continues to this day.

Vision of a national educational network

The most recent development in South African educational technology policy has been the establishment of a vision to develop a national education network. This vision emerged from earlier attempts at exploring the viability of establishing a dedicated educational broadcasting service, and was a joint exercise of the national Departments of Education and Communication. Essentially, the vision proposes that the government should establish an educational technology network that incorporates four core functions:

- Content acquisition and dissemination;
- Communication;
- Administration and management; and
- Network roll-out and maintenance.

The report on this vision notes that, notwithstanding clear trends of convergence in the functionality of ICTs and broadcasting technologies, there will remain a vibrant and distinct terrestrial broadcasting sector in South African communications for the foreseeable future. It proposes that the SABC television and radio services continue to include a range of educational and educative programming on existing channels and stations as they do currently, expanding and augmenting these services as finance becomes available to do so. Thus, while there is a growing focus on supporting structured education in areas such as schooling and adult education, there is also a

181

wealth of informal educative programming on both radio and television that harnesses many of the greatest potential strengths of educational broadcasting.

The concept of an educational technology network implies a need to roll out technological infrastructure on a large scale. In this regard, the report proposes judicious investments in networking teaching and learning sites (including schools, adult learning centres, health clinics, multi-purpose community centres and a range of other potential sites) around cluster hubs. Via a wide area network, these hubs would provide access to network servers for the teaching and learning sites connected to them. They would provide connected sites with the full functionality of a distributed computer network, including access to websites, email facilities and centrally stored database systems.

Several projects now being launched either at provincial level or through the involvement of private sector partners have brought in sizable investments. In 2000, SchoolNet SA, for example, was managing projects that led to the installation of networked computer laboratories in over 300 schools. Gauteng Online.Com, a provincial project of the Gauteng Department of Education, constitutes a R500 million provincial investment in ICT between 2001 and 2003, while there are similarly ambitious plans presented in the Khanya Project of the Western Cape Department of Education.

ICT forum

The above processes led to the establishment of a national ICT forum, which was jointly launched by the Departments of Education and Communication early in 2001. This forum intended to bring together private and public sector players to support implementation of the vision of a dedicated national education network.

Legislative context

Since 1995, the government has undertaken a thorough programme of legislative reform in education. Secondary education in South Africa today is governed by a comprehensive set of legislation, including:

- South African Council for Educators Act 31 of 2000;
- Education Laws Amendment Act 48 of 1999;
- Further Education and Training Act 98 of 1998;

182

- Employment of Educators Act 76 of 1998;
- Education Laws Amendment Act 100 of 1997;
- Abolition of Corporal Punishment Act 33 of 1997;
- South African Schools Act 84 of 1996; and
- National Education Policy Act 27 of 1996.

At the time of the study, no specific provisions were made in the legislation for the use of ICTs in education. However, the national curriculum documentation confirms the use of ICTs as one of several strategies that may be used in the achievement of educational outcomes (e.g. TELI), as discussed above.

Project background

Conceptualising and launching of the project

SchoolNet SA had its forerunners in a few local NGOs founded by teachers with the aim of providing computers and Internet access to schools. However, most of the NGOs suffered from lack of funding and infrastructural support. To secure and extend their work, the local NGOs considered the establishment of a national umbrella organisation and approached the IDRC for support. During 1997, the IDRC brought together possible partners and started negotiations between the local NGOs and the government. It was eventually decided that the CETDE would coordinate the initiative and SchoolNet SA would be set up as an independent entity. Its mandate stipulates that the organisation should stimulate ICTs in education and the support of educational systems in four main areas:

- Connectivity and technology;
- Human resources development;
- Online content and material in function of the curriculum; and
- Marketing and promotion.

The organisation was unique in the South African context in that it was managed by an executive council comprising representatives from NGOs, the CETDE, the Department of Arts, Culture, Science and Technology, the Department of Communication, and the Department of Trade and Industry. Initially, SchoolNet's funding largely originated from donors and international

183

organisations. By 2001, however, much of the funding came from the private sector, either in terms of direct funding or through delivered services and infrastructure. Since its inception, the IDRC has funded SchoolNet SA, financially and in kind. Contributions in kind included the housing of the secretariat within the IDRC's Regional Office for Southern Africa (ROSA) in Johannesburg, and administrative support associated with the financial management of the project.

Through its operations, the organisation has shown that partnerships between the public and private sectors can yield considerable benefits. SchoolNet SA has been able to promote and widen the use of computers and the Internet in schools.

SchoolNet SA's development during the period under evaluation (early 1997 to July 2000) can be categorised into three stages:

1) The first period up to November 1997 was characterised by disparate, grassroots school networking initiatives in a few provinces. In November 1997, the National Schools Network (NSN), which was informally constituted, met to discuss the possibility of establishing a formal national school networking agency to pursue the development of ICT use in education countrywide. SchoolNet SA was established out of this meeting, leading to the second period, which was a planning phase;

2) A business plan was developed by SchoolNet SA and presented to the IDRC in July 1998 for funding approval; and

3) This was the first phase of 24 months leading up to July 2000.

Project objectives

The global objectives for SchoolNet SA were conceptualised around three core theme areas. These were further subdivided as follows:

- *To develop provincial structures and networks in the nine provinces.* In the two provinces with appropriate provincial networks, SchoolNet would support existing structures and use well-established schools as pilots and reference sites for the next activities. In the four provinces with emerging networks or existing initiatives, SchoolNet would build upon existing structures and establish new provincial School Net structures, implement connectivity projects, establish training and resources centres and run training and human resource development projects. In the other three provinces, SchoolNet would establish relationships with provincial government and NGOs to initiate the formation of school networking structures;

- *To develop human resources at the provincial level.* The model for implementing human resource development would be based on the WorLD training programme. Various training schemes would be implemented at the provincial, district and school levels. Training would be provided in basic ICT literacy, use of ICTs in education (using WorLD and other appropriate material), technical ICT support and information technology facilities management and sustainability; and
- *To provide national support in the areas of learning and teaching resources, connectivity and technology, and human resources development.* This would include the promotion of appropriate ICT-based learning and teaching resources, exploration of alternative ICT infrastructural and connectivity options, coordination of relevant training resources, and research to determine best practices for implementation.

These objectives formed the core of activities during the first phase of SchoolNet SA. Specific objectives were to pilot a provincially based school connectivity implementation model in four provinces – the Eastern Cape, KwaZulu-Natal, Northern Province and North West province (SchoolNet Proposal 1998). The implementation strategy is described in terms of these specific objectives in Section 7.3 below.

Monitoring and evaluation of SchoolNet activities

SchoolNet SA aimed to assess its overall achievements through ongoing monitoring and evaluation of its outcomes through the following measurements:

- Four functioning provincial school network organisations, established with the involvement of the stakeholders;
- A model for expansion into other provinces and into other countries in Africa;
- A number of functioning connectivity hubs and training sites able to provide appropriate support to surrounding schools;
- A number of connected schools participating in ICT learning projects as contemplated in the broader SchoolNet SA programme;

185

- The value of the key teacher concept in providing connectivity in support of teachers involved in teacher development programmes;
- The value of a geographical approach to access in providing connectivity within reasonable travel distances of target teachers and learners, e.g. through telecentres or education resource centres; and
- A technology map of the minimum hardware and support requirements for achieving various ICT-based education outcomes, as well as the constraints determined by the lack of resources available for technology in the country.

To evaluate the project, SchoolNet planned to access:

- The prospects for sustainability, i.e. continued use of ICT facilities after one to two years;
- Educational outcomes from the use of the ICT facilities, and the extent to which these matched the targeted learning areas and supported the work of other projects involved; and
- The technical success of the project, i.e. the extent to which the provided Internet connectivity was used.

Some of the projects undertaken by SchoolNet SA have warranted detailed, independent evaluations. For example, the Telkom 1000 School Internet Project (described later in this chapter), as well as a project in collaboration with the Open Society Foundation (also described later), was evaluated by outsourced, specialist evaluation agencies. SchoolNet SA has evaluated other projects internally on an ongoing basis, both during implementation as well as upon completion of projects and interventions.

This chapter does not address each outcome or project individually. Rather, it provides a snapshot of the context and the achievements of the project in the light of the broader scope of the Acacia initiative. The report also reveals how each of these envisaged outcomes have been met.

SchoolNet activities

Projects and related activities

SchoolNet South Africa's success can be largely attributed to the support it received from an extensive number of partners. Table 7.1 provides a summary overview of these partners and the projects that they funded(SchoolNet South Africa 2000).

SchoolNet SA was pivotal in establishing and shaping SchoolNet Africa,[16] an initiative to support national school networking programmes in African countries. SchoolNet SA participated in a regional networking workshop in Cape Town in October 1999, which led to the Cape Town Declaration. Representatives were nominated to present the conclusions of the workshop at the African Development Forum held in Ethiopia in November 1999, which identified SchoolNet Africa as a development priority. In addition, SchoolNet SA played an important role in the formation of SchoolNet Namibia through working with the Namibian SchoolNet director and being involved in initial planning activities.

SchoolNet SA also contributed towards the research design and interpretation of data of a "Computers in Schools" survey commissioned by the IDRC from the Education Policy Unit at the University of the Western Cape. This report, published in May 2000, provides a snapshot of the state of computer technology and ICT use in schools in 1998, with valuable data on many aspects of computer provisioning and use.[17]

SchoolNet SA technical services

SchoolNet SA, in response to requests from schools for specialised email and Internet services that would meet the specific needs of educators, established a number of technical services to underpin its school networking activities. These activities generate revenue for SchoolNet SA, and the SchoolMail service is provided on a subscription basis.

SchoolMail

SchoolNet provides the SchoolMail service, which was launched in September 1998 and is operated by the Western Cape Schools Network (WCSN). SchoolMail is a multi-user dialup service that provides more effective and cheaper access to e-mail for schools than standard services available through ISPs. Established with support from Uniforum and the Internet Service Providers' Association (ISPA), the service uses the dialup networks of MWeb and Telkom's SAIX. Server hosting is donated by Intekom and UUNet.

Table 7.1: Summary of SchoolNet SA project activities and partners

Project/ Partner	Project Value	Duration	Scope/Target	Outcomes/Comments
Telkom 1000 Schools Internet Project[1]	ZAR 3 225 132	Sept. 1999 to May 2000	Provide basic ICT training for 2 000 teachers in schools that received computers and Internet access from Telkom, technical support to 850 schools, and logistical support.	• Undertaken in all nine provinces • Two teachers trained in each of 1 034 schools • 88 trainers, mainly teachers • Short two-day courses and preparation of training manuals and CD-ROMs
Nortel Phumelela Networks Project[2] supported by Nortel, Internet Solution (IS), Novell SA and Toshiba[3]	ZAR 1 500 000	July 1999 to July 2001	Establish three Internet-connected community computer facilities in Gauteng, Eastern Cape and Northern Province, with appropriate training and support staff.	• Hub sites located in communities, but with a focus on schools • Leased line access for two years • Flagship is the Katlehong Resource Centre – 50 teachers and 18 NGOs trained in basic ICT literacy • Each NGO was provided with an email address • Canadian Netcorps volunteer deployed to work with two technical interns and manage the centre • Plans under way to develop management capacity

Open Society Foundation for South Africa	ZAR 750 000 (Limpopo and Eastern Cape)	February 1999 to August 2000	Undertake a pilot project in four schools in the Eastern Cape, and enhance the teaching of maths, science and English through the use of ICTs. Use ICTs to support education management and administration at district and regional levels.	• 24 teachers trained in subject-related content and the Internet • Eight maths teachers received specialist training in Geometer's sketchpad and Excel • Computers were installed • Workshops were held to determine ICT needs in school district offices • ICT training in four districts • Developed in close collaboration with the provincial Department and other related educational programmes – DDSP and EMDP
World Bank–World Links for Development (WorLD)	US$ 40 000	June 1997 to June 2001	Install and support computer networks in 15 schools and two online training centres, and provide ongoing teacher training and support to these and an extended group of schools.	• SchoolNet's first project was active in the North West, Eastern Cape and KwaZulu-Natal • Phase 1 training: Basic ICT literacy • Phase 2 training: Skills to participate in collaborative projects with schools and students from other countries; basic technical training on networks to equip teachers with some knowledge of troubleshooting • 333 educators and managers trained in eight training events

Table 7.1: Summary of SchoolNet SA project activities and partners (continued)

Project/ Partner	Project Value	Duration	Scope/Target	Outcomes/Comments
				• Considerable difficulties with refurbished computers, commitment from school management and teachers
Think Quest,[4] Advanced Network and Services (international), Telkom SA (South Africa)	ZAR 150 000 annually	Annually	Expand and support the participation of South African learners in ThinkQuest; grow a repository of educational material accessible by learners worldwide.	• In 1999, 139 team members from South Africa entered the contest, primarily working locally with team-mates • Training programmes include research methods, locating and referencing information on the Internet, and website construction and design.
Volunteer and Internship Project – NetCorps, VSO Canada, IDRC Acacia	CAD 260 900	February 2000 to February 2001	Place and support 18 Canadian volunteers in South Africa, and appoint six local interns for one year; provide employment and work experience for Canadian and local youths and build capacity.	• Volunteers were hosted by SchoolNet and placed in all nine provinces • South African interns were placed alongside Canadian volunteers allow exchange of skills and knowledge

Global Teenager project – International Institute for Communications and Development (IICD)	US$ 55,000	February 2000 to June 2001	Implement computer networks in four schools in Gauteng and North West; support participation of schools in Global Teenager projects through collaborative email-based projects.	• Project revolves around learners and teachers from schools in various countries collaborating in I*EARN Learning Circles Projects[5] • Worked in partnership with WorLD-supported teachers • Four new Global Teenager project sites were developed

1 Telkom 1000 Project, http://www.telkom1000.schoolnet.org.za

2 Nortel Phumelela Networks Project, http://www.school.za/projects/nortel

3 Nortel Networks is a global corporation involved in telephony, data, e-business and wireless solutions for the Internet. Internet Solution's key business focus is on network and systems integration and on the technologies associated with e-commerce, voice/data convergence and customer management.

4 ThinkQuest is an international Web development competition that has achieved international collaboration and participation, and requires teams of high school students to develop educationally useful websites. SchoolNet SA was appointed as the national partner in South Africa, with Telkom SA as the major sponsor. ThinkQuest International is available at http://www.thinkquest.org, while the local version is available at http://www.thinkquest.org.za

5 The International Education and Resource Network (I*EARN) is a non-profit global network that enables young people to use the Internet and other new technologies to engage in collaborative educational projects that both enhance learning and make a difference in the world, http://www.iearn.org/

During 2000, a substantial number of new schools joined the SchoolMail service through the Telkom 1000 Project.

Table 7.2: Number of SchoolMail addresses per province, as on 1 September 2000

Province	SchoolMail accounts
Eastern Cape	101
Free State	141
Gauteng	277
KwaZulu-Natal	57
Mpumalanga	61
Northern Cape	71
Northern Province	73
North West	105
Western Cape	771
Total	1,657

Domain administration

SchoolNet is responsible for managing the second-level Internet domain name "school.za", and for ensuring appropriate management of the third-level provincial domains (such as ecape.school.za). Domain names allow schools to have their own unique and permanent Internet locator, which is independent of the particular ISP or access technology that they use. Domain registration is a free service for schools.

Website hosting

Provincial schools networks provide website hosting services for member schools, as a benefit of membership.

Leased-line connectivity

The WCSN and the Gauteng Schools Network (GSN) provide leased-line connectivity to schools, reselling bandwidth from a commercial ISP. As at the end of March 2000, both networks provided Internet connectivity to 27 sites with a combined total bandwidth of 448 kilobytes per second.

A significant number of schools, especially in provinces other than Gauteng and the Western Cape, obtain leased-line connectivity directly from commercial ISPs. The extent of such school connectivity was not surveyed.

NetDay

NetDay,[18] a non-profit section 21 organisation that empowers schools and assists with accessing ICTs, was started by SchoolNet SA and Sun Microsystems. Sun Microsystems provides funding to ensure that low-cost solutions are provided to schools and management to guarantee the success of the organisation. The project is not restricted to a few partners, as all corporate citizens can be involved in the deployment of computers and related technologies to schools. The concept originated in America in 1995, and has since spread to more than ten countries, including South Africa.

NetDay's main aim is to provide low-cost technology solutions to schools, community-based organisations and community facilities through:

- Refurbishing of old computers;[19]
- Implementation of low-cost networking options using new and refurbished equipment; and
- Technical skills development.

There have been many challenges, particularly the opening of the first operations and refurbishing facility at Springs College for reconditioning old computers. As part of a solution for schools, the organisation includes an empowerment component that teaches refurbishment skills. NetDay encourages interns to write examinations towards receiving A+ certification. Four technical interns were trained in 1999/2000.

NetDay installations throughout the country include the networking of computers (cabling), provision of SchoolMail and Internet access, and basic training in maintenance and use.

Provincial project activities

SchoolNet SA's activities are in progress in all nine provinces of South Africa, as outlined below.

Eastern Cape[20]

- Activities centred on the Telkom 1000 Schools Internet Project, working with the provincial Department of Education;
- A local coordinator was appointed to supervise training and on-site technical needs, and is assisted by a Canadian volunteer;
- No definitive data exist on the number of schools with access to ICTs, but 89 further schools were added; and
- There is one community hub site at Qunu, with 24 Pentium computers and an integrated services digital network (ISDN) line.

Free State

- 133 schools were provided with one computer each, including training; and
- A further 30 schools were connected to the Internet by March 2000, as part of the Telkom 1000 Schools project.

Gauteng

- The number of schools increased to 266 in 2000 due to the Telkom 1000 Project; and
- Three Canadian volunteers were based in Pretoria, Johannesburg and Katlehong. The Katlehong Resource Centre was established.

KwaZulu-Natal

- SchoolNet KZN[21] opened an office at the South African College for Open Learning (SACOL) in Pietermaritzburg, with a part-time administrator. The provincial Department of Education provided most of the administrative support;
- Schools' membership grew from 48 to 210, mainly through the Telkom 1000 Project. All schools with telephones were approached to apply for membership;
- Several training courses were offered to teachers (in the afternoons and over weekends) at two schools. By the end of 1999, 52 teachers had been trained;
- Training for 20 WorLD schoolteachers was conducted at SACOL. Projects were posted on the SchoolNet KZN and WorLD websites; and

- SchoolNet KZN was contacted to provide training at the Manguzi Community Centre.

Limpopo

- SchoolNet activities were kick-started through Telkom 1000 Schools, the Open Society Foundation and Nortel-Phumelela projects;
- In each district, an ICT coordinator worked with the provincial education representative; and
- An additional 63 schools received computers and were linked to the Internet.

Mpumalanga

- SchoolNet Mpumalanga was established in June 1999 at the offices of the Mpumalanga Department of Education, with a full-time official in the service of SchoolNet SA; and
- The Department of Education became involved in the SCOPE[22] project, bringing 13 new computer facilities to schools and teachers in the province.

Northern Cape

- The Telkom 1000 Schools Project provided new computers to 96 schools; and
- Sixty-four schools gained Internet access.

North West

- The Mmabatho High School Community Information Technology Training Centre was launched in February 2000. The WorLD project added 70 computers to schools in 1999. Five schools were provided with full computer centres; and
- The national Department of Education committed one full-time person to the WorLD project, assisted by Canadian volunteers.

Western Cape[23]

- The WCSN grew from 250 to over 1 000 schools by 2000; School networking activities expanded to include training, a help-desk, and educational projects and partnerships with donor organisations;
- The Western Cape Educational Department (WCED) Telecommunications Project provided hardware, training and Internet connectivity to some 200 schools throughout the province in 1999;
- A further 517 schools were connected through the Telkom 1000 project and others;
- Partnerships were formed in 1999 with Schools' Online (the Mayor's office in San Francisco), Community HEART, Old Mutual and several other corporate organisations; and
- A partnership was formed between the WCED and WCSN to establish the Khanya project, a plan for the implementation of educational ICT in all schools in the Western Cape.

Conference activities

Since 1999, SchoolNet SA has been involved in organising an annual conference aimed primarily at school-based educators. The 1999 Millennium Minds Conference, attended by more than 800 delegates, was held in Cape Town, and organised jointly by the WCSN and SchoolNet SA. The conference catered for a wide range of participants and included pre-conference training sessions for teachers new to technology. Millennium Minds enjoyed strong support from the corporate sector, with key information technology companies participating through sponsorship, in-kind donation of services and infrastructure, and programme involvement.[24]

SciFest is the annual festival of science and technology held in Grahamstown. SchoolNet SA has participated in SciFest in partnership with companies such as Microsoft, InfoSat, Pinnacle Micro and Intelligence Publishing, resulting in increased awareness and grassroots demand for ICT by teachers and learners. During SciFest 99, SchoolNet trained 300 teachers and learners on the basic use of the Internet in education.

Research process

The evaluation study for SchoolNet SA followed the generic research methodology outlined in Chapter 2. A matrix was developed, showing the relationship between the four theme areas and the five evaluation areas – this is presented in Appendix 2. Descriptions of SchoolNet SA's activities and projects, as contained in its annual report for the period 1 March 1999 to 31 March 2000, were also reviewed.

Paper-based questionnaires were completed by a sample of learners and educators in each of the five selected provinces – Western Cape, Eastern Cape, North West, Gauteng and KwaZulu-Natal. Ten schools were selected, two in each of the five research provinces. The most important criterion was that they should illustrate the variety of the different projects that SchoolNet had undertaken up to July 2000. Historically disadvantaged schools were selected, which is SchoolNet SA's focus area for interventions in ICT. No schools from privileged areas were included. The questionnaires were completed during the site visits. The educator questionnaire was piloted at the Millennium Minds in September 2000, albeit unsatisfactorily.

In addition, interviews were conducted with:

- Specialists and school networking managers within and outside of SchoolNet SA, including managers from each of the five selected provincial school networking bodies;
- Two educators per school – in some cases this was an educator, in others the principal or a member of the school's administrative personnel.
- Ten learners from each school, selected by the computer educators and who were all involved in ICTs at their schools. Learners responded in a separate session to the educators, in order to avoid the possibility of responses being influenced by the physical presence of an educator. The learner questionnaire posed limited direct questions about SchoolNet SA, because it was assumed that learners would have had little, if any, opportunity to interact with SchoolNet SA as an organisation; and
- *Partners,* although only two responded.

An email survey was sent to all questionnaire respondents asking for a brief description of what they had done on their computers during the previous week. It was hoped that the nature and extent of the responses could be compared with claims made in the questionnaire. The response level was poor, with a 5.7 per cent response from learners and a higher response rate of 43.7 per cent from educators. More than 31 per cent of the learners' emails came back undelivered.

The scope of the study did not allow for a nationally representative sample to be identified. This aspect should be noted as a limitation of the research and be attended to in a more comprehensive research study in the future.

Research findings

School context

During the final feedback workshop for this evaluation study, a visit was organised to a nearby school in Katlehong. The excursion provided some interesting observations that illustrate the challenges posed at the school level in establishing a SchoolNet site, and the contextual issues that must be addressed during implementation.

At Katlehong High School:

- Not one of the 11 computers had been connected to the electrical power supply and there was no network in place;
- Despite great excitement and animation from the principal about the possibilities that computers could provide, no computer lessons had in fact begun at the school for the academic year 2001. These were due to start only the following week;
- The computers were not used at all during the school day from 08:00 to 14:00 on the grounds that is was impossible to share the 11 computers fairly between the 1,600 learners in the school. Lessons were offered to groups of 11 students after school hours in the form of a three-month course in basic computer literacy;
- Students had to pay ZAR 100 each for the course on a first-come, first-serve basis. The course ran on two afternoons per week, with the laboratory closed to learners on the remaining days of the week. All but one student that had been accepted for the course were in Grade 12, which suggests that their seniority in the school played a role. The one exception was a Grade 11 student who was the acknowledged computer expert of the school;
- The reason given by the student group for attending the course was their desire to improve their academic results quickly, given that the

school-leaving examinations were approaching in October. They possessed a mistaken confidence that a three-month crash course in computer literacy would improve their results in conventional subject disciplines such as mathematics and English;

- During the visit to the school, two interns from the Katlehong resource centre arrived to undertake some maintenance work on a computer. The opportunity to speak to them was utilised, during which they delivered a scathing attack on the local teachers who, despite training and retraining, had to be shown how to log into the system and surf the Web every time they returned to the centre;
- There was a perception that the science teachers could make the best use of information technology;
- Educators that had been trained by SchoolNet SA saw themselves as fortunate in having had that opportunity and indicated a need for training on the Internet; and
- Educators felt that the principal had no real understanding of computers.

Institutional structures and processes

Within SchoolNet SA

Comments were made that SchoolNet SA's first-phase activities were characterised by repeated cycles of crisis. The result was hastily and incorrectly chosen schools, inappropriate management of pilot projects, and hurried materials development. These factors meant that the process was often compromised, which led to the evaluation of materials that were already compromised. The crisis-mode operation was seen to be the result of a lack of organisational capacity, as SchoolNet SA could only employ capacity after a contract was signed. The comment was made that SchoolNet SA's "hands were tied" because of contractual obligations and that it needed capacity to work outside of donor funding. This would enable it to build a vision outside of the confines of contract outcomes.

External institutions

Outside of the organisation, SchoolNet SA has experienced several instances where specific institutional structures were a hindrance in promoting the use of ICTs in schools. For example, in the North West province, there is an overlap in directorates, resulting in information technology being located within finance. Education is not a priority area, at the time of the study, no policy had been developed to address the use of ICTs in education. In Gauteng, teachers were not involved in the planning and implementation of school networking activities, which resulted in slow implementation.

There have also been situations where the non-resolution of conflicts has led to non-delivery on connectivity projects. In the Eastern Cape, for example, some lessons around conflict management were learnt. In the early overtures from WorLD, there was disagreement between the Eastern Cape Schools Network (ECSN) and the provincial Department of Education on the selection process for WorLD schools. While ECSN wanted the provincial Department to make choices, it suggested a guideline that schools should be close to existing centres of activity. The Department, on the other hand, insisted on redress of the imbalances of the past. Teacher volunteers were not prepared to visit remote areas that required travel of several hundred kilometres at their own expense. The result was that the Department selected facilities in rural areas that were not supported by the existing volunteer body and which subsequently collapsed. In one case, the Department selected a school without electricity and a telephone line in the confident belief that SchoolNet SA would be compelled to provide the required infrastructure. The result was the delivery of unusable equipment to the school.

Policy

SchoolNet has not been especially active in this area and there were few tangible outcomes. Key informants had mixed responses to the effects of SchoolNet SA in this area. SchoolNet SA staff themselves believed that the policy component of the educator development framework had been its greatest success.

The nature and extent of the policy-related activities of SchoolNet SA varied from province to province. In most cases, there were no direct influences on policy development but rather guidance and leadership on how things could be done. The WCSN, however, was instrumental in developing policy for the province, especially in the Khanya project. This developed from a bottom-up, needs-driven approach that fed into the policy development process. The organisation played a mediating role between the real needs of schools and the Department of Education, especially with regard to the information technology unit and the curriculum unit.

In contrast, the relationship between SchoolNet SA and the Department of Education in the Eastern Cape was problematic. There was strong resistance to the suggestions of SchoolNet SA about shaping policy regarding ICTs in education in the province. The provincial thrust was on the implementation of connectivity with no human resource base to deal with anything beyond this level.

SchoolNet SA's first experience of the policy arena was with the WorLD project, the first programme that SchoolNet SA implemented. SchoolNet SA developed acceptable user policies with guidelines on when to use computers, cost-saving modalities and so on. It also developed school charters to guide schools as community centres, in keeping with the Department's nine-point plan for educational renewal in South Africa. Sustainability models were developed to guide schools on how to keep their computer centres running efficiently.

These types of activities have enabled SchoolNet SA to feed into the policy development process in education in South Africa. Its advocacy role was to show the potential of and to provide case studies on using ICTs in education. Its role as a provider of grassroots information fed into the value chain, and in this way influenced policy development.

Connectivity and access

SchoolNet SA's position regarding connectivity objectives is that of demonstrating the educational use of ICTs and of advocating their use (SchoolNet 2000). It does not see its role as increasing the availability of technology, but rather as providing examples of technology implementation in disadvantaged schools. The government is seen as the main provider of technology in the future. This section draws together the research data describing the first phase of SchoolNet SA's efforts to provide universal connectivity for schools.

The delivery performance of SchoolNet SA as at July 2000 was easily measurable against the expected outputs in the area of connectivity, most of which were achieved through the initiation and development of partnerships:

- Technical support to 850 schools through the Telkom 1000 project;
- Community computer centres in Gauteng and the Northern Province;

- Four district offices in the Northern Province connected in a pilot project for supporting education management;
- Computer networks in 16 schools with WorLD;
- Online training centres in KwaZulu-Natal and North West with WorLD;
- Four schools equipped with computer networks through the Global Teenager project;
- Technical support via 18 Canadian and six local interns through NetCorps;
- Local support for school networking through the development of the provincial networks;
- SchoolMail in 1,657 schools; and
- Hardware and connectivity through NetDay.

A number of interview respondents expressed their views on the effects of the connectivity drive, but they tended to focus on the bigger picture that might impact on connectivity efforts in the future. Some of the comments made by key stakeholders are listed below:

- SchoolNet SA influenced Uniform, the Internet Service Providers Association (ISPA), Telkom, the Department of Communication and the South African IT Industry Strategy Project (SAITIS) in the way they think about school connectivity. This had some impact on lowering barriers to entry, according to the Executive Director of SchoolNet SA;
- Connectivity efforts raised awareness among educators about technologies available to them;
- In some cases, the drive for connectivity led to the development of interschool partnerships between the "haves" and the "have-nots," which gained international exposure. These were two-way processes of ICT and cultural exchange that had unintended positive consequences; and
- Sponsorship of the outputs through long-term partnerships with technology companies was important.

These incidental benefits show that the connectivity outputs became closely linked to the advocacy and awareness drive of SchoolNet SA. Other respondents spoke more specifically of the effects of the connectivity effort:

- It was important that teachers and learners actually put networks in place, getting hands-on experience; and
- Some respondents mentioned being disappointed with the low level of connectivity after the completion of large projects such as Telkom 1000 and WorLD. In Gauteng, connectivity in general was still very low and schools seemed afraid to sign up with the provincial networks for fear of reduced service quality, compared with connections obtained through conventional commercial channels.

During the site visits, educators in connected schools were asked to give an indication of the relative value of the communication possibilities that computers bring. On average, communication was ranked third after the administrative and subject-related use of computers. Of the educator respondents, 71 per cent had operational email facilities in their school. All these respondents claimed that SchoolNet SA had played an enabling role in providing this access. In a test of educator claims of regular use of computers, an email was sent to all the educator respondents with email addresses some months after the site visits. A response was requested. Almost 50 per cent replied to the request, which may be considered a fairly favourable response ratio considering that, on average, only 24 per cent of the respondents saw communication as the primary function of the computers in their schools. The response rate compares favourably with a similar exercise conducted in a well-resourced government secondary school that claims to be a national leader in the use of ICTs in education.

In a similar exercise conducted with the learners in the schools that were visited, the picture was quite different. Of the 35 learners from Grades 8-11 with email addresses, only two responses were received, and these arrived some two months after they had been sent. In the original questionnaires, some 75 per cent of these learners indicated that they used the computers more than once a week for more than one hour at a time. Over half indicated that they use the Internet and email. The low response rate (two learners, or 8 per cent of those with email addresses) to this exercise did not confirm the claims of the learners.

This finding matched the results of a quick survey at a leading school. Emails were sent to every learner and educator in the school that had an email address. Despite the availability of unlimited email addresses to the school, which runs its own Web server on campus, the total number of allocated email addresses was 23. This was made up of three learners and

20 educators. A total of four responses was received, all from educators; that is, a response rate of zero for learners and 20 per cent for educators – even the principal did not respond. This is lower than the 47 per cent for educators and 8 per cent for learners in the historically disadvantaged schools represented in the case study. One can therefore surmise that the non-response may be due to factors other than mere non-use of the facilities at their disposal.

Capacity building and training

The following outcomes were achieved during the first phase:

- Training was provided to 2,000 teachers through the Telkom 1000 project;
- In association with Nortel, two online community centres were established in Gauteng and Northern Province, to be used for training;
- A management support project in North West province included training for regional and district office personnel;
- In association with WorLD, two online training centres were established in KwaZulu-Natal and North West province for the provision of teacher training and support;
- Teachers in the four schools that were equipped with computer networks through the Global Teenager project were trained and supported;
- Some 800 delegates, mostly teachers, attended a variety of courses and presentations at the annual SchoolNet SA conference;
- Some 300 learners and teachers were trained at SciFest in Grahamstown in 1999;
- The provincial school networks were developed to provide teacher training; and
- The educator development framework was completed,[25] thereby laying the foundation for future educator development and training. Some key informants regard this as the most significant development of SchoolNet SA in the field of educator training.

Key informants' general impression of SchoolNet SA's educator training intervention was positive. Responses did, however, tend to enumerate the types of intervention that took place and the number of educators involved, as opposed to the effects on the process of integration of ICTs into education. The preoccupation with numbers of educators trained, as against how the training was being used, is reflected in many of the comments. The Telkom 1000 project was repeatedly mentioned in the interviews, for example in the North West province and in the Western Cape, where it led to the termination of existing training programmes because of the additional pressure that Telkom 1000 brought to bear on training capacity in the province.

The Gauteng Schools Network tried hard to explain the educational applications of ICTs, rather than just where to click and push. A key informant in the Western Cape suggested that, from her own observations, it takes three years to internalise knowledge of computers before teachers can use them in the classroom. As a result, successes will only be seen over the next few years.

Although there are no data on the impact of the training, the experience of SchoolNet SA has been that face-to-face workshop training had a limited effect because it did not respond to teachers' requirements and did not provide long-term support.

An important effect of the training interventions is the close partnerships that have developed with crucial agencies such as the national Department of Education and the CETDE, because it led to the funding of educator resources development. The effects of educator training interventions are therefore not to be found in the classroom alone, but also at the partner level.

Conferences

SchoolNet SA conferences have been a high-profile focal point for educator training. The Millennium Minds conference provided basic skills training, as did SciFest over a period of a full week. SchoolNet SA has provided training for almost 3,000 teachers. Staff felt that the organisation had done well, having produced materials for self-study and established a teacher development model on well-articulated principles.

Quality and scope of training

A key informant stated that the Telkom 1000 training was not as good as they would have liked, but that it brought a measure of control. She added that teachers were very enthusiastic after the training but that a two-day training course was unlikely to impact on their teaching. In KwaZulu-Natal, the SchoolNet Project had not run as many workshops as they would have liked. They nevertheless tried to provide basic skills and integration skills, as well as technical skills, so that teachers did not become "victims of the machine".

Some other opinions expressed by key informants were the following:

- SchoolNet SA training projects had been good and were a good place for schools to develop basic literacy;
- The Telkom 1000 training was inadequate because it provided no educational context, although it did fulfil the need for basic training. New materials should be developed and made available at no cost for anyone to use. SchoolNet SA believes that the Educator Development Framework would go some way towards meeting this need; and
- A representative from the national Department of Education stated that what SchoolNet SA did with its target audience in Telkom 1000 training was "amazing". The selection of schools was, however, a barrier because SchoolNet SA was not involved in the selection process and its criteria had been set aside. Were it not for external factors in the political realm, the impact of the training could have been far greater. The greatest impact of the intervention, in this key informant's view, was the advocacy role of SchoolNet SA in promoting the value of ICT training for educators.

Levels of computer proficiency

Educators from the selected schools saw themselves as sufficiently well trained in the use of computers and confirmed unanimously that this status was attributable to the role played by SchoolNet SA. In contrast, only 39 per cent of the learner respondents believed their educators to be well trained in the use of computers.

Several informants indicated that the timeframe for training was too short. It was very difficult for educators to continue with what they were taught, and the training had been more successful with those teachers who already had some computer knowledge. Another respondent argued that educators needed time to internalise the training and that it was unrealistic to get people who had never used a computer before up to speed. He pointed out that it was a crash course and a great deal of knowledge would be forgotten. Although the materials were valuable, the educators needed the opportunity to practise their skills until they had become comfortable with them.

This was a handicap of the Telkom 1000 project, as training could not be a one-off intervention, but had to be ongoing and followed up.

Content and curriculum development

Effects in the area of content and curriculum are less tangible than the more easily quantifiable areas such as connectivity and educator training. SchoolNet SA staff suggested that the main impact during the first phase was impressing on the Departments of Education that content and curriculum are not about lessons per se and that "the use of ICTs extends beyond general learning and teaching". The notions of online schools, portals and so on would be tested in the second phase in 2001. SchoolNet SA did not invest heavily in this area, the primary reason being that content development is expensive and requires considerable expertise. There are also a large number of third-party content developers that could engage in this task more effectively.

Informants in a number of provinces were asked about local initiatives. Their responses confirmed that content and curriculum development did not enjoy the same attention as other SchoolNet SA theme areas. For example, in North West province, the Directorate of Communication and Exams of the provincial Department of Education has a technology education dimension that deals with content. In Gauteng, there was a candid: "Nothing. We don't have the resources." In a similar vein, the Western Cape stated that there was a great need to do a lot of work and it was a priority area, but had not been given much attention. This was largely due to lack of funding. There have been some limited efforts by individuals to put science material on a website, but SchoolNet SA has not pursued this initiative.

The overall picture is promising when one considers what is happening and what is planned, rather than what is not happening. The South African coordinator of ThinkQuest explained that this global competition is part of an effort to develop websites with educational content around locally relevant ideas.

Provincial initiatives

Some ideas have also been discussed in the Western Cape around a template for teacher-based curriculum development, where content can be placed on a website for other teachers to use. However, to access online content educators need access to the Internet and the Web.

In KwaZulu-Natal a partnership has been developed with a national training company that offers free content to implement the International Computer Drivers Licence (ICDL) with school-type content. This project at the private Hilton College is part of the community outreach initiative, but was still very much in the formative stage at the time of the study. The school is also developing a basic course around conventional educational knowledge and how information technology can be brought into it.

A KwaZulu-Natal departmental official seconded to assist SchoolNet SA is involved in planning the materials for teacher development in collaboration with TELI. She used a WorLD training project to pilot the materials and came up with four collaborative projects, which are posted on the SchoolNet KZN website.[26] There are, however, complaints that the schools have all been let down by connectivity, echoing the point made by other informants. From these repeated observations on connectivity, it could be argued that SchoolNet SA has opted for the correct strategy in looking to connectivity first, even though some practitioners did not fully agree.

In the Eastern Cape, the SchoolNet maintains a list server of schools that are known to have connectivity – this is used for mail shots. They also maintain a website with links to SchoolNet SA, but it is very static. The previous SchoolNet coordinator did not believe that content and curriculum development was feasible at provincial level and argued that such an effort must be nationally coordinated and aimed at teachers on the ground.

The WCDE is following up with an expert as regards implementation planning. Comments from informants in this province suggest that teaching materials need to be put on the Web, so that weaker teachers can have the materials that they need to teach and learners can access it directly if they need to do so. SchoolNet SA was investigating the idea of a portal with maths, science and English content – a one-stop shop – with access to lessons, question papers, answers and so on. SchoolNet SA has entered into a partnership with the Learning Channel, in which it will take material written by good teachers and digitise it. This is built on the SchoolNet SA training model in which teachers must become content developers.

Looking to the future, it was suggested that the national Department of Education should put the curriculum on the Web, so that teachers could download it. This would not be prescriptive and would be underpinned by a theoretical framework. There could also be resources to complement the curriculum when this vision was implemented.

The initiation of the Telkom 1000 project in June 1999 was seen as a turning point, as it was the first time that SchoolNet SA had the funding to emphasise educational solutions as part of the "ICT in education" package. The importance of partnerships was seen as critical to the development of content and the curriculum. For example, the SCOPE project in Umtata has been a pilot for curriculum materials in English and mathematics, and the Khanya project in the Western Cape was initially a connectivity project but now focuses on curriculum and content development.

No single issue stood out as a primary lesson in the area of content and curriculum, probably because this theme area was still being formulated into a coherent form of practice. On the other hand, a SchoolNet SA staff member identified limited access to technology and the Internet as notable constraints.

Respondents held a variety of opinions, possibly reflecting their personal areas of interest, rather than the macrolevel issues at stake:

- The focus of the content and curriculum intervention should be more cognitive and academic, not technological;
- Things need to move much faster to speed up delivery of content and curriculum;
- In curriculum development a major public-private partnership is needed;
- Projects that research ICT-based content and learning need stable and controlled environments so that they do not interfere with educational processes; and
- Teachers seem motivated to learn about ICT application skills, but less so to explore curriculum applications of ICTs.

Conclusions and recommendations

This concluding section briefly reviews some of the areas in the first phase of activities until July 2000 that warrant special mention. This is over and above the other areas already discussed above.

Incubate within an existing organisation

The concept of SchoolNet SA was spawned independently of the primary donor agency, the IDRC, but it was incubated within its administrative and support structures. This seems to have had a strong impact on the initial successes of SchoolNet SA and in particular on its ability to be successful from the start. A possible disadvantage relates to the degree of perceived autonomy of SchoolNet SA in its actions. SchoolNet SA is currently housed on its own premises and is a separate legal entity. However, it continues to receive core funding for certain operational costs, while the majority of project costs are covered in partnership agreement with organisations other than the IDRC.

Create an organisation with a clear and narrower focus

SchoolNet SA's activities have been largely project driven, with little evidence of a coherent strategic vision. While this approach was acceptable during the first phase where institutional survival was the driver, it is not an appropriate approach for future phases. Research needs to be conducted on scaling the initiative from project to programme, including workable sustainable models; models that allow for project and programme level work to co-exist; and even the development of existing projects into independent programme-level initiatives.

The broad range of SchoolNet SA activities was also questioned and the recommendation was made that SchoolNet needs to focus on a few narrowly defined areas. Possible areas of exclusion would be policy and content development, the latter because so many other players are already involved in this field.

Raise Awareness and play an advocacy role

SchoolNet SA has played a leading role in raising awareness of the use and importance of ICTs in education. It is seen as a strategic partner of the national Department of Education. The advocacy role can be extended to other government departments using the leverage already established.

Create close working relationships with policy partners

SchoolNet's extensive experience with policy partners has led to the conclusion that close working relationships with policy-making entities such as provincial and national government departments are important. Good project implementation should contribute to the formulation of appropriate future policy, but policy formulation should not be a goal for SchoolNet SA in itself. The close involvement of policy makers in implementation processes is probably the single most enabling factor in the policy development around the

210

use of ICTs in education. However, capacity constraints within policy-making entities, where the portfolio is understaffed or staff lack ICT experience, have been a problem.

Identify champions

Many of the study informants reiterated the role played by champions. This is applicable at every level of the organisation, from the executive director to individual educators. Motivated educators were a powerful force in the realisation of SchoolNet SA's objectives, and required little intervention from the national level.

Provide dedicated full-time staff

One of the problem areas mentioned repeatedly by informants was the lack of appropriate staff to run the activities of SchoolNet SA nationwide. The high percentage of volunteer staff (usually teachers) presented difficulties when their regular workloads became too heavy. This was particularly noticeable in cases where schools relied on volunteer teachers for technical support.

Noticeable differences were reported when full-time staff were employed, for instance in KwaZulu-Natal, the Department of Education seconded a staff member to SchoolNet SA. As a result, activities in that province gained ground. Similarly, in Gauteng, a full-time administration officer was appointed to handle the day-to-day paperwork. This freed up the volunteers to become more involved in the delivery of projects. Likewise, the Western Cape with its full-time personnel showed high levels of activity and output.

At the level of the national executive body, the fully-fledged management element of the organisation handles all the financial administration, technical services, new project development and partnerships. Notable aspects were the calibre of staff in the first phase of SchoolNet SA, the availability of technical skills, business acumen and partnership development skills, and an understanding of the education sector in South Africa.

Move towards equity between advantaged and disadvantaged schools

Considering South Africa's history of apartheid and the need to accelerate the development of historically disadvantaged schools, SchoolNet SA has

211

made a conscious effort to address connectivity in these areas. For example, the Telkom 1000 project focuses almost exclusively on this sector. Twinning of schools has been used to good effect in the equity drive, particularly in the Western Cape and KwaZulu-Natal. Important models for the role that privileged schools can play are being tested, and researchers believe that this is an area that should be developed further.

Develop more test cases to prove the benefits of integrating ICTs into the curriculum

ICT implementation in education often shows a disjuncture between the ICTs themselves and their use in education. Ways need to be sought to integrate them effectively into the curriculum. The linkages need to be made explicit and this is a potential area for future research. It also suggests close partnering with Departments of Education because of the implications for curriculum-based development models. More test cases need to be undertaken to prove the benefits of ICTs in education, and such interventions must have visible cost benefits.

Notes

1   Central Intelligence Agency, CIA – *The World Factbook,* http:/www.odci.gov/cia/publications/factbook/
2   World Population Bureau. (2001). Population Data Sheet, http://www.prb.org/Content/NavigationMenu/Other_reports/2000-2002/sheet4.html
3   BMI-Techknowledge (2001). Communication Technologies Handbook 2001.
4   Cellular Statistics – Africa, http://www.cellular.co.za/stats/stats-africa.htm
5   BMI-Techknowledge (2001), op. cit.
6   Figures refer to the number of children in the defined age category that should be attending school. Higher figures indicate the enrolment of children outside the expected age grouping. See World Bank, www4.worldbank.org/afr/stats/adi2002/default.cfm
7   CIA, The World Factbook.; for map see: http://home.global.co.za/~mercon/map.htm
8   Human Sciences Research Council (HSRC) and National Department of Education. (1996). 1996 Schools Register of Needs. Pretoria: HSRC.

9   A model that generally emerged in more privileged areas, and that allowed the governing bodies of schools to make a wide range of decisions on the structures, staffing, funding and school fee structures of schools.

10   James, T. (Ed.). (2001). Educational Technology Policy in Southern Africa. In *An Information Policy Handbook for Southern Africa*. Ottawa: IDRC. A detailed description of the educational technology processes, written by Neil Butcher, is provided in this publication and is not repeated here. See also the website, http://www.dbsa.org/publications/ictpolsa/

11   Telkom 1000 Project, http://www.telkom1000.schoolnet.org.za

12   Nortel Phumelela Networks Project, http://www.school.za/projects/nortel

13   Nortel Networks is a global corporation involved in telephony, data, e-business and wireless solutions for the Internet. Internet Solution's key business focus is on network and systems integration and on the technologies associated with e-commerce, voice/data convergence and customer management.

14   ThinkQuest is an international Web development competition that has achieved international collaboration and participation, and requires teams of high school students to develop educationally useful websites. SchoolNet SA was appointed as the national partner in South Africa, with Telkom SA as the major sponsor. ThinkQuest International is available at http://www.thinkquest.org, while the local version is available at http://www.thinkquest.org.za

15   The International Education and Resource Network (I*EARN) is a non-profit global network that enables young people to use the Internet and other new technologies to engage in collaborative educational projects that both enhance learning and make a difference in the world, http://www. iearn.org/

16   More information on SchoolNet Africa is available at http:// www.schoolnetafrica.org

17   The report can be viewed at http://www.schoolnet.org.za/schoolsurveys

18   NetDay, http://www.netday.org.za

19   In 1999, over 800 computers were donated to the project by the government and private sector organisations. These machines all vary in terms the extent of refurbishing required.

20   The Eastern Cape provincial school network's website can be viewed at http://www.ecape.school.za

21   KwaZulu-Natal's provincial school network website: http:/www.kzn.school.za

22 SchoolNet brokered an agreement with the national Department of Education and the Finnish-funded SCOPE project to jointly develop a set of materials for delivering mentor-supported distance education to teachers. The SAIDE manages this project.

23 The WCSN's provincial school network website can be viewed at http://www.wcape.school.za

24 The proceedings are available online at http://archive.wcape.school.za/conf99/

25 www.school.za/edict

26 KwaZulu-Natal provincial school network website, http://www.kzn.school.za

Chapter 8

Schoolnet Uganda – CurriculumNet

Anne Ruhweza Katahoire, Grace Baguma and
Florence Etta

Country context

Introduction

Unlike the other school networking projects included in this evaluation study,
Acacia has not directly supported SchoolNet Uganda, although it has been
engaged in the exchange of experiences with Acacia. The Acacia Initiative
is, however, supporting a pilot CurriculumNet project in Uganda being implemented by the National Curriculum Development Centre (NCDC). This
project deploys a mechanism for delivery of the Uganda primary and secondary school curriculum via computer-based tools and communication
networks. The pilot project is a research and experience-gaining exercise
to test the economic, technical and operational feasibility of ICTs as teaching and learning support mechanisms in the core subject areas of the educational system.

The CurriculumNet initiative aims to determine the value added by ICTs
to the educational process in Uganda. It is expected that ICT facilities will
enhance intra- and interschool learning, and that students from different
schools will collaborate in the learning process by using ICTs to interact
with each other. It was hoped that the CurriculumNet project would benefit
from the existing experiences of SchoolNet Uganda in this area, and that

---

Box 1 : Uganda in brief

Area: 236 040 sq km

Location: Eastern Africa, west of Kenya

Capital: Kampala

Population: 23 985 712 (July 2001 est.)

Age:
0–14 years: 51.08%
5–64 years: 46.78%
65+ years: 2.14% (2001 est.)
Life Expectancy: Total population (43.37 years); Male (42.59 years);
Female (44.17 years) [2001 est.]

Literacy: 61.8% of adult population (1995)[1]

Official Language: English

Telecommunications:
Landlines: 80 868 (1998)[2]
Mobiles: 280 000 (Nov. 2001)[3]

School Enrolments[4]
Primary: 74% of schoolgoing age
Secondary: 12% of schoolgoing age

Evaluation Survey
Name of Project: SchoolNet Uganda / CurriculumNet
Implementing Agency: SchoolNet Uganda

Beneficiaries: 14 schools
Sample Size:
No. of Schools: 5
No. of Learner Questionnaires: 141
No. of Interviews: 18
No. of Email questionnaires: 30

Period of Evaluation: November to December 2000

---

these experiences would serve as a useful input not only for the CurriculumNet Project, but also for other school networking projects in Africa and elsewhere. Hence the inclusion of SchoolNet Uganda in this pan-African evaluation study.

ICTs in Ugandan schools

Formal education in Uganda has its origins in missionary activity from the turn of the 19th century. The formal education system consists of seven years of primary education, four years of secondary education and two years of advanced-level education. After seven years of primary education, students undertake a Primary Leaving Examination (PLE). Those who continue into secondary education have four years studying for O- (ordinary) level examinations, provided by the Uganda National Examinations Board (UNEB). A further two years are available for study towards A-level (Advanced) examinations also provided by the UNEB.

Despite political disruption and the substantial decline in the economy, the education system has grown dramatically, as shown by the growth in government-aided primary schools. Since the introduction of Universal Primary Education (UPE), the enrolment in primary schools in Uganda has more than doubled. By the year 2000, student enrolments in primary schools had risen to more than 6.5 million from a figure of about 1.3 million in 1980. To accommodate this burgeoning population of schoolgoing children, the number of primary schools rose from 4,276 in 1980 to 9,500 by 1997. Slightly fewer than half (3,164,092) of primary school pupils were females. The total number of teachers teaching in primary schools in 1999 was 110,298.

The secondary school system, which in the past formed a relatively small sector of the total education provision, has grown even more rapidly in recent years. According to 1994 government statistics, there were 666 government-aided schools, 44 per cent of the pupils being female. Of the students who successfully leave primary school, only about 25 per cent complete their secondary education and, of these, only about a fifth complete the Uganda Advanced Certificate of Education. In 1999, the total number of teachers in secondary schools was 22,599.

The Ministry of Education and Sport divides secondary schools into government-aided and private schools, the difference being the state funding to the former. In essence, the extent of such funding for aided schools is a minimal proportion of any school budget, hence the distinction is minor.

217

Another way of classifying the schools is by origin. The oldest secondary schools were founded by missionaries. Because of their history, these institutions are by far the best equipped, though not necessarily the best run or the most successful. Another group of schools were those developed in the 1960s and 1970s under international donor funding programmes. These schools are sometimes termed "IDA schools" after the International Development Agency's programme that sponsored them. These sites have sound buildings, some of which have suffered seriously due to civil strife and neglect. Others were looted during the wars and have therefore been left with low levels of equipment. More recently, both government-aided and private schools have been established but these institutions were severely affected by the current state of the economy – they are sometimes referred to as "Third World schools". A review of government statistics indicates that most O-level secondary schools are mixed day schools (73 per cent), while girls' boarding schools are more numerous than boys or mixed boarding schools (a 2:1 ratio). With the growth and development of secondary education in Uganda, different types of curricula at different levels of the secondary school have emerged over time.

The rapid growth in demand for secondary education in Uganda and the severe financial constraints on government expenditure caused by the prolonged economic crisis have resulted in substantial increases in family and community financing of secondary education. The number of secondary schools increased sharply in the 1980s, but many of these schools had inadequate physical facilities and could not afford to pay teachers adequate salaries or provide textbooks or materials. As a result, all schools, whether government-aided or private, now rely mainly on fees, contributions by parent-teacher associations (PTAs) and other charges to cover costs. There are still hundreds of schools without laboratories, science equipment or an adequate supply of textbooks. In addition, Uganda's secondary education system continues to face the same challenges as many other developing countries – how to provide better quality education and greater relevance of education, with limited resources, to an increasing number of students. Financial problems and civil unrest have made Uganda's situation particularly difficult.

Secondary school management is in the hands of the Boards of Governors and PTAs, who liaise with the head teachers and staff. Boards of Governors were established in 1962 and are the supreme body responsible for assisting the head teacher to run the school in accordance with government policies and procedures. The PTAs, in contrast, are voluntary organisations but must be recognised by the Ministry of Education and Sport. PTAs play a major role in aiding, constructing and developing schools. There are some important executive differences between the two bodies: PTAs are allowed to levy extra school income above government funding, while Boards of Governors have no fundraising powers. The latter have powers to probe into the professional conduct of PTAs and approve PTA recommendations concerning finances, discipline and development projects. From this point of view, there is limited government control over the day-to-day operations of schools. Both manpower and physical resources for each school are catered for through both bodies and there is thus both the potential and the reality of wide differences in provision between schools, and between districts and regions.

Project background

Conceptualising and launching the project

SchoolNet Uganda is an outgrowth of what was originally the World Links for Development (WorLD) programme[5] in Uganda – Uganda was the first pilot country. The effort began in 1996 with the School-to-School Initiative (STSI), a programme focused primarily on helping students develop basic computer skills and communicate via the Internet. Under the pilot, three senior secondary schools in Kampala with about 930 students in all, received the necessary hardware and software for training and establishing connections. These schools were Gayaza High School, Namilyango College and Mengo Senior Secondary School,[6] all situated within a 10–15 km radius of Kampala. They were chosen in accordance with the following criteria:

- Existence of telecommunications infrastructure;
- Existence of a burglar-proofed room;
- Opportunity for long-term self-sustainability;
- Interest of the local community; and
- Capacity to innovate.

In 1998 the programme expanded to include ten schools and trained 55 teachers and administrators. Attempts were made to engage in collaborative distance learning activities with American schools, but none of these were fully realised. At the time of the evaluation study in December 2000, the WorLD programme was being implemented in 20 schools, all with vary-ing levels of connectivity and equipment. Ten other schools were also being considered for inclusion.

WorLD has combined efforts with I*EARN and Schools Online USA to form an Alliance for Global Learning. In this Alliance, Schools Online USA provides the equipment, WorLD provides staff development expertise and training materials, and I*EARN provides collaborative project opportunities. SchoolNet Uganda has implemented the programme of the Alliance for Glo-bal Learning in secondary schools in Uganda.

SchoolNet Uganda is piloting very small aperture terminals (VSATs) in ten rural areas. It also organises training programmes and workshops for the professional development of teachers in the use of computers. The train-ing is organised in phases, where at least two teachers and the head teacher from each of the participating schools are encouraged to participate. Ac-cording to the National Coordinator, approximately 120 teachers and ad-ministrators had gone through the first two phases of this training at the time of this study.

Project objectives

The purpose of SchoolNet Uganda is to promote and support the develop-ment of the educational use of the Internet in Ugandan schools. Its aims are to:

- Coordinate the use of information technology in schools;
- Consolidate and share the experiences of ICT use in education for the benefit of other schools;
- Support educators and learners through:

  o Provision of leadership, expertise and resources;
  o Development of effective partnerships in the areas of Internet con-nectivity and appropriate technology;
  o Development of online electronic content, teaching and learning re-sources;
  o Human resource development and capacity building; and
  o Advocacy for ICTs in schools.

Beneficiaries

The listed members of SchoolNet Uganda, in total 14 schools, are Bombo Secondary School, Bukoyo Secondary School, Busoga College Mwiri, Gayaza High School, Iganga Secondary School, Kibuli Secondary School, Kings College Budo, Kitante Hill School, Lubiri Secondary School, Makerere College School, Mengo Senior School, Nabisunsa Girls School, Namilyango College and St James Secondary School.

Institutional structures and staffing

SchoolNet Uganda was launched as an NGO in 1999. The proposal to establish this NGO arose from the experiences and needs assessed by the WorLD programme in providing Internet access to secondary schools in Uganda.

By 2000, SchoolNet Uganda was not yet fully functional as an organisation in that its constitution had not yet been operationalised. No annual general meeting had been convened since it was launched and, as a result, the organisation had no executive body. The member schools had not yet started paying their annual subscriptions as stipulated in the constitution. SchoolNet Uganda therefore relies entirely on donor funding. It has a secretariat funded by the Alliance for Global Learning. This funding pays for two members of staff – the National Coordinator and the Technical Coordinator.

Monitoring and evaluation – The WorLD project evaluations

The WorLD programme has conducted two evaluations of its projects in Uganda. In the last evaluation conducted in 2000, the student to computer ratio in Ugandan WorLD schools was 70:1, which was below the average ratios in Africa and in other WorLD programme countries.

The report observed that Ugandan schools were above the African and WorLD averages in the following areas:

- Teachers and students in Uganda spent more time using ICT in schools;
- Ugandan students use ICT in more sophisticated ways with greater frequency. ICT use was, however, concentrated in subjects such as computer science and word processing;
- Schools in Uganda frequently used instructional practices that encouraged student autonomy;

221

- Ugandan students were also reported to be participating in learning activities that exposed them to subject matter content and that promoted interaction between students and teachers; and
- Ugandan students exhibited higher levels of collaboration.

Areas where Ugandan schools scored lower than the African and WorLD averages are the following:

- Although training workshops were held for teachers and administrators primarily by World Bank staff, there was little variety in the training support received by the teachers;
- Informal teacher-to-teacher training was reported to be occurring in the schools, but fewer than 25 per cent of the teachers reported having received informal training. The training topics included using hardware, application and Internet software, and designing and leading collaborative projects;
- A lower percentage of females participated in WorLD activities;
- Technology skills and attitudes had increased significantly because of the WorLD programme but were still at low levels;
- Communication and information reasoning skills were also influenced by the WorLD programme but were lower than average; and
- Most students in Uganda were reported to exhibit some awareness of and improved attitudes towards different cultures.

The students were also reported to display high levels of positive attitudes towards schooling. The major barriers to implementation highlighted in the report included hardware/software deficiencies, infrastructure/connectivity problems, the lack of a national policy on computer use, and the lack of time in the school schedule.

The research process in Uganda

The evaluation study in Uganda focused primarily on SchoolNet Uganda's activities and addressed Research Questions #3 and #4, as outlined in Chapter 2:

- What are the common themes, trends and lessons emerging from school networking that can guide future SchoolNet projects and evaluation activities?
- What areas require further investigation and what evaluation agenda is proposed for the subsequent phases of IDRC's evaluation and research?

Since previous evaluations had already been undertaken by WorLD, the present study focused particularly on the users of ICTs in the school environment. It did not cover in any detail the aspects of project planning and implementation, institutional mechanisms and management structures.

The methodology comprised the following:

Research instruments

A national workshop was held in September 2000 for familiarisation with and adaptation of the instruments. During the national workshop, the research team and other stakeholders were introduced to the design, methodology and instruments for the study. Using the input from the different stakeholders, the instruments were adapted to the national setting and then pilot tested in one of the SchoolNet schools near Kampala. As a result of the pilot test, changes were made to the pre-tested instruments and two additional instruments were designed.

A decision was made to design separate instruments for school administrators and the SchoolNet Uganda National Coordinator, since the information needed from the two sources was very different. The instrument for area specialists was divided into separate response sections for the various types of specialists – policy makers, curriculum developers, connectivity specialists and so on. An additional instrument was designed to collect information on the school profiles.

Sampling of schools and respondents

Two of the schools sampled, Gayaza High School and Namilyango College, were included because they were among the first three pilot schools to be connected to the Internet in November 1996 by the WorLD programme. The other two sample schools, Nabisunsa Girls School and Kings College Budo, were connected in 1998. Two of the schools were girls' schools, one was a boys' school and the other was mixed. All were boarding schools.

223

About 30 students were sampled from each school using random sampling – this included both computer users and non-users. In total, 141 learner questionnaires were analysed.

Four educators were also selected from each of the sample schools, giving a total of 16 educators. In addition, another seven educators from other SchoolNet Schools participated. In total, 23 educator responses were analysed.

Data collection

Preliminary visits were made to each of the schools to introduce the exercise and schedule appointments. The learner questionnaires were administered with little difficulty and overall the exercise lasted between 30 and 45 minutes in each of the schools. Educator questionnaires, however, were difficult to obtain due to end-of-year activities. Likewise, there were problems in interviewing the school coordinators and the head teachers for the same reasons. In total, 18 interviews were conducted (Table 8.1). In addition, 30 email questionnaires were returned by educators for analysis.

Table 8.1: Number of interviews conducted

Head teachers	4
School coordinators	5
Members of the National Steering Committee	3
Ministry of Education ICT Task Force	2
National Coordinator	1
Technical Coordinator	1
Director, NCDC (Curriculum Developer)	1
ICT specialist	1

Findings

The major issues in this evaluation were connectivity, access to ICTs, and the professional development of teachers. From an institutional perspective, the main issues were sustainability, management and ownership.

This section firstly examines the types of learners and educators inter-viewed in the four sample schools. Thereafter the issues raised above will be discussed.

Beneficiaries

Schools

All four schools sampled in this study are located within a 25 km radius of Kampala, the capital city of Uganda:

- Namilyango College is found in Mukono district, 16 km along the main Kampala–Jinja highway. This boys' boarding school has approximately 1,100 students, with a teaching staff of 61. It is the oldest boarding secondary school in Uganda, founded in 1902 by the Mill Hill Fathers.
- Gayaza High School is situated about 17 km north of Kampala. It has a student population of approximately 1,050 students, with 60 teaching staff. Gayaza is the oldest girls' boarding school and was established in 1905 by the Church Missionary Society.
- Kings College Budo is located on Budo Hill, approximately 25 km from Kampala on the Kampala–Masaka highway. Budo was founded in 1906, also by the Church Missionary Society, and has a student population of 1,200 and a teaching staff of 70.
- Nabisunsa Girls School is situated 7 km on the Kampala-Jinja high-way. It was founded in the late 1950s by three prominent Muslim lead-ers, namely Haji Kakungulu, Haji Gava and Haji Kasule. It is one of the first Muslim girls' secondary schools in the country. The school has a population of 1,100 students and 60 teaching staff.

The student populations in all four schools reflect the growing need and demand for secondary education in Uganda. All are government schools and rank among the top ten best performing schools in the national O- and A-level exams. These schools admit the best-performing pupils in the PLEs.

Unlike in the past, most students admitted to these schools are from Kampala and the surrounding districts. Very few students are from upcoun-try. They generally come from middle-class families, with very few from low-income families. The students' backgrounds influence their exposure and access to ICTs. They are more likely than students in rural areas to have had prior access to computers; to continue to have access to them either at home or in the numerous cafes that are being established; and to be trained in ICTs elsewhere than at school. Their parents are also more likely to appreciate the use of ICTs, and to be able to contribute towards the purchase and maintenance of computers in schools.

Learners

There were more or less equal numbers of males and females in the sample (n = 141). Learners ranged from 13 to 21 years, with a mean age of 16.5 years. Slightly more than half the learners were A-level students, the rest being O-level students.

Educators

The majority of educators sampled were male (74 per cent, n = 23). The experience in all the schools sampled, even the girls' schools, was that there were more male than female teachers engaged in the use of computers. Of the 23 educators interviewed, there were 12 teachers, 8 heads of department and three head teachers.

The educators had varying years of teaching experience, ranging from less than a year to more than ten years. The majority had three or more years of teaching experience. All the educators were graduates, with four holding a Master's degree and two a postgraduate diploma.

Partnerships

The educators indicated that both parents and other community members were involved in the ICT development in their schools (Figures 8.1a and b).

Connectivity and access

Telecommunications

One of the criteria for the selection of schools to participate in the WorLD programme was the existence of telecommunications infrastructure within the school. The WorLD programme provided email and Internet access to schools through the purchase of Internet services from ISPs and the contracting of local firms to provide ongoing support. According to the National Coordinator of SchoolNet Uganda, most schools did not initially have the

Figure 8.1a: Parents involvement in ICT development in schools

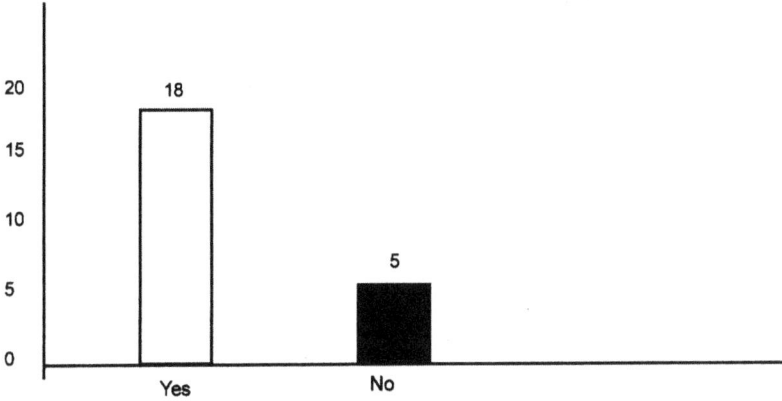

Figure 8.1b: Community involvement in ICT development in schools

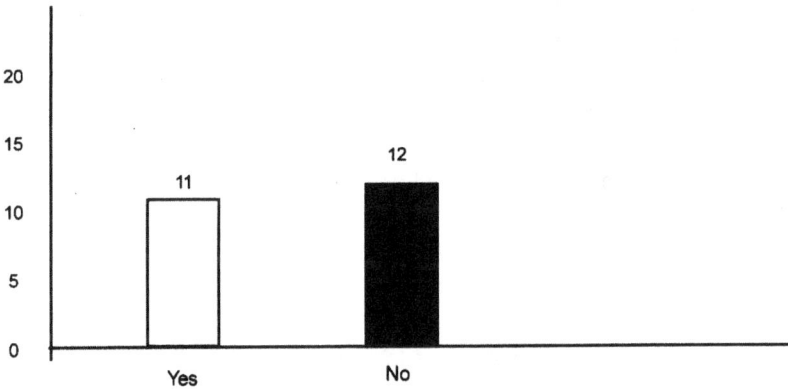

financial resources or the expertise needed to enter into these negotiations and to make appropriate choices. The Technical Coordinator of SchoolNet reported that out of the 20 schools participating in the WorLD programme, six were using spread-spectrum wireless connectivity. Four of the schools were using a dial-up cellular connection (using a mobile phone), six others were dialling up via landlines, and the other four were to pilot the use of VSATs.

SchoolNet Uganda initially negotiated with a local cellular phone company, CelTel, to provide schools with some free airtime. The company agreed to give one hour of free airtime daily for one year. Two of the schools in the study benefited from this arrangement.

The level of connectivity was found to vary from school to school, depending on the communication infrastructure available. Two of the sampled schools in this evaluation study had spread-spectrum wireless connectivity, the other two were using dial-up cellular and landline connections but found them both unsatisfactory and expensive. The landlines were reported to be unreliable due to traffic congestion and there were frequent communication breakdowns, especially during the rainy seasons and morning hours. The cellular phones, on the other hand, were said to be very slow and their costs were much higher than those of landlines.

King's College Budo suspended its Internet connection for almost a year and was exploring the possibilities of installing a wireless connection. The School Coordinator explained that the school was initially happy with its connection via the cellular phone. Although it was slow, they were able for the first time to surf the Web, communicate using email, work on collaborative projects and access all types of useful information through the Internet. Unfortunately, the bills sent to the school after a year's connection were very discouraging. The school then changed from cellular to a landline, but the telephone bill became too expensive and they were cut off. At the time of this study, the school had not had access to the Internet since January 2000, but was in the process of installing a wireless connection. It was evident, however, that within the one year that it was connected the school had made several advances which included:

- Opening active email addresses for about 350 students and almost all the teachers;
- Providing a forum for students to discover and apply their talents in computer network administration, Web design and general skills through the computer club;
- Carrying out educational tele-collaborative projects;
- Developing authoring capacities among students by publishing club magazines and the *Budonian*; and
- Designing and maintaining the Budo website (done by the students).

228

Nabisunsa Girls School also made use of a wireless connection, while Gayaza and Budo were hoping to move in the same direction. In the past, SchoolNet Uganda had met 50 per cent of the costs for installing wireless connections for some of the schools. The Technical Coordinator of SchoolNet Uganda revealed that it was no longer able to meet these costs, and the schools would have to meet the entire cost themselves.

The National and Technical Coordinators of SchoolNet both indicated that SchoolNet was preparing the ground to pilot VSAT technology in some rural schools. Among the issues that this pilot phase would address were whether VSAT technology was workable within the Ugandan context, whether the equipment required was affordable and sustainable, and whether the schools could meet the recurrent costs. SchoolNet Uganda also wished to explore further whether ISPs could be persuaded to offer special educational rates to schools. For example, AFSAT and SANYUTEL charged US$150 per month for wireless connectivity and some schools such as Makerere College School and Mengo Secondary School were already benefiting from these concessions. SchoolNet Uganda was also exploring the possibilities of the private sector assisting with some of the connectivity issues.

During the interviews with head teachers and teachers it was observed that, although Internet services were a valuable resource, the integration of ICTs in education was a very expensive venture. Arrangements for maintaining equipment and plans to ensure sustainability were issues for the four surveyed schools. While the initial equipment for most of the schools was supplied free of charge by the WorLD programme, some of the computers had since broken down, some had to be repaired and others had to be replaced. All four schools had developed contingency plans for replacing the old computers with new ones, and for increasing the number of computers available in the school.

The costs of connectivity have also been prohibitive and frustrating for some schools. The four schools sampled in the study recognised that they were responsible for the management and sustainability of their computer labs and for the purchase of software, teaching and learning materials. All the schools, with the exception of one, levied some amount of money (ranging from 10,000 to 20,000 shillings) each term from each student, which went towards these costs. The target for three of the schools was to buy at least one computer a term, but this was not always possible.

Those schools on wireless connection, such as Namilyango and Nabisunsa, explained that they could now afford to pay for connectivity, which came to about US$ 150 a month. This, they explained, was more manageable compared with the dial up system. Three of the schools were also raising extra revenue by training people from the surrounding communities, but their charges remained minimal, as they perceived this training to be a community service more than a fundraising activity. The money generated from these kinds of initiatives went towards maintenance and repair costs.

Access to computers

Educators and learners were asked how well equipped their schools were in terms of computers. Some 74 per cent of educators believed their laboratories were well equipped. Learners generally (65 per cent) perceived their facilities to be well equipped, compared with 21 per cent who said they were very well equipped, and 14 per cent who did not feel that they were well equipped at all. These perceptions, however, need to be understood in a context where the schools were moving from a position of having had no computers at all to a position of having access to some computers within the school.

All four schools had bought additional computers, adding to those donated by the WorLD programme, an indication that they had appreciated the value of access to computers. Two of the schools then had between 16 and 20 computers, while another school had more than 21 computers. All these schools had a budget for the purchase of at least one computer per term and for maintenance.

While two-thirds of the students indicated that there was no computer that they could use within walking distance of their home, 75 per cent indicated that there was a computer that they could use within 5-10 minutes walking distance of their classroom. Slightly more than half the learners said they used the computer more than once a week.

While none of the schools had a computer in the classroom, all the teachers indicated that they had access to a computer within walking distance of their homes. When asked where this computer was located, they all indicated that it was within the school. This is not surprising given that these were all boarding schools and the majority of educators resided within the school compound. Educators ranked in order of importance three important uses of the computers at school: learning tasks, followed by the preparation of tests, and then email.

Patterns of use

Learners

More than 83 per cent of the sampled learners could use a computer. Of the remaining 17 per cent, over half of the learners said they could not use one, and the remainder that they did not have time. Nabisunsa Girls School charges a separate fee for computer training, which makes such training less accessible to some students. The Coordinator explained that the school was forced to charge a fee of 30,000 shillings per student per term for computer training in order to raise money to pay the teacher who was brought in from outside to teach the girls. The head teacher explained that the policy would change in future, and instead of charging individual learners an amount would be levied on all learners as part of their school fees. This was the system employed in the other three schools. The experience was that computers were more accessible to students and staff at such schools. Ten of the students who indicated that they did not use computers explained that they had not had the time because they had been busy preparing for their final exams.

Those learners who used computers were asked to indicate the year they started doing so. The majority indicated that they had started using a computer during the last two to three years. Of the 119 learners, more than half (81) had learned to use them at school. Thirty-one students acquainted themselves with a computer at home, while seven learnt how to do the same at the computer centre.

Learners were also asked to indicate where they learned most about computers. Figure 8.2 shows the results.

More than half the learners indicated that most of what they knew about computers was learned at school, followed by 40 per cent who learnt most at home. Other sources of knowledge were the cyber cafe, computer club, community centre and friends and family.

Figure 8.2: Places where learners learnt the most about computers

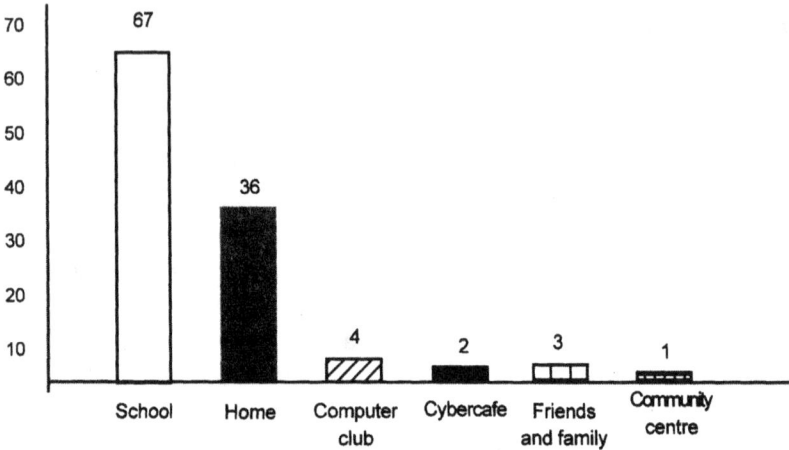

Learners indicated that they had been using computers for durations ranging from one to nine years (Figure 8.3). The mean was three years, with a standard deviation of 2.9.

Figure 8.3: Duration of learners' computer use

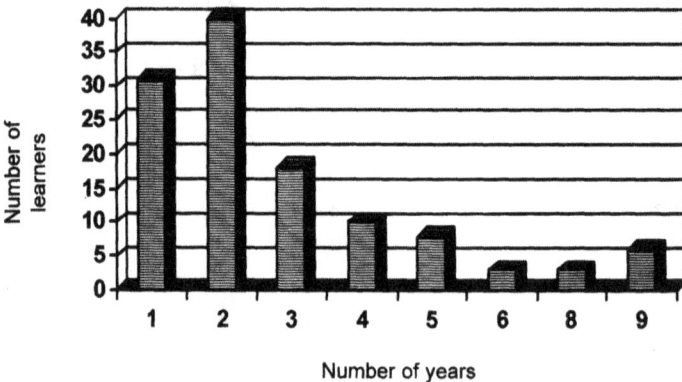

Nearly half the learners (73) indicated that they spent one to two hours each week in school learning and using the computer. Forty-two learners spent less than one hour, 19 none at all, and eight over two hours. In all four schools computer training for students had been added to the school time-table and some free time was made available for students to use the Inter-net and to send email.

These findings confirm those reported in the WorLD evaluation report that students in Uganda spent more time using ICTs in school than the average for Africa and the WorLD programme. This is an indication that the initial introduction of learners to computers by the WorLD programme has had a catalytic effect and has stimulated a demand for greater access to computers and computer training.

Educators

Some 83 per cent of educators indicated that they were fully computer liter-ate, with the rest indicating that they were fairly literate. None of the educa-tors indicated that they were not computer literate, an indication that they all had been exposed to computer training of some sort. When asked how often they used computers, their responses ranged from daily to about once a week. Slightly more than half of the educators used computers daily.

Although some educators initially shied away from using computers, the majority enjoyed using them and would actually like to learn about how to do so, as shown in Table 8.2. Educators used computers mainly for teach-ing, followed by student learning and communication. They were used very little for administrative tasks.

What is of interest, however, is that the email questionnaire sent out to 30 teachers yielded a zero response. The teachers had indeed received the questionnaire because the National Coordinator indicated that he had received it and it was sent using a list address. The reasons for this zero response therefore remain unclear. The majority of educators indicated that their schools had access to the Internet (83 per cent) and email (95 per cent).

Community

Two of the schools reported that they made their computers accessible to the neighbouring communities during the holidays at a minimal cost, which was used to cover a contribution towards the maintenance and costs of the computers. In both cases the schools offered computer training to teachers in neighbouring primary schools and in one instance to a women's group.

Table 8.2: Teachers' perceptions of using ICTs

I was afraid of using computers	10	43
I have never been afraid of computers	6	26
I enjoy using computers	15	65
I would like to learn about computers	14	61
I would like to learn more about computers	10	43
Total	**23**	–

Levels of computer proficiency and confidence

Learners' assessment of their computer proficiency

The assumption was that the more accessible computers were made to learners and educators, the more computer proficient they would become. Learners and educators were therefore asked to give an assessment of their computer proficiency. Most learners rated their proficiency as "well" to "very well". Learners were also asked to compare their computer proficiency with that of other students and teachers in their school (Figures 8.4a and b).

While the majority of learners assessed themselves as being more proficient than other students in their classes, they assessed themselves as being generally less proficient than their teachers. This was somewhat surprising, given the fact that more than half of the students (68 per cent) indicated that they did not know whether their teachers were well trained in computers. The majority of the learners (86 per cent) also indicated that their teachers did not use computers during teaching.

Most learners used computers for schoolwork. Those learners who used the Internet indicated that they did so mainly for personal reasons, including email and entertainment, as opposed to school projects (Figure 8.5).

An attempt was made to establish whether there were any associations between the age and gender of the learners and variables such as the use of computers; where computer skills were learnt; how often learners used computers; where they used them most; the actual use of the Internet; how

Figure 8.4a: Computer proficiency compared with teachers at school

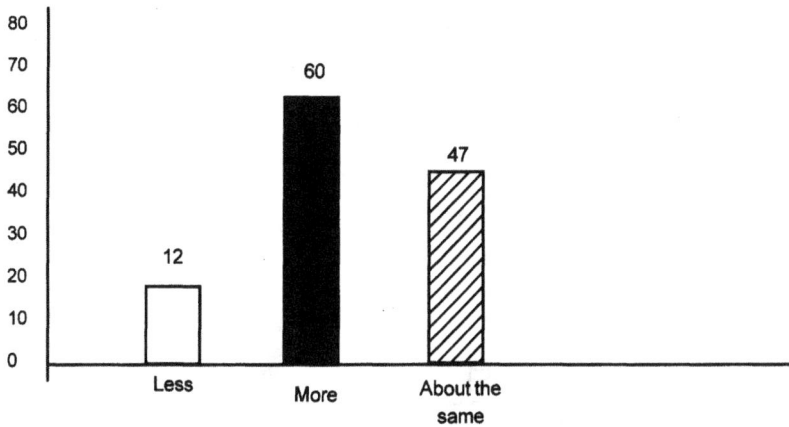

Figure 8.4b: Computer proficiency compared with students in class

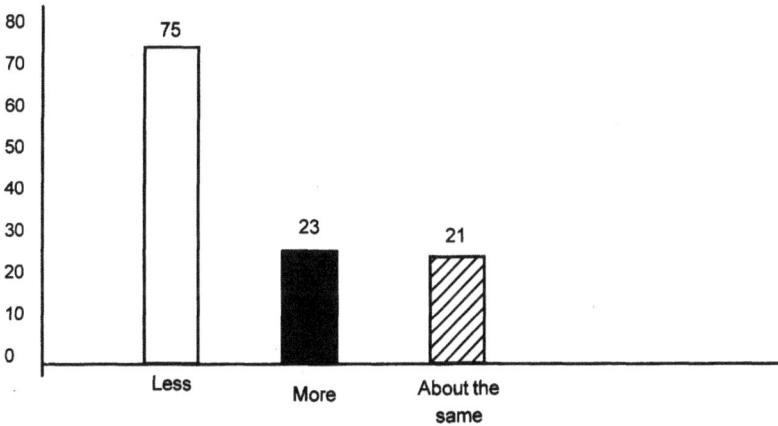

well learners could use computers; and the time spent learning and using the computers. Tables 8.3 to 8.6 present associations that were significant from the cross-tabulations.

Figure 8.5: Use of the Internet by learners

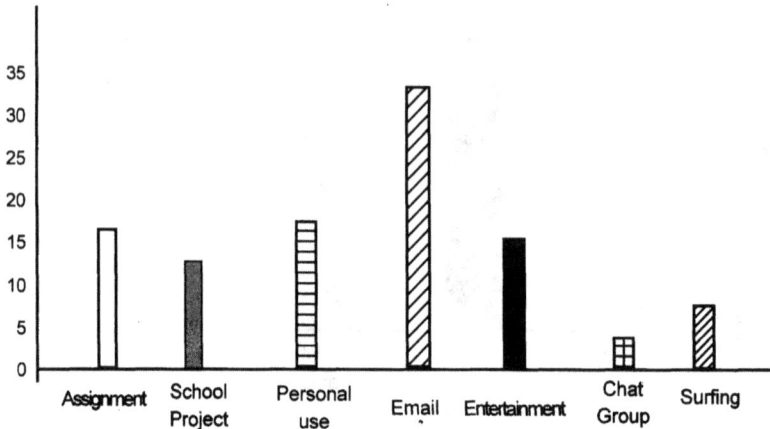

There was a significant association between learners' age and how well they used computers. While the sample had more of the age group 13–17 years using computers than the older learners aged 18 years and more, there were significantly more older than younger learners indicating that they could use the computer very well.

There was also a significant association between learner's age and the time spent using the computers, with older learners (18+) spending significantly more time at the computer than younger learners. This might be the reason why the older learners were more computer proficient. It was a policy in some of the schools to give A-level students more time on the computers than O-level students.

There was a significant association between gender and the use of computers, with significantly more male than female learners using computers. These findings are similar to findings from elsewhere in Africa and the world over. This issue needs to be addressed at the school level, with more girls being encouraged to use computers. Further research is needed to establish the reasons why girls do not take an active interest in the use of computers, even in cases where they have access to them.

Table 8.3: Cross-tabulation of the age of learners by how well they used a computer

Age of Learners	Well	Very Well	Total
13–17 years	56(72.7%)	21(27.3%)	77(100%)
18+ years	22(52.4%)	20(47.6%)	42(100%)
Total	78(65.5%)	41(34.5%)	119(100%)

Notes: X^2 = 4.982; S = 0.03; df = 1; n = 119.

Table 8.4: Cross-tabulation of the age of learners by time spent using a computer

Age of Learners	None	< 1 Hour	1-2 hours	Other	Total
13–17 years	17(17.7%)	24(25%)	47(49%)	8(8.3%)	96(100%)
18+	2(4.3%)	18(39.1%)	26(56.5%)	–	46(100%)
Total	19(13.4%)	42(29.6%)	73(51.4%)	8(5.6%)	142(100%)

Notes: X^2 = 10.326; S = 0.016; df = 3; n = 142.

Table 8.5: Cross-tabulation of the gender of learners by the use of computers

Gender	Yes	No	Total
Male	65(91.5%)	6(8.5%)	71(100%)
Female	54(76.1%)	17(23.9%)	71(100%)
Total	119(83.8%)	23(16.2%)	142(100

Notes: X^2 = 6.278; S = 0.012; df = 1; n = 142.

Table 8.6: Cross-tabulation of gender by the purpose for which learners use the Internet

Responses	Male	Female	Total
Don't use the Internet	8 (12.3%)	18 (33.3%)	26 (21.8%)
Assignments	13 (20.6%)	3 (5.7%)	16 (13.4%)
School Projects	8 (12.7%)	4 (7.5%)	12 (10.1%)
Personal Use	10 (15.9%)	5 (9.4%)	15 (12.6%)
Email	12 (19%)	21 (39.6%)	33 (27.7%)
Entertainment and chat groups	11 (17.5%)	3 (5.7%)	14 (0.12%)
Surfing	3 (4.8%)	1 (1.9%)	4 (3.4%)
Total	65 (54.6%)	54 (45.4%)	119 (100%)

Notes: $X^2 = 25.865$; $S = 0.001$; $df = 8$; $n = 119$.

Table 8.6 presents a cross-tabulation of gender by purpose for which learners use the Internet. Again, there was a significant association between the gender of the learners and use of the Internet, with female learners using the Internet less than male learners.

This again is an issue that requires further research and needs to be addressed at the school level. In the light of findings such as these, schools need to come up with strategies for encouraging girls to use computers.

Educators' assessment of their computer proficiency

Educators were asked to rate their computer skills against those of students and colleagues at their schools. Slightly more than a quarter of the teachers felt that they were less competent than their students. Most educators indicated that they were about as competent as their colleagues.

Figure 8.6a: Educators' assessment of their proficiency with computers (compared with colleagues)

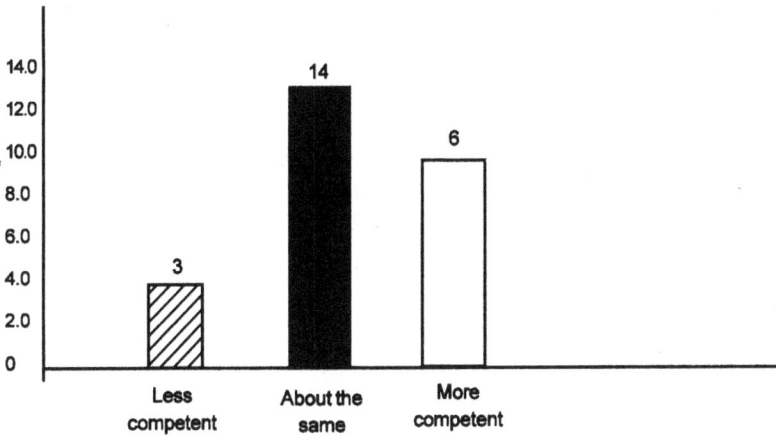

Figure 8.6b: Educators' assessment of their proficiency with computers (compared with learners)

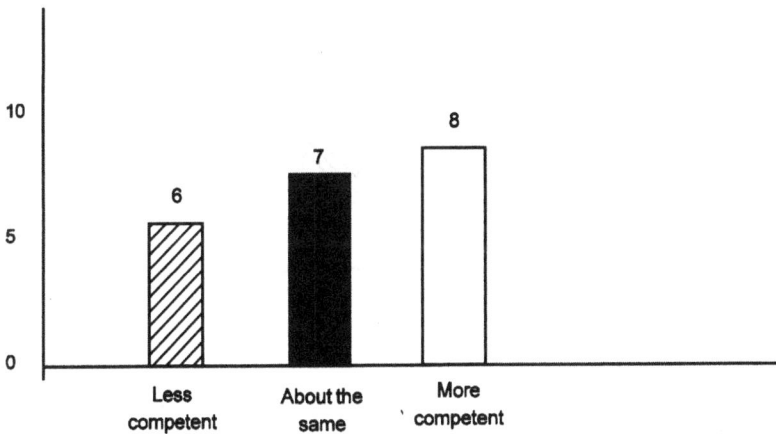

Levels of confidence in using ICTs

The majority (74 per cent) of educators indicated that they used the computer as an educational tool and that their levels of confidence were generally good. However, about a third were not that confident, which might explain the learners' observations that the majority of teachers did not use computers during their teaching. As previously noted in the WorLD evaluation report (2000), the training support received by teachers in Uganda was seen to be inadequate, as was the informal teacher-to-teacher training that was occurring in the schools – fewer than 25 per cent of the teachers sampled in the WorLD evaluation reported having received informal training. The topics that most teachers had been exposed to during training included using hardware, using application and Internet software, and designing and leading collaborative projects. More training may, therefore, be needed in this area.

Figure 8.7: Level of confidence in the use of ICTs
as an educational tool

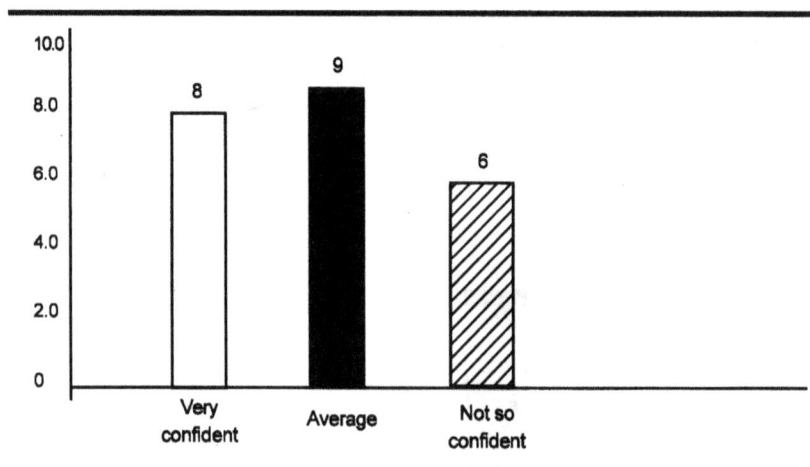

Capacity building and training

Educators were asked to indicate who played the primary role in their training on the computer. Figure 8.8 shows their responses.

All educators felt they had influenced the ICT knowledge of their learners. The same number of educators also indicated that the use of ICTs had a positive influence on teaching and learning in their classrooms. Slightly fewer than 75 per cent indicated that they integrated ICTs into the various subjects they taught, although this does not seem to correlate with the perceptions of learners.

SchoolNet Uganda has run training programmes for teachers on the integration of technology into the curriculum, which a few of the interviewed teachers indicated they had attended. According to them, these courses covered several topics including Web-based tutorials and resources, use of the Web as a teaching resource, the newsletter as a powerful tele-collaborative teaching tool, and writing and creating HTML files as a way of creating teaching resources. One of the teachers explained that they were exposed to a large variety of online tutorials in the major computer applications. Another remarked that he realised that most of the teaching guides needed to teach computer software were available on the Internet, and could be used to make handouts or to teach with them directly. Another teacher explained that, as part of their training, they surveyed a variety of web pages that could be used to teach various science and language subjects. They also had to create a WorLD schools newsletter for the participating schools as a way of practising how to help students' tele-collaborate and improve their language skills. Most teachers mentioned that they were exposed to the basic skills of creating web pages. As a result of this training, two of the schools went ahead to establish their own websites.

Figure 8.8: Sources of ICT training

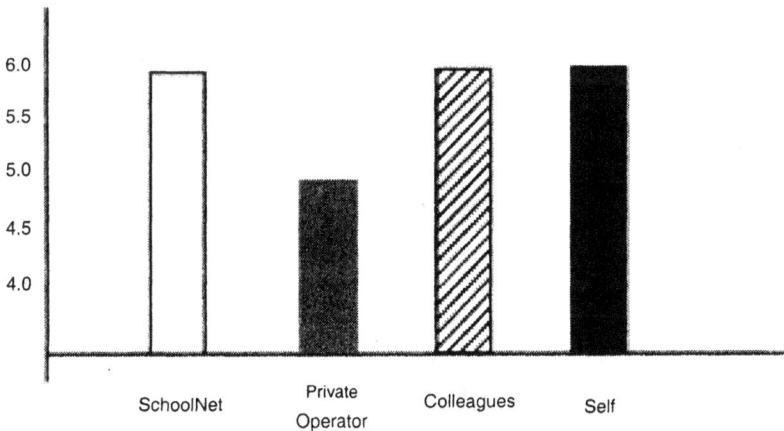

The School Coordinator at Budo had developed a computer resource centre and a computer teacher's guide and teaching syllabus. The teacher's guide covers, among other topics, an introduction to computer basics, learning about software, together with details on what was to be covered. This same teacher had trained all the teachers in the school in computer basics, creating learning materials, using PowerPoint and HTML, and creating small websites and a resource centre.

Some 31 per cent of the educators indicated that the use of ICTs had had some negative influence on the teaching and learning in their classroom, in that learners could access slightly desirable (and undesirable) information on the Internet. Educators felt that they sometimes had very limited control over this.

Content and curriculum development

The majority (87 per cent) of the educators indicated that their schools had been involved in content development activities for ICTs in education. Several had been involved in the development of the ICT curriculum for secondary schools under the auspices of the NCDC. Some efforts were also being made to integrate ICTs in education into their schools, for example at Kings College Budo and Namilyango College.

The NCDC is the statutory body charged with the development and implementation of the primary, secondary and tertiary school curricula in Uganda. NCDC's Director noted that an O-level syllabus for computer studies was in its final stages and awaiting approval from the Academic Board of the Ministry. According to the Director, SchoolNet Uganda had put a framework in place that CurriculumNet could build on and use. Educators believed that by making computer studies an examinable course, parents would be more willing to contribute towards the upkeep of the computer laboratories.

Several schools in the country have been engaged in collaborative learning using the Internet and email. At Kings College Budo, for example, 60 students were engaged in a wetlands project, which involved the study of wetlands in Uganda and Australia in collaboration with Comperdown College, Australia. PowerPoint presentations were made and a website produced. The wetland project continued until the end of 2001.

Another 60 students were involved in a project called "Technical-based Learning in School Science" (TBLISS), in partnership with the New York

Institute of Technology. PowerPoint presentations on water science were made and a website set up.

Twenty students were involved in a project on African refugees, in collaboration with Lubiri Senior Secondary School and Mengo Secondary School. Another project entitled, "Flowers and Friendships", involving ten students was carried out jointly with schools in Romania. A CD on flowers and a website were produced. The TBLISS project was extended to the year 2000, due to relocation of the Programme Director to the Queen's College, New York. Through this project the school was expecting some video conferencing equipment to be donated by the Project Director. New projects being considered included the study of the United Nations and its functions, which is a collaborative project between Kings College Budo and Ashbrook School in Hgatonia, North Carolina, under the guidance of the University of North Carolina. Another project is "Connecting Maths to Our Lives", which is done in joint partnership with schools all over the world, directed by Orillas in Puerto Rico. "Advanced Joint English Teaching" is done in collaboration with schools in Britain and Taiwan.

Namilyango College was also actively engaged in the use of the Internet and students developed and maintained a website for the school. Because of the school's wireless connectivity, the students and teachers could surf the Web at any time and had unlimited access to the Internet. The School Coordinator and head teacher of Namilyango observed, however, that their connection through AFSAT, the ISP, was very slow. The school was working on three tele-collaborative projects: with Instituto Olivetti, Ivera (Italy); with the Centre of Education, Siberia (Russia); and with Canadian and South African schools. Namilyango has been invited to participate in the 21st Century Schoolhouse Project representing Uganda (and Africa). Among the tele-collaborative projects completed by the school are a project on wetland management, malaria and waste management.

Policy

There is no definitive national ICT policy in place. The Ministry of Education and Sport is, however, engaged in a process to develop a viable ICT policy for education. A number of workshops have been held that have generated a multiplicity of ideas on how best ICT can be integrated in education to enhance the delivery of education services. One of the major recommendations has been the urgent need to evolve an ICT policy for the education sector. Having such a policy in place is viewed as central to coordinating government integration efforts.

In August 2000, the Ministry of Education and Sport established an education ICT task force for the purpose of formulating and implementing an ICT policy for the Ministry. It is also responsible for managing, monitoring and evaluating all ICT activities in the Ministry. Its specific tasks are to:

- Formulate an ICT policy for the Ministry of Education;
- Initiate ICT activities and projects;
- Review and direct new and ongoing ICT activities and projects;
- Perform monitoring and evaluation;
- Disseminate information; and
- Publicise the ICT policy for the Ministry of Education internally and among stakeholders in the education sector.

The International Institute for Communication and Development (IICD), a Dutch NGO, is supporting these efforts by the Ministry of Education and Sport. There are other ICT policy initiatives under the auspices of the Uganda Council for Science and Technology, Uganda Investment Authority and the Infodev Information Infrastructure Agenda Project, which is sponsored by the World Bank. The question remains, however, how best these different efforts can be linked together to share resources and avoid duplication.

Effects of the project

Achievement of project goals and objectives

Learner participation in SchoolNet Uganda

The majority (76 per cent) of learners indicated that they had not heard of SchoolNet Uganda and 91 per cent had never participated in any such activities. This is not entirely surprising, given that SchoolNet Uganda had not interacted directly with learners but focused on educators. Learners most likely did not know about its facilitative role in the provision of computers and access to the Internet. It is possible, however, as suggested earlier, that learners are not familiar with the name, since the WorLD programme in Uganda was originally known as the "School to School Initiative". This is an aspect that SchoolNet Uganda might need to address more seriously.

Educators' knowledge of SchoolNet Uganda

Most educators (91 per cent), on the other hand, had heard of SchoolNet Uganda. Some 83 per cent also indicated that they had participated in SchoolNet activities, such as a number of training programmes it had organised. In addition, nearly three-quarters of the educators indicated that SchoolNet Uganda had played a role in facilitating their schools' access to email and the Internet (Figures 8.9a and b).

Figure 8.9a: The role of SchoolNet Uganda in access to Email

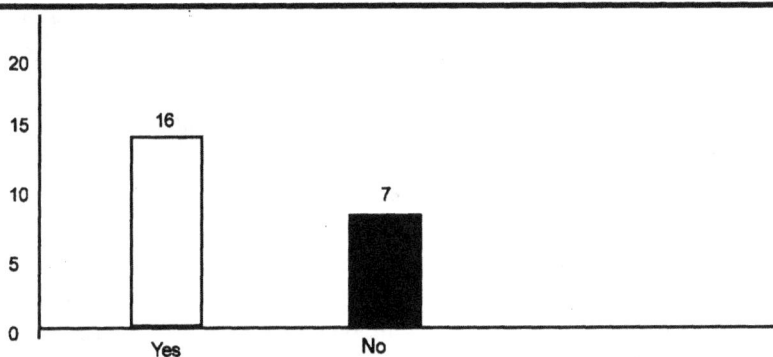

Figure 8.9b: The role of SchoolNet Uganda in access to the Internet

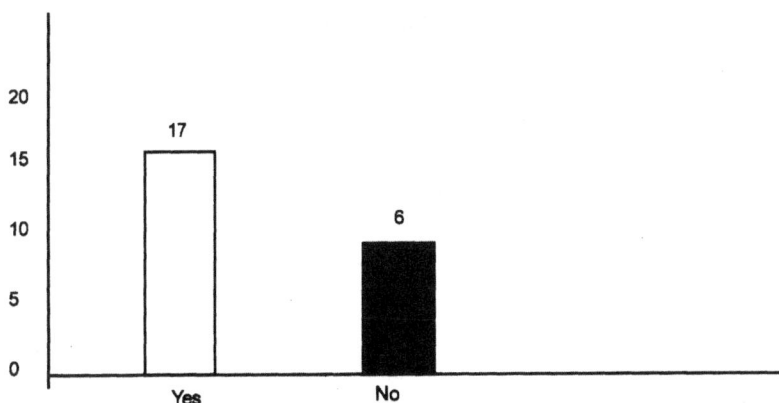

Nearly all educators (91 per cent) indicated that SchoolNet Uganda had played an influential role in the ICT knowledge of the learners. The use of ICTs had had a positive influence on teaching and learning in their classrooms and SchoolNet Uganda's role in these developments was acknowledged.

Conclusions and recommendations

Institutional structures and staffing

- SchoolNet Uganda has not had an active steering committee for more than a year. The steering committee should be reactivated so that the SchoolNet can play its rightful role;
- Ways need to be found to support the ICT coordinators in schools. Schools need to reduce the other duties of teachers to enable them to spend more time training other educators and learners;
- Schools need to come up with sustainability plans that reflect innovative ways of raising funds to continue operating and expanding their computer laboratories. There is a need to demonstrate that school networking can work, and that it is manageable and sustainable if it is to take root in schools; and
- Some of the schools run training programmes for community members during holidays. Depending on the different locations of schools (urban or rural) and the socio-economic status of the surrounding community, the training of community members, especially in rural areas, is likely to remain more of a community service than an income-generating activity. If a school aims to raise funds through these kinds of initiatives, it is likely to experience some frustrations, especially in areas where people are relatively poor and the demand for computer training is limited. There will also be areas where people cannot afford to pay much for these kinds of services, much as they would like to undergo such training. If the school's aim is to provide a community service, then the training for community members may have to be highly subsidised in most cases. The question, however, remains, subsidised by whom? This raises the concomitant question of the extent to which schools can afford to offer these kinds of services to their surrounding communities, and at whose expense they should be rendered. The issue of long-term sustainability is also raised.

Partnerships

- There is a need to sensitise parents through workshops organised by schools, to expose them to the benefits of ICTs and what they are paying for;
- There is a need for schools to extend their partners beyond the parent community, thus building local partnerships to mobilise resources; and
- Schools could lobby large organisations for donations of ICT equipment, as well as approach the government to waive taxes on ICTs. Although SchoolNet Uganda could pursue this, individual schools should still take responsibility for mobilising their own resources.

Connectivity

Connectivity was recognised as a concern and the problems of using a dial-up connection were highlighted. Even those schools that were using wireless connections complained about the low bandwidth. There was also the problem of licensing fees that had to be paid. It was pointed out that there was a need to:

- Explore in detail the various technical options available and affordable to schools so that they could make informed choices with regard to connectivity;
- Speed up the process of formulating the ICT policy in order to address the problems relating to licensing; and
- Explore more seriously the different connectivity options that could be used by different schools, keeping in mind the issues of cost, reliability and efficiency. There is a need not only for technical studies but also for feasibility studies to minimise the kinds of frustrations experienced by schools and in order to promote sustainability.

Access

Some of the computers available in the schools were slow, and more reliable and fast machines are needed. The maintenance of already existing computers also posed a problem. It was recommended in this case that:

- Schools needed to look into mechanisms for purchasing new and faster computers; and
- Regarding problems of maintenance, schools should try to develop their own maintenance capacity and seek outside help only when necessary.

Some computer laboratories were small, with only a limited number of computers, which impeded their effective use to some extent. Some learners and educators lacked interest and did not make use of the computers available to them in the schools. More males than females were utilising the available computers in the schools. On the basis of these observations the following recommendations were made:

- There is need for greater sensitisation of educators and learners to the benefits of ICTs;
- More training programmes should be organised for both educators and learners to expose them to the potential that computers have in an educational setting;
- Schools should explore the possibilities of acquiring bigger rooms to house their laboratories, and should come up with plans and strategies for buying new computers and even soliciting donations; and
- In relation to gender and age differences in ICT usage, schools should come up with workable strategies for enabling and encouraging females to take part more actively.

Capacity building and teacher training

- Teachers still lacked skills to integrate information technology in the curriculum – more teacher training is needed;
- There is a need for further in-depth research into the possible reasons why female pupils and teachers tend to use computers less than males. Reasons for this reluctance are not very clear and need to be understood if the gender imbalance in the use of computers is to be addressed;
- It cannot be assumed that the potential positive changes that can be brought about by the integration of ICTs in education will necessarily be welcomed and embraced by all educators. Some educators may not be interested, or are yet to be convinced. It is, therefore, important

to identify and build a cadre of educators who will be the prime movers of ICTs in schools;

- The integration of ICTs involves a shift from teacher-centred methodologies to learner-centred approaches. This necessitates a shift not only in methodology but also in attitudes and, eventually, in the philosophy of education. Educators need to be retrained to think differently about their pedagogical role. They also need to be encouraged to create their own content. These are areas in which educators may need further training; and
- Further explorations are needed into ways and means in which ICTs can be popularised and made available to all at a reasonable cost. Questions of equity in this respect also need to be investigated further.

Content development

Much of the content now available through the Internet was developed elsewhere and is not always relevant to the local situation. It was recommended that the Ministry of Education should set up a website with relevant information. The Ministry should also encourage educators to develop their own local content and post it to this site.

Notes

1   African Development Bank, African Statistics, *http://afdb.org/african_countries/information_comparison.htm*

2.   Central Intelligence Agency, *CIA – The World Factbook, http://www.odci.gov/cia/publications/factbook/*

3.   Cellular Statistics – Africa, *http://www.cellular.co.za/stats/stats-africa.htm*

4.   World Bank, based on UNESCO figures, *http://www4.worldbank.org/afr/stats/adi2000/default.cfm*

5.   WorLD is a World Bank-funded global programme that provides Internet connectivity and trains teachers, teacher trainers and students in developing countries in the use of technology in education. WorLD also links students and teachers in secondary schools in developing countries, for collaborative learning via the Internet.

6.   WorLD, 2000, *World Links for Development Country Reports: Brazil, Chile, Colombia, Ghana, Mauritania, Mozambique, Paraguay, Peru, Senegal, South Africa, Uganda and Zimbabwe 1999–2000.* Washington, DC: World Bank.

Appendices

Appendix I: Additional Research Questions

Below is a list of some the detailed areas that were explored in each of the evaluation studies. Appropriate instruments were designed in each country on the basis of these questions.

Context

Questions in this section typically included the following areas:

* What are the social, political and economic features at the country level that might affect and impact on the project?
* What was the educational context of the project?
* How has the context changed over time?
* Was anything in place prior to the IDRC investment? If so, what?
* What are the characteristics of other projects or initiatives for introducing ICTs into schools, if any? (State similarities and differences.)

Infrastructure and Connectivity

The questions in this category sought to understand the nature of the physical infrastructure, with specific reference to the conditions of school buildings and access to electricity and telephones. Here the intention was to ascertain the extent to which the infrastructure might have enabled or hindered the implementation of the project.

Some typical questions included the following:

* What are the technological facilities available at the school?
* How accessible are these facilities to users?

- What major technical problems have been identified?
- Who are the users? (profile, number)
- Why do they use these facilities?
- Are other partners involved in the project? If yes, what is their contribution?
- What are the difficulties faced with regard to connectivity?

Content Development

- Is there an official curriculum for ICT use in schools?
- What curriculum is used in the schools?
- Does the curriculum contain any new activities?
- Who designed the curriculum?
- What changes have there been in school management, teaching, learning or other project areas?

Teacher Training

- What is the profile of ICT trainers?
- Where were teachers trained?
- What is the curriculum for training? Is it an official curriculum?
- Is the material used appropriate for the training?
- Have there been any difficulties?

Policy

- What legislation and/or policy frameworks inform the education system, or address the use of ICTs in education?
- If legislation and a policy framework existed, how enabling or hindering were they to the process of starting up school networking projects?
- How does the project specifically link to the national policy?
- How does the project contribute towards national policy, or how does national policy influence the project?

Planning

The questions sought to understand why the project was perceived as a need:
- Why was the project started?
- Who started it?

- What were the project's objectives?
- What was the IDRC's contribution?
- Who were the project partners?
- What were the intended project activities?
- What evaluation and monitoring processes were planned?
- What were the start-up costs (including hidden costs)?
- What plans are there to sustain the project beyond donor support?

Project Activities and Implementation

- Were adequate facilities and resources available to ensure that the project was effectively implemented?
- What were the costs for delivering the project? Who carried those costs and why?
- What were the main tasks and who was responsible for carrying them out?
- Were tasks and responsibilities carried out effectively and efficiently?
- What factors enabled or hindered implementation of the project?
- Who were the project beneficiaries?
- What services were offered?
- What activities were carried out?
- Who were the project partners?
- What evaluation and monitoring processes were in place?

Effects of the Project

Questions in this category sought to understand the extent to which the project had met its objectives:

- What difference did it make in the lives of the beneficiaries and their work environment?
- How did the target audience and others benefit from the project?
- Did the project lead to the development of new activities in schools?
- How has the project been received by its beneficiaries?
- To what extent have the project objectives been met?
- What changes have occurred since the IDRC investment?

Lessons Learnt

The questions in this section sought to explore the lessons that the SchoolNet project managers had learned from the implementation of the project:

• What factors have enabled the project to reach its objectives?
• What factors hindered the project in reaching its objectives?
• What was unexpected or difficult during the start-up phase?
• What would be done differently if start-up was repeated?

Appendix 2: Schoolnet South Africa research question matrix

	Connectivity	Teacher Training	Content	Policy
	Context: What is the infrastructural context within which the SchoolNet Project (SNP) is operating?	Context: • What is the nature of the teacher training system? • To what extent does it incorporate ICT training?	Context: • What is the nature of curriculum and education content development in the country? • Does it take into account ICT platforms? • Who are the key role players in content development?	Context: • What is the status of ICT policy in the country? • Does it incorporate ICT application in education? • What effect has this had on the SNP? • Has the SNP played any role in ICT policy in education?
Subquestions	Planning: • How have computerisation and connectivity in schools been planned by the project? • From where were computers sourced?	Planning: • How has teacher training been planned? • How are teachers selected for training?	Planning: Has the SNP planned any content-related programmes?	Planning: Has the SNP planned to influence ICT in education policy?

Appendix 2: Schoolnet South Africa research question matrix (Continued)

Connectivity	Teacher Training	Content	Policy
Delivery: • How many schools have been computerised and connected by the project? • What kinds of computers exist in schools and do they all work?	Delivery: • How many teachers have been trained? • What were their levels of ICT capability? • What courses were available for training?	Delivery: • How have content-related programmes been delivered? • Who were the main users of the content and how was the content used?	Delivery: • Has ICT policy in education been implemented? • What role has the SNP played in this?
Effects: What have been the effects of connectivity in schools?	Effects: • How have teachers responded to the training? • What effects have teacher training programmes had on teachers?	Effects: What were the effects of the SNP's content programmes?	Effects: What have been the effects of ICT policy in education or the absence thereof?
Lessons: What lessons can be learned from the connectivity experience?	Lessons: What lessons can be learned from the teacher training experience in the project?	Lessons: What lessons can be learned from the SNP's experience in content development?	Lessons: What lessons can be learned for SNPs with regard to involvement in education policy and ICTs?

Data Sources	• Project management • Telecom operators • Internet service providers	• Project management • Teacher trainers • Teachers	• Project management • Curriculum specialists • Teachers	• Project management • Department of Education
Data-gathering Techniques	• Document analysis • Interviews	• Document analysis • Interviews • Questionnaires	• Document analysis • Interviews • Questionnaires	• Document analysis • Interviews

Bibliography

African Development Bank (AFDB), African Statistics, http://afdb.org/african_countries/information_comparison.htm

African Development Bank, http://www.afdb.org

African Development Bank, African Development Forum, 1999, http://www.afdb.org

Anderson, G., 1990, *Fundamentals of Educational Research*. London: Palmer Press.

Balfour, Williamson & Co. Limited, 1995, *Uganda Secondary Education Subsector Studies*. Balfour, Williamson & Co. Limited.

BMI-Techknowledge, 2001, *Communication Technologies Handbook 2001*.

Cellular Statistics – Africa, http://www.cellular.co.za/stats/stats-africa.htm

Central Intelligence Agency, *CIA – The World Factbook*, http://www.odci.gov/cia/publications/factbook/ and http://www.cia.gov/cia/publications/factbook/geos/sg.html

CIUEM, Status of the proposal: *Introduction of Information and Communication Technologies in Secondary Schools and Teacher Training Institutions in Mozambique*, File 97-8921.

Cross, M., 2000, *Education in Mozambique*.

Eastern Cape provincial school network website: http://www.ecape.school.za

Eduardo Mondlane University Centre of Informatics, 1998, *Introduction of Information and Communication Technologies (ICT) in Secondary Schools (Pre-University Schools) in Mozambique*, Maputo. (Final Version, February.)

GEEP, 1995, *Survey on Adolescent Sexuality among Students*.

GEEP, www.refer.sn/sngal_ct/rec/geep

Howell, C. & Lundall, P., 2000, *Computers in Schools: A National Survey of Information Communication Technology in South African Schools*. Education Policy Unit. Cape Town: University of the Western Cape, *http://www.school.za/schoolsurveys/suveys_index.htm*

259

http://education.pwv.gov.za/teli2/default.htm

http://www.cia.gov/cia/publications/factbook/geos/sg.html

http://www.education.gouv.sn/stat.htm

http://www.odci.gov/cia/publications/factbook/

http://www.prb.org/Content/NavigationMenu/Other_reports/2000-2002/ sheet4.html

Human Sciences Research Council (HSRC) and National Department of Education, 1996, *1996 Schools Register of Needs*. Pretoria: HSRC.

Human Sciences Research Council (HSRC) and National Department of Education, 1996, *Telecommunications Potential in South African Schools*. Pretoria: HSRC.

INGC Situation Report, *http://www.mozambique.mz/floods/02082000/htm*

INGC Situation Report: *Mozambique Devastated by Floods, http:// www.mozambique.mz/floods/experi5.htm*

International Development Research Centre (IDRC), 1996, *Communities and the Information Society: A Canadian Initiative for the Millennium*. Ottawa: IDRC.

International Development Research Centre (IDRC), 2000, *Computers in Schools, http://www.schoolnet.org.za/schoolsurveys/index.htm*

International Development Research Centre (IDRC), 2000, *School Networking in Africa Compendium*. Ottawa: IDRC.

International Development Research Centre (IDRC). Acacia National Strategies: Mozambique-IDRC Study/Acacia Initiative in preparation for the workshop entitled "Towards the Information Society", convened in Maputo in February 1997 and sponsored by both the IDRC and the World Bank, *http://www.idrc.ca.acacia./outputs/op-mozam.htm*

International Development Research Centre (IDRC). *Acacia Prospectus*. Ottawa: IDRC.

International Development Research Centre (IDRC). *SchoolNet South Africa Project Summary (98-8905)*. Internal unpublished document.

International Education and Resource Network (I*EARN), *http:// www.iearn.org/*

Isaacs, S. & Sibthorpe, C., 2000, *Report on IDRC School Networking in Africa Workshop*, Okahandja, Namibia, 17-20 July.

James, T. & Hesselmark, O., 2001, *A Country ICT Survey for Mozambique*, www.sida.se

James, T. (Ed.)., 2001, Educational Technology Policy in Southern Africa. In

An Information Policy Handbook for Southern Africa. Ottawa: IDRC, *http://www.dbsa.org/publications/ictpolsa/*

Jensen, M., 2002, *The African Internet – A Status Report, http://www3.sn.apc.org/africa/afstat.htm*

Joint Technical Mission, 2000, *Knees, Blackboards, and Logs.* Unpublished paper.

KwaZulu-Natal provincial school network website: http://www.kzn.school.za

Lave, J. & Wenger, E., 1991, *Situated Learning: Legitimate Peripheral Participation.* Cambridge: Cambridge University Press.

Marquard, S., 1996, *1996 School Connectivity Review.*

Ministère des Finances, de l'Economie et du Plan du Sénégal. (1999). *Direction de la Prévision et de la Statistique: Situation économique du Sénégal année.*

Ministry of National Education (Senegal). *Plan décennal de l'éducation et de la formation,* http://www.education.gouv.sn/pdef.htm

Ministry of National Education (Senegal). Student Statistics, http://www.education.gouv.sn/stat.htm

Ministry of the Interior (Senegal), 1994,. *Rapport d'avant-projet du schéma régional d'aménagement du territoire: Direction de l'aménagement du territoire.*

Mozambique Commission for Information and Communication Technology Policy, 1998, Minutes of the Meeting of the Mozambique Acacia Advisory Committee held on 14 October 1998. Minutes drawn from http://www.mozambique.mz/informat/maacs/encotel.htm

Mozambique Commission for Information and Communication Technology Policy, 2000, *Draft Policy for Information and Communication.* As approved by the Council of Ministers on 30 May 2000 and in a national debate between 18 June and 28 July, 2000, http://www.onfopol.mz

Mutume, G., 2000, *Education – South Africa: Fewer Funds for a System in Shambles,* http://www.oneworld.org/ips2/feb98/southafrica_educ.html

NetCorps Canada International, http://www.netcorps-cyberjeunes.org/english/main_e.htm

NetDay, http://www.netday.org.za

Nortel Phumelela Networks Project, http://www.school.za/projects/nortel

NUA, http://www.nua.ie/surveys/how_many_online/index

Programme décennal pour l'éducation et la formation (PDEF), Component 2: Improving the quality of teaching/learning.

Proposal for the development of SchoolNet SA, Version 1.0a, 6 July 1998.

SchoolNet Africa, http://www.schoolnetafrica.org

SchoolNet SA and Western Cape SchoolNet, 1999, Millennium Minds Conference, Cape Town. Proceedings are available online at http://archive.wcape.school.za/conf99/

SchoolNet South Africa, 1998,. *Proposal to IDRC for the development of SchoolNet SA*, Version 1.0a, 6 July.

SchoolNet South Africa, 2000, *Annual Report for 1 March 1999–31 March 2000,* http://www.schoolnet.org.za

SchoolNet South Africa, 2000, *Educator Development Framework.*

SchoolNet South Africa, 2000,. *Annual Report for 1 March 1999 – 31 March 2000, http://www.schoolnet.org.za*

Sherry, L., 1998, An Integrated Technology Adoption and Diffusion Model. *International Journal of Educational Telecommunications,* 4(2/3): 113-145.

South African Department of Education, *TELI framework,* http://education.pwv.gov.za/teli2/default.htm

South African government, http://www.gov.za

South African government, *South Africa Yearbook 2000/01,* http://www.gov.za/yearbook/education.html

South African Institute for Distance Education (SAIDE), 2000a,. *Evaluation of the Telkom One Thousand Schools Internet Project: A Focus on SchoolNet SA's Involvement.* Braamfontein, South Africa: SAIDE.

South African Institute for Distance Education (SAIDE), 2000b, *Piloting Professional Development of Teachers in Use of IT in the Classroom: Evaluation of a SCOPE/SchoolNet Pilot Project.* Braamfontein, South Africa: SAIDE.

South African map, see: *http://home.global.co.za/~mercon/map.htm*

Sow, M., 2000,. *Education pour tous* (Education for All), Bilan à l'an 2000, National Report for Senegal.

Telkom 1000 Schools Internet Project evaluation, *http://telkom1000.schoolnet.org.za*

ThinkQuest International, http://www.thinkquest.org and http://www.thinkquest.org.za

UNESCO, http://www2.unesco.org/wef/countryreports/senegal/contents.html

UNICEF Balance Sheet of Human Progress in Africa, http://www.unicef.org/miscellaneous/balance.htm

United Nations Development Programme (UNDP), 1992, *United Nations*

Human Development Report, 1992: Global Dimensions of Human Development. New York: UNDP, p. 29.

United Nations Development Programme (UNDP), 2000, *United Nations Human Development Report 2000: Human Rights and Human Development.* New York: UNDP.

United Nations Human Development Report, 2000, *Human Rights and Human Development.* New York: UNDP.

United Nations Human Development Report, 2001, 'Making New Technologies Work for Human Development', Section E-1-1, http://www.undp.org/hdr2001/

United Nations Human Development Report, 2001, *Making New Technologies Work for Human Development, Section E-1-1,* http://www.undp.org/hdr2001/

United States Internet Council, 2000, *2000 Report of the US Internet Council.*

Universidade Eduardo Mondlane Centro De Informatica, 1997, *CIUEM: Introduction of Information and Communication Technologies in Secondary Schools and Teacher Training Institutions in Mozambique, Appraisal,* IDRC file 97-8921.

Universidade Eduardo Mondlane Centro De Informatica, 1999, *Internet Para as Escolas (SchoolNet Project) Report of the Pedagogical Training Workshop II,* Maputo, 20 April.

Western Cape provincial school network website: *http://www.wcape.school.za*

Whyte, A., 2000, *An Evaluation of Telecentres: Guidelines for Researchers.* Ottawa: IDRC.

World Bank Group, 2000, Infodev Working Papers, June 2000. *The Networking Revolution: Opportunities and Challenges for Developing Countries.* Global Information and Communications Technologies Department, http://www.infodev.org/library/WorkingPapers/NetworkingRevolution.doc

World Bank, based on UNESCO figures, http://www4.worldbank.org/afr/stats/adi2000/default.cfm.

World Bank, based on UNESCO figures. http://www4.worldbank.org/afr/stats/adi2000/default.cfm

World Bank, http://www4.worldbank.org/afr/stats/adi2000/default.cfm

World Bank, *http://www4.worldbank.org/Afr/stats/adi2002/default.cfm*

World Bank, www4.worldbank.org/afr/stats/adi2002/default.cfm

World Population Bureau, 2001, Population Data Sheet, http://www.prb.org/

Content/NavigationMenu/Other_reports/2000-2002/sheet4.html

WorLD, 2000,. *World Links for Development Country Reports: Brazil, Chile, Colombia, Ghana, Mauritania, Mozambique, Paraguay, Peru, Senegal, South Africa, Uganda and Zimbabwe 1999-2000.* Washington, DC: World Bank.

The Publishers

The **International Development Research Centre** is a public corporation created by the Parliament of Canada in 1970 to help developing countries use science and technology to find practical, long-term solutions to the social, economic, and environmental problems they face. Support is directed toward developing an indigenous research capacity to sustain policies and technologies developing countries need to build healthier, more equitable, and more prosperous societies.

IDRC Books publishes research results and scholarly studies on global and regional issues related to sustainable and equitable development. As a specialist in development literature, IDRC Books contributes to the body of knowledge on these issues to further the cause of global understanding and equity. IDRC publications are sold through its head office in Ottawa, Canada, as well as by IDRC's agents and distributors around the world. The full catalogue is available at http://www.idrc.ca/booktique/.

The **Council for the Development of Social Science Research in Africa** (CODESRIA) is an independent organisation whose principal objectives are facilitating research, promoting research-based publishing and creating multiple forums geared towards the exchange of views and information among African researchers. It challenges the fragmentation of research through the creation of thematic research networks that cut across linguistic and regional boundaries.

CODESRIA publishes a quarterly journal, *Africa Development*, the longest standing Africa-based social science journal; *Afrika Zamani*, a journal of history; the *African Sociological Review*, *African Journal of International Affairs (AJIA)* and *Identity, Culture and Politics: An Afro-Asian Dialogue*. Research results and other activities of the institution are disseminated through 'Working Papers', 'Monograph Series', 'New Path Series', 'State-of-the-Literature Series', 'CODESRIA Book Series', and the *CODESRIA Bulletin*.

www.ingramcontent.com/pod-product-compliance
Lightning Source LLC
Chambersburg PA
CBHW061139220326
41599CB00025B/4294